SHERLOCK HOLMES

The Published Apocrypha

Yours very truly
A Conan Doyle

SHERLOCK HOLMES

The Published Apocrypha

by

SIR ARTHUR CONAN DOYLE

AND ASSOCIATED HANDS

Selected and Edited by Jack Tracy

Houghton Mifflin Company Boston

1980

Also by Jack W. Tracy

THE ENCYCLOPAEDIA SHERLOCKIANA
SUBCUTANEOUSLY, MY DEAR WATSON
CONAN DOYLE AND THE LATTER-DAY SAINTS

Library of Congress Cataloging in Publication Data

Doyle, Arthur Conan, Sir, 1859–1932.
  Sherlock Holmes, the published apocrypha.

  1. Detective and mystery plays, English. 2. Detective and mystery stories, English. 3. Doyle, Arthur Conan, Sir, 1859–1932—Parodies, travesties, etc. I. Tracy, Jack, 1945-   II. Title.
PR4622.S4 1980   823'.8   80–16328
ISBN 0–395–29454–1

Printed in the United States of America

S 10 9 8 7 6 5 4 3 2 1

"The Field Bazaar" was first published in *The Student* (University of Edinburgh) for November 1896 • "How Watson Learned the Trick" was first published in *The Book of the Queen's Doll's House Library* (1924) edited by E. V. Lucas • "The Adventure of the Two Collaborators" was first published in *Memories and Adventures.* Copyright © 1923 by A. Conan Doyle • "The Man with the Watches" and "The Lost Special" were first published in the *Strand* magazine for July and August 1898. First book publication: *Round the Fire Stories,* 1908 • *Sherlock Holmes* was first performed 6 November 1899 at the Garrick Theatre, New York. Publication: Samuel French, 1922. Copyright © 1922 by Samuel French, Ltd. Copyright © 1949 (in renewal) by Denis P. S. Conan Doyle and Hartford National Bank & Trust Company • *The Painful Predicament of Sherlock Holmes* was first performed 24 March 1905 at the Metropolitan Opera House, New York • *The Speckled Band* was first performed 4 June 1910 at the Adelphi Theatre, London. Publication: Samuel French, 1912. Copyright © 1912 by Samuel French, Ltd. Copyright © 1940 (in renewal) by Jean Conan Doyle • *The Crown Diamond* was first performed 2 May 1921 at the Hippodrome, Bristol, England • "Plot for a Sherlock Holmes Story" was first published in *Conan Doyle: His Life and Art* (1943) by Hesketh Pearson • "The Case of the Man Who Was Wanted" was first published in *Cosmopolitan* for August 1948. Copyright © 1948 by Denis P. S. Conan Doyle, Executor of the Estate of the late Sir Arthur Conan Doyle.

This book is dedicated, in great admiration, to
JOHN BENNETT SHAW
respected Sherlockian,
keeper of the lumber room,
and The Hans Sloan of His Age

Contents

Introduction

It is one measure of Sherlock Holmes's enormous popularity that he is literature's most imitated character. Virtually from the moment of his creation, Sir Arthur Conan Doyle's master detective has been the subject of more satires, parodies, pastiches, and dramatic adaptations than even the most avid "Sherlockian" can count. The total in Ronald B. De Waal's *The World Bibliography of Sherlock Holmes and Dr. Watson* (1974) is eight or nine hundred, and the number is forever rising.

According to the researches of Anthony Boucher, the earliest Sherlockian spoof appeared in *The Idler* for May 1892 — a magazine to which Conan Doyle contributed many of his non-Holmes works. Mark Twain also wrote one of the first — and worst. August Derleth's serious pastiches featuring Solar Pons have developed a fandom of their own, and Robert L. Fish's outrageous Schlock Homes has a legion of loyal followers. The Holmes novels by Nicholas Meyer have inspired a whole new industry of pseudo-Sherlockian ripoffs of various degrees of awfulness.

In 1944 the Conan Doyle Estate suppressed by threat of legal action an anthology of pastiches assembled by Ellery Queen called *The Misadventures of Sherlock Holmes.* Two or three years later there was a half-hearted attempt to halt publication of the *Baker Street Journal* on the grounds that the Sherlockian periodical infringed upon the Sherlock Holmes copyright. But the Estate soon relented, and Sir Arthur's son Adrian Conan Doyle wrote an outstanding series of pastiches entitled *The Exploits of Sherlock Holmes* in collaboration with John Dickson Carr.

Adrian was in excellent company — for not even Sir Arthur Conan Doyle himself had escaped the temptation to mimic his own creation.

In addition to the four novels and fifty-six short stories which comprise the "complete" Sherlock Holmes, Doyle wrote nine other works in which the great detective figures. One has been irretrievably lost. Two remain unpublished at the insistence of his heirs. The remaining six are collected in this volume for the first time.

Just as the sixty "complete" tales are known as "The Canon" or "The Sacred Writings," Sherlockians have designated these other pieces "The Apocrypha." Doyle wrote them — there is no question of that — but for various reasons he never saw fit to collect them, and they have remained in obscurity, known only to those few Sherlockians whose mutual avocation it is to know about such things.

And until now their anthologization was not possible. Sir Arthur was his own worst critic — in more ways than one, because his self-judgment was not always very good. He bitterly resented the unauthorized publication of those works he considered unworthy, and following his death in 1930 his children became even more protective, aggressively limiting which of their father's writings might reach the public. For nearly forty years Sherlockians railed, helplessly and politely, at these "recalcitrant heirs," but recently the copyrights were sold, and the new proprietors are more open to reason. The required permission has at last been granted.

Five additional pieces are included in this volume. One is by Doyle, the others by different hands. Each belongs for reasons of its own. Each has its own introduction in which those reasons are set forth in some detail.

This book is subtitled "The *Published* Apocrypha." There are still the *unpublished* Apocrypha — two tantalizing works in Sir Arthur Conan Doyle's own hand — which remain suppressed. They are *The Angels of Darkness,* a three-act play, written in 1890, based on the Mormon flashback in *A Study in Scarlet,* set in San Francisco, and having Doctor Watson for its principal character; and *The Stonor Case,* a "first version" of the 1910 drama *The Speckled Band. The Angels of Darkness* was discovered about 1946. *The Stonor Case* was seen by Pierre Nordon while he was researching his 1966 biography of Doyle.

So the *unpublished* Apocrypha remain so. "My father did not wish it published, nor did my brothers, and nor do I," Dame Jean Conan Doyle, the last surviving direct descendent, has written to us. With the appearance of this volume, fans and scholars of Sherlock Holmes have much to be thankful for — and much to look forward to.

The Parodies

Sherlock Holmes first appeared in A STUDY IN SCARLET *and* THE SIGN OF THE FOUR, *two novels published in 1887 and 1890. During 1891–93 his adventures ran in the* STRAND *magazine in England and various publications in the United States.*

Holmes's unprecedented popularity wearied his creator, who preferred to make his mark with a series of heavily-researched historical novels such as MICAH CLARKE, THE WHITE COMPANY, *and* THE REFUGEES. *"I think of slaying Holmes," Arthur Conan Doyle wrote his mother as early as November 1891, "and winding him up for good."*

"You won't!" the horrified woman wrote back, presaging the anguish of Holmes's followers the world over. "You can't! You mustn't!"

But he did. In the December 1893 issues of the STRAND *and* McCLURE'S, *he laid Sherlock Holmes to rest beneath the "dreadful cauldron" of Reichenbach Falls and got on with other things.*

The decision was final, he assured the hordes of questioners. There would be no more of Sherlock Holmes.

Conventional wisdom has it that he finally relented with THE HOUND OF THE BASKERVILLES, *which ended its serialization in the* STRAND *and came out in book form in 1901. In truth his resolve failed much earlier, if only fleetingly, when he wrote "The Field Bazaar" for* THE STUDENT *of November 1896.*

THE STUDENT *was the undergraduate magazine of Edinburgh University, Doyle's own* alma mater. *The circumstances in which it was composed were precisely those described in "The Field Bazaar" itself. The humour of the piece is so gentle that it is barely parody at all—and so affectionate as to belie forever the notion that Doyle had come to hate his famous detective.*

Twenty-five years later he was asked to contribute his talents to another worthy project—though one of considerably different

3

scale. He received a personally-written letter from Princess Marie Louise, asking him to participate in the creation of the library of the Queen's Dolls' House.

The Queen's Dolls' House was conceived in 1920 as a gift from the British people to Her Majesty Queen Anne, wife of King George V, to be presented as "a token or symbol of national goodwill realized through the generous workmanship of many hands." Designed by Sir Edwin Lutyens, who had previously been the chief architect of the city of New Delhi, it was "a model twentieth-century residence, to the exact scale of one inch to the foot, and as complete and perfect in every detail as British art and craftsmanship could make it."

When finished four years later, the miniature mansion measured 100 by 62 inches by 39 inches in height and had been designed and decorated in extraordinary beauty. "The human note is never forgotten," though,. THE TIMES reported in May 1924. The electric lights worked, every water tap and kitchen drain functioned. "In a manservant's bedroom, equipped simply but adequately, there is also the essential trouser press! And it works! . . . On [the Queen's] dressing table are all the brushes and other equipment necessary for the adornment of beauty. . . . The King has tiny sporting guns which fire real cartridges. The jam-pots in the kitchen are filled with real jam, and the bottles in the cellar enclose vintage wine. In the garage are five cars perfect in scale. Their petrol consumption—for the envy of full-grown people—is twenty thousand miles to the gallon."

Even in the midst of all this artistry, the library stood out. Here were found diminutive sculptures and hung postage-stamp-sized paintings done expressly for the Queen's Dolls' House by British masters. A collection had been assembled of a number of the novelty "tiny books" already existing. WHO'S WHO, WHITAKER'S ALMANACK, *railway guides, and a selection of popular magazines had been photographically reduced to the dimensions—about one-and-a-half by two inches—of the house.*

But the majority of the books in the library, some two hundred of them, were "diminutive editions of manuscript from the hands of living authors," the result of Princess Marie Louise's letters. "The authors were asked to. contribute, in [previously-prepared] volumes of appropriately small dimensions, some of their work: either an original composition for the occasion, or a passage from their already published works which seemed to them worthy of being thus perpetuated," wrote Stephen Gaselee in THE BOOK OF THE QUEEN'S DOLLS' HOUSE LIBRARY. *They responded willingly, and little hand-written books were prepared by the likes of Rudyard Kipling, Thomas Hardy, Anthony Hope, Joseph Conrad, J. M. Barrie, G. K. Chesterton, Clemence Dane, Somerset Maugham, May Sinclair—and, of course, Sir Arthur Conan Doyle.*

Doyle chose to write an original Sherlock Holmes parody which he titled "How Watson Learned the Trick," a pleasant spoof of those powers of observation and deduction which had by then become universally famous. It was published in THE BOOK OF THE QUEEN'S DOLLS' HOUSE LIBRARY *in 1924, in a limited edition of 1500 copies, and has been reprinted in various periodicals over the years.*

The third piece in this section was written not by Doyle but by J. M. Barrie, the creator of PETER PAN. *It deserves inclusion nonetheless, for Doyle called it "the best of all the numerous parodies" on Holmes and thought so much of it that he gave it the place of legitimacy by including it in his autobiography,* MEMORIES AND ADVENTURES.

Barrie was probably Doyle's closest "literary" friend. They met in the early 1890s, when as emerging young writers they both played on the cricket team of THE IDLER, *a self-indulgent little magazine for and about the world of English letters. Barrie had recently achieved acclaim with* AULD LICHT IDYLLS, *a whimsical volume of sketches of Scottish village life, and Doyle was basking under the double suns of* THE WHITE COMPANY *and the Sherlock Holmes stories then running in the* STRAND.

The two Scotsmen made a curious pair—"a fir tree and a pencil," one writer described them—Barrie small, delicate, and dapper, Doyle burly and jovial. Anthony Hope, who was to write THE PRISONER OF ZENDA *and was another of* THE IDLER'S *circle, complained that Doyle had the best of two worlds: he not only wrote good books but he looked as if he'd never even read one. Barrie, on the other hand, was the very type of the effete littérateur.*

But when Barrie was commissioned by Richard D'Oyley Carte to write a comic opera libretto and found himself unable to complete the work, it was to Conan Doyle he appealed. Doyle journeyed up to Suffolk, where his friend was lying ill from a combination of bronchitis and nervous exhaustion, and agreed to finish up the dialogue and lyrics for the last half of the play. He had already resolved to kill Sherlock Holmes off in the STRAND *and was looking for new worlds to conquer. He barged into theatrical life with all the good-natured bluster he brought to everything he did.*

So JANE ANNIE; OR, THE GOOD CONDUCT PRIZE, *with music by Ernest Ford, opened at the Savoy Theatre on 13 May 1893. It was an utter disaster. There was not a witty line nor a memorable tune in the whole dismal show, and it has been forgotten except by the few students of theatrical history who amuse themselves at trying to guess which author was responsible for which bit of errant humour. The great mystery seems to be how* JANE ANNIE *lasted a full seven weeks before closing forever.*

It was one of the few failures either of them ever experienced, but it was a bitter blow at the time. "We were well abused by the critics," Doyle recalled in his autobiography, "but Barrie took it all in the bravest spirit," sending Doyle "The Adventure of the Two Collaborators," written on the flyleaves of one of his books, as a token of his "debonnaire courage."

Neither their careers nor their friendship suffered because of JANE ANNIE, *and some years later, according to* MEMORIES AND ADVENTURES, *it was a chance remark of Doyle's, concerning a strange dream he had had, which inspired Barrie's masterpiece,* THE ADMIRABLE CRICHTON.

The Field Bazaar

"I should certainly do it," said Sherlock Holmes.

I started at the interruption, for my companion had been eating his breakfast with his attention entirely centred upon the paper which was propped up by the coffee pot. Now I looked across at him to find his eyes fastened upon me with the half-amused, half-questioning expression which he usually assumed when he felt that he had made an intellectual point.

"Do what?" I asked.

He smiled as he took his slipper from the mantelpiece and drew from it enough shag tobacco to fill the old clay pipe with which he invariably rounded off his breakfast.

"A most characteristic question of yours, Watson," said he. "You will not, I am sure, be offended if I say that any reputation for sharpness which I may possess has been entirely gained by the admirable foil which you have made for me. Have I not heard of debutantes who have insisted upon plainness in their chaperones? There is a certain analogy."

Our long companionship in the Baker Street rooms had left us on those easy terms of intimacy when much may be said without offence. And yet I acknowledge that I was nettled at his remark.

"I may be very obtuse," said I, "but I confess that I am unable to see how you have managed to know that I was. . .I was. . ."

"Asked to help in the Edinburgh University Bazaar."

"Precisely. The letter has only just come to hand, and I have not spoken to you since."

"In spite of that," said Holmes, leaning back in his chair and putting his finger tips together, "I would even venture to suggest that the object of the bazaar is to enlarge the University cricket field."

I looked at him in such bewilderment that he vibrated with silent laughter.

7

"The fact is, my dear Watson, that you are an excellent subject," said he. "You are never *blasé*. You respond instantly to any external stimulus. Your mental processes may be slow but they are never obscure, and I found during breakfast that you were easier reading than the leader in the *Times* in front of me."

"I should be glad to know how you arrived at your conclusions," said I.

"I fear that my good nature in giving explanations has seriously compromised my reputation," said Holmes. "But in this case the train of reasoning is based upon such obvious facts that no credit can be claimed for it. You entered the room with a thoughtful expression, the expression of a man who is debating some point in his mind. In your hand you held a solitary letter. Now last night you retired in the best of spirits, so it was clear that it was this letter in your hand which had caused the change in you."

"This is obvious."

"It is all obvious when it is explained to you. I naturally asked myself what the letter could contain which might have this effect upon you. As you walked you held the flap side of the envelope towards me, and I saw upon it the same shield-shaped device which I have observed upon your old college cricket cap. It was clear, then, that the request came from Edinburgh University — or from some club connected with the University. When you reached the table you laid down the letter beside your plate with the address uppermost, and you walked over to look at the framed photograph upon the left of the mantelpiece."

It amazed me to see the accuracy with which he had observed my movements. "What next?" I asked.

"I began by glancing at the address, and I could tell, even at the distance of six feet, that it was an unofficial communication. This I gathered from the use of the word 'Doctor' upon the address, to which, as a Bachelor of Medicine, you have no legal claim. I knew that University officials are pedantic in their correct use of titles, and I was thus enabled to say with certainty that your letter was unofficial. When on your return to the table you turned over your letter and allowed me to perceive that the enclosure was a printed one, the idea of a bazaar first occurred to me. I had already weighed the possibility of its being a political communication, but this seemed improbable in the present stagnant conditions of politics.

"When you returned to the table your face still retained its expression and it was evident that your examination of the photograph had not changed the current of your thoughts. In that case it must itself bear upon the subject in question. I turned my attention to the photograph, therefore, and saw at once that it consisted of yourself as a member of the Edinburgh University Eleven, with the pavilion and cricket-field in the background. My small experience of cricket clubs has taught me that next to churches and cavalry ensigns they are the most debt-laden things upon earth. When upon your return to the table I saw you take out your pencil and draw lines upon the envelope, I was convinced that you were endeavouring to realise some projected improvement which was to be brought about by a bazaar. Your face still showed some indecision, so that I was able to break in upon you with my advice that you should assist in so good an object."

I could not help smiling at the extreme simplicity of his explanation.

"Of course, it was as easy as possible," said I.

My remark appeared to nettle him.

"I may add," said he, "that the particular help which you have been asked to give was that you should write in their album, and that you have already made up your mind that the present incident will be the subject of your article."

"But how—!" I cried.

"It is as easy as possible," said he, "and I leave its solution to your own ingenuity. In the meantime," he added, raising his paper, "you will excuse me if I return to this very interesting article upon the trees of Cremona, and the exact reasons for their pre-eminence in the manufacture of violins. It is one of those small outlying problems to which I am sometimes tempted to direct my attention."

How Watson Learned the Trick

Watson had been watching his companion intently ever since he had sat down to the breakfast table. Holmes happened to look up and catch his eye.

"Well, Watson, what are you thinking about?" he asked.

"About you."

"Me?"

"Yes, Holmes, I was thinking how superficial are these tricks of yours, and how wonderful it is that the public should continue to show interest in them."

"I quite agree," said Holmes. "In fact, I have a recollection that I have myself made a similar remark."

"Your methods," said Watson severely, "are really easily acquired."

"No doubt," Holmes answered with a smile. "Perhaps you will yourself give an example of this method of reasoning."

"With pleasure," said Watson. "I am able to say that you were greatly preoccupied when you got up this morning."

"Excellent!" said Holmes. "How could you possibly know that?"

"Because you are usually a very tidy man and yet you have forgotten to shave."

"Dear me! How very clever!" said Holmes. "I had no idea, Watson, that you were so apt a pupil. Has your eagle eye detected anything more?"

"Yes, Holmes. You have a client named Barlow, and you have not been successful in his case."

"Dear me, how could you know that?"

"I saw the name outside his envelope. When you opened it you gave a groan and thrust it into your pocket with a frown on your face."

"Admirable! You are indeed observant. Any other points?"

"I fear, Holmes, that you have taken to financial speculation."

"How *could* you tell that, Watson?"

"You opened the paper, turned to the financial page, and gave a loud exclamation of interest."

"Well, that is very clever of you, Watson. Any more?"

"Yes, Holmes, you have put on your black coat, instead of your dressing gown, which proves that you are expecting some important visitor at once."

"Anything more?"

"I have no doubt that I could find other points, Holmes, but I only give you these few, in order to show you that there are other people in the world who can be as clever as you."

"And some not so clever," said Holmes. "I admit that they are few, but I am afraid, my dear Watson, that I must count you among them."

"What do you mean, Holmes?"

"Well, my dear fellow, I fear your deductions have not been so happy as I should have wished."

"You mean that I was mistaken."

"Just a little that way, I fear. Let us take the points in their order: I did not shave because I have sent my razor to be sharpened. I put on my coat because I have, worse luck, an early meeting with my dentist. His name is Barlow, and the letter was to confirm the appointment. The cricket page is beside the financial one, and I turned to it to find if Surrey was holding its own against Kent. But go on, Watson, go on! It's a very superficial trick, and no doubt you will soon acquire it."

The Adventure of
the Two Collaborators
by J. M. Barrie

In bringing to a close the adventures of my friend Sherlock Holmes I am perforce reminded that he never, save on the occasion which, as you will now hear, brought his singular career to an end, consented to act in any mystery which was concerned with persons who made a livelihood by their pen. "I am not particular about the people I mix among for business purposes," he would say, "but at literary characters I draw the line."

We were in our rooms in Baker Street one evening. I was (I remember) by the centre table writing out "The Adventure of the Man without a Cork Leg" (which had so puzzled the Royal Society and all the other scientific bodies of Europe), and Holmes was amusing himself with a little revolver practice. It was his custom of a summer evening to fire round my head, just shaving my face, until he had made a photograph of me on the opposite wall, and it is a slight proof of his skill that many of these portraits in pistol shots are considered admirable likenesses.

I happened to look out of the window, and perceiving two gentlemen advancing rapidly along Baker Street asked him who they were. He immediately lit his pipe, and, twisting himself on a chair into the figure 8, replied:

"They are two collaborators in comic opera, and their play has not been a triumph."

I sprang from my chair to the ceiling in amazement, and he then explained:

"My dear Watson, they are obviously men who follow some low calling. That much even you should be able to read in their faces. Those little pieces of blue paper which they fling angrily from them are Durrant's Press Notices. Of these they have obviously hundreds about their person (see how their pockets bulge). They would not dance on them if they were pleasant reading."

I again sprang to the ceiling (which is much dented), and shouted: "Amazing! but they may be mere authors."

"No," said Holmes, "for mere authors only get one press notice a week. Only criminals, dramatists and actors get them by the hundred."

"Then they may be actors."

"No, actors would come in a carriage."

"Can you tell me anything else about them?"

"A great deal. From the mud on the boots of the tall one I perceive that he comes from South Norwood. The other is as obviously a Scotch author."

"How can you tell that?"

"He is carrying in his pocket a book called (I clearly see) 'Auld Licht Something.' Would any one but the author be likely to carry about a book with such a title?"

I had to confess that this was improbable.

It was now evident that the two men (if such they can be called) were seeking our lodgings. I have said (often) that my friend Holmes seldom gave way to emotion of any kind, but he now turned livid with passion. Presently this gave place to a strange look of triumph.

"Watson," he said, "that big fellow has for years taken the credit for my most remarkable doings, but at last I have him — at last!"

Up I went to the ceiling, and when I returned the strangers were in the room.

"I perceive, gentlemen," said Mr. Sherlock Holmes, "that you are at present afflicted by an extraordinary novelty."

The handsomer of our visitors asked in amazement how he knew this, but the big one only scowled.

"You forget that you wear a ring on your fourth finger," replied Mr. Holmes calmly.

I was about to jump to the ceiling when the big brute interposed.

"That Tommy-rot is all very well for the public, Holmes," said he, "but you can drop it before me. And, Watson, if you go up to the ceiling again I shall make you stay there."

Here I observed a curious phenomenon. My friend Sherlock Holmes *shrank*. He became small before my eyes. I looked longingly at the ceiling, but dared not.

"Let us cut the first four pages," said the big man, "and proceed to business. I want to know why—"

"Allow me," said Mr. Holmes, with some of his old courage. "You want to know why the public does not go to your opera."

"Exactly," said the other ironically, "as you perceive by my shirt stud." He added more gravely, "And as you can only find out in one way I must insist on your witnessing an entire performance of the piece."

It was an anxious moment for me. I shuddered, for I knew that if Holmes went I should have to go with him. But my friend had a heart of gold. "Never," he cried fiercely, "I will do anything for you save that."

"Your continued existence depends on it," said the big man menacingly.

"I would rather melt into air," replied Holmes, proudly taking another chair. "But I can tell you why the public don't go to your piece without sitting the thing out myself."

"Why?"

"Because," replied Holmes calmly, "they prefer to stay away."

A dead silence followed that extraordinary remark. For a moment the two intruders gazed with awe upon the man who had unravelled their mystery so wonderfully. Then drawing their knives—

Holmes grew less and less, until nothing was left save a ring of smoke which slowly circled to the ceiling.

The last words of great men are often noteworthy. These were the last words of Sherlock Holmes: "Fool, fool! I have kept you in luxury for years. By my help you have ridden extensively in cabs, where no author was ever seen before. *Henceforth you will ride in buses!*"

The brute sunk into a chair aghast.

The other author did not turn a hair.

>   *To A. Conan Doyle,*
>   *from his friend*
>   *J. M. Barrie.*

The Stories of Mystery

Conan Doyle never regretted doing away with Holmes. Neither did his popular appeal seem to suffer as a result.

He was the creator and chief practitioner of a wholly new kind of magazine fiction—the series of self-contained short stories featuring a single character—which he had invented for Sherlock Holmes and which had supplanted the serialized novel, in the STRAND *at least, as the dominant fictional form. Now he wrote a historical novel in this episodic form—*RODNEY STONE, *about prizefighting life in Regency England—which also ran in the* STRAND. *For the same magazine he created Brigadier Gerard, a cavalry officer in Napoleon's army, "who thought so much of himself, but still more of this Emperor," and whose exploits appeared off and on for fifteen years.*

In 1898 he began a new variation on this technique. He conceived the ROUND THE FIRE *stories as twelve tales, unrelated except for their shared themes of the bizarre and mysterious, which would appear from the beginning under a common title. Two of the stories in this "planned anthology" were "The Man with the Watches" and "The Lost Special."*

In them Doyle gently abused his great detective by having an unnamed "amateur reasoner of some celebrity" present a solution to each mystery which turned out to be completely in error. The logical progressions, the familiar catch-phrases, the "condescending didacticism" made it obvious that the author of these letters to the London newspapers was intended to be none other than Sherlock Holmes—and it is equally apparent that "one of the acutest brains in England," who conceived the insoluble riddle of "The Lost Special," was Professor Moriarty. This was made much of by Edgar W. Smith, for many years the guiding spirit of the Baker Street Irregulars, the national society of Holmes devotees, and founder in 1949 of the BAKER STREET JOURNAL.

"The Man with the Watches" and "The Lost Special," Smith argued, should be "subsumed" into the official Sherlock Holmes Canon. His agitation, however, came to little. They had both been published in the ROUND THE FIRE STORIES *in 1908, not in any of the Holmes collections. Doyle himself had never considered them part of the "complete" Sherlock Holmes any more than he had "The Field Bazaar" or "How Watson Learned the Trick." Other Sherlockians wrote to refute Smith's claims with equally facile counter-arguments, and after his death in 1960 the whole good-humoured controversy blew over.*

Herewith their Apocryphal nature is re-asserted. The two stories' real significance, it would seem, is their appearance in the STRAND *for July and August 1898. Nearly five years after "The Final Problem" and the supposed death of his detective creation, Conan Doyle could still neither forget Sherlock Holmes nor even resist the urge to write about him.*

The Man with the Watches

There are many who will still bear in mind the singular circumstances which, under the heading of the Rugby Mystery, filled many columns of the daily Press in the spring of the year 1892. Coming as it did at a period of exceptional dulness, it attracted perhaps rather more attention than it deserved, but it offered to the public that mixture of the whimsical and the tragic which is most stimulating to the popular imagination. Interest drooped, however, when, after weeks of fruitless investigation, it was found that no final explanation of the facts was forthcoming, and the tragedy seemed from that time to the present to have finally taken its place in the dark catalogue of inexplicable and unexpiated crimes. A recent communication (the authenticity of which appears to be above question) has, however, thrown some new and clear light upon the matter. Before laying it before the public it would be as well, perhaps, that I should refresh their memories as to the singular facts upon which this commentary is founded. These facts were briefly as follows: —

At five o'clock upon the evening of the 18th of March in the year already mentioned a train left Euston Station for Manchester. It was a rainy, squally day, which grew wilder as it progressed, so it was by no means the weather in which anyone would travel who was not driven to do so by necessity. The train, however, is a favourite one among Manchester business men who are returning from town, for it does the journey in four hours and twenty minutes, with only three stoppages upon the way. In spite of the inclement evening it was, therefore, fairly well filled upon the occasion of which I speak. The guard of the train was a tried servant of the company—a man who had worked for twenty-two years without blemish or complaint. His name was John Palmer.

The station clock was upon the stroke of five, and the guard was about to give the customary signal to the engine-driver, when he

19

observed two belated passengers hurrying down the platform. The one was an exceptionally tall man, dressed in a long black overcoat with an astrakhan collar and cuffs. I have already said that the evening was an inclement one, and the tall traveller had the high, warm collar turned up to protect his throat against the bitter March wind. He appeared, as far as the guard could judge by so hurried an inspection, to be a man between fifty and sixty years of age, who had retained a good deal of the vigour and activity of his youth. In one hand he carried a brown leather Gladstone bag. His companion was a lady, tall and erect, walking with a vigorous step which outpaced the gentleman beside her. She wore a long, fawn-coloured dust-cloak, a black, close-fitting toque, and a dark veil which concealed the greater part of her face. The two might very well have passed as father and daughter. They walked swiftly down the line of carriages, glancing in at the windows, until the guard, John Palmer, overtook them.

"Now, then, sir, look sharp, the train is going," said he.

"First-class," the man answered.

The guard turned the handle of the nearest door. In the carriage, which he had opened, there sat a small man with a cigar in his mouth. His appearance seems to have impressed itself upon the guard's memory, for he was prepared, afterwards, to describe or to identify him. He was a man of thirty-four or thirty-five years of age, dressed in some grey material, sharp nosed, alert, with a ruddy, weather-beaten face, and a small, closely cropped black beard. He glanced up as the door was opened. The tall man paused with his foot upon the step.

"This is a smoking compartment. The lady dislikes smoke," said he, looking round at the guard.

"All right! Here you are, sir!" said John Palmer. He slammed the door of the smoking carriage, opened that of the next one, which was empty, and thrust the two travellers in. At the same instant he sounded his whistle, and the wheels of the train began to move. The man with the cigar was at the window of his carriage, and said something to the guard as he rolled past him, but the words were lost in the bustle of the departure. Palmer stepped into the guard's van as it came up to him, and thought no more of the incident.

Twelve minutes after its departure the train reached Willesden Junction, where it stopped for a very short interval. An examination of the tickets has made it certain that no one either joined or left it at this time, and no passenger was seen to alight upon the platform. At 5.14 the journey to Manchester was resumed, and Rugby was reached at 6.50, the express being five minutes late.

At Rugby the attention of the station officials was drawn to the fact that the door of one of the first-class carriages was open. An examination of that compartment, and of its neighbour, disclosed a remarkable state of affairs.

The smoking carriage, in which the short, red-faced man with the black beard had been seen was now empty. Save for a half-smoked cigar, there was no trace whatever of its recent occupant. The door of this carriage was fastened. In the next compartment, to which attention had been originally drawn, there was no sign either of the gentleman with the astrakhan collar or of the young lady who accompanied him. All three passengers had disappeared. On the other hand, there was found upon the floor of this carriage —the one in which the tall traveller and the lady had been—a young man, fashionably dressed and of elegant appearance. He lay with his knees drawn up, and his head resting against the further door, an elbow upon either seat. A bullet had penetrated his heart, and his death must have been instantaneous. No one had seen such a man enter the train, and no railway ticket was found in his pocket, nor were there any markings upon his linen, nor papers which might help to identify him. Who he was, whence he had come, and how he had met his end were each as great a mystery as what had occurred to the three people who had started an hour and a half before from Willesden in those two compartments.

I have said that there was no personal property which might help to identify him, but it is true that there was one peculiarity about this unknown young man which was much commented upon at the time. In his pockets were found no fewer than six valuable gold watches, three in the various pockets of his waistcoat, one in his ticket-pocket, and one small one set in a leather strap and fastened round his left wrist. The obvious explanation that the man was a pick-pocket, and that this was his plunder, was discounted by the fact that all six were of American make, and of a type which is rare in England. Three of them bore the mark of the Rochester Watchmaking Company; one was by Mason, of Elmira; one was unmarked; and the small one, which was highly jewelled and ornamented, was from Tiffany, of New York. The other contents of his pocket consisted of an ivory knife with a corkscrew by Rodgers, of Sheffield; a small circular mirror, one inch in diameter; a re-admission slip to the Lyceum theatre; a silver box full of vesta matches, and a brown leather cigar-case containing two cheroots—also two pounds fourteen shillings in money. It was clear then that whatever motives may have led to his death, robbery was not among them. As already mentioned, there were no markings upon the man's linen, which appeared to be new, and no tailor's name upon his coat. In appearance he was young, short, smooth cheeked, and delicately featured. One of his front teeth was conspicuously stopped with gold.

On the discovery of the tragedy an examination was instantly made of the tickets of all passengers, and the number of the passengers themselves was counted. It was found that only three tickets were unaccounted for, corresponding to the three travellers who were missing. The express was then allowed to proceed, but a new guard was sent with it, and John Palmer was detained as a witness at Rugby. The carriage which included the two compartments in question was uncoupled and side-tracked. Then, on the arrival of Inspector Vane, of Scotland Yard, and of Mr. Henderson, a detective in the service of the railway company, an exhaustive inquiry was made into all the circumstances.

That crime had been committed was certain. The bullet, which appeared to have come from a small pistol or revolver, had been fired from some little distance, as there was no scorching of the clothes. No weapon was found in the compartment (which finally disposed of the theory of suicide), nor was there any sign of the brown leather bag which the guard has seen in the hand of the tall gentleman. A lady's parasol was found upon the rack, but no other trace was to be seen of the travellers in either of the sections. Apart from the crime, the question of how or why three passengers (one of them a lady) could get out of the train, and one other get in during the unbroken run between Willesden and Rugby, was one which excited the utmost curiosity among the general public, and gave rise to much speculation in the London Press.

John Palmer, the guard, was able at the inquest to give some evidence which threw a little light upon the matter. There was a spot between Tring and Cheddington, according to his statement, where, on account of some repairs to the line, the train had for a few minutes slowed down to a pace not exceeding eight or ten miles an hour. At that place it might be possible for a man, or even for an exceptionally active woman, to have left the train without serious injury. It was true that a gang of platelayers was there, and that they had seen nothing, but it was their custom to stand in the middle between the metals, and the open carriage door was upon the far side, so that it was conceivable that someone might have alighted unseen, as the darkness would by that time be drawing in. A steep embankment would instantly screen anyone who sprang out from the observation of the navvies.

The guard also deposed that there was a good deal of movement upon the platform at Willesden Junction, and that though it was certain that no one had either joined or left the train there, it was still quite possible that some of the passengers might have changed unseen from one compartment to another. It was by no means uncommon for a gentleman to finish his cigar in a smoking carriage and then to change to a clearer atmosphere. Supposing that the man with the black beard had done so at Willesden (and the half-smoked cigar upon the floor seemed to favour the supposition), he would naturally go into the nearest section, which would bring him into the company of the two other actors in this drama. Thus the first stage of the affair might be surmised without any great breach of probability. But what the second stage had been, or how the final one had been arrived at, neither the guard nor the experienced detective officers could suggest.

A careful examination of the line between Willesden and Rugby resulted in one discovery which might or might not have a bearing upon the tragedy. Near Tring, at the very place where the train slowed down, there was found at the bottom of the embankment a small pocket Testament, very shabby and worn. It was printed by the Bible Society of London, and bore an inscription: "From John to Alice. Jan. 13th, 1856," upon the fly-leaf. Underneath was written: "James. July 4th, 1859," and beneath that again: "Edward. Nov. 1st, 1869," all the entries being in the same handwriting. This was the only clue, if it could be called a clue, which the police obtained, and the coroner's verdict of "Murder by a person or persons unknown" was the unsatisfactory ending of a singular case. Advertisement, rewards, and inquiries proved equally fruitless, and nothing could be found which was solid enough to form the basis for a profitable investigation.

It would be a mistake, however, to suppose that no theories were formed to account for the facts. On the contrary, the Press, both in England and in America, teemed with suggestions and suppositions, most of which were obviously absurd. The fact that the watches were of American make, and some peculiarities in connection with the gold stopping of his front tooth, appeared to indicate that the deceased was a citizen of the United States, though his linen, clothes, and boots were undoubtedly of British manufacture. It was surmised, by some, that he was concealed under the seat, and that, being discovered, he was for some reason, possibly because he had overheard their guilty secrets, put to death by his fellow-passengers. When coupled with generalities as to the ferocity and cunning of anarchical and other secret societies, this theory sounded as plausible as any.

The fact that he should be without a ticket would be consistent with the idea of concealment, and it was well known that women played a prominent part in the Nihilistic propaganda. On the other hand, it was clear, from the guard's statement, that the man must have been hidden there *before* the others arrived, and how unlikely the coincidence that conspirators should stray exactly into the very compartment in which a spy was already concealed! Besides, this explanation ignored the man in the smoking carriage, and gave no reason at all for his simultaneous disappearance. The police had little difficulty in showing that such a theory would not cover the facts, but they were unprepared in the absence of evidence to advance any alternative explanation.

There was a letter in the *Daily Gazette*, over the signature of a well-known criminal investigator, which gave rise to considerable discussion at the time. He had formed a hypothesis which had at least ingenuity to recommend it, and I cannot do better than append it in his own words.

"Whatever may be the truth," said he, "it must depend upon some bizarre and rare combination of events, so we need have no hesitation in postulating such events in our explanation. In the absence of data we must abandon the analytic or scientific method of investigation, and must approach it in the synthetic fashion. In a word, instead of taking known events and deducing from them what has occurred, we must build up a fanciful explanation if it will only be consistent with known events. We can then test this explanation by any fresh facts which may arise. If they all fit into their places, the probability is that we are upon the right track, and with each fresh fact this probability increases in a geometrical progression until the evidence becomes final and convincing.

"Now, there is one most remarkable and suggestive fact which has not met with the attention which it deserves. There is a local train running through Harrow and King's Langley, which is timed in such a way that the express must have overtaken it at or about the period when it eased down its speed to eight miles an hour on account of the repairs on the line. The two trains would at that time be travelling in the same direction at a similar rate of speed and upon parallel lines. It is within everyone's experience how, under such circumstances, the occupant of each carriage can see very plainly the passengers in the other carriages opposite to him. The lamps of the express had been lit at Willesden, so that each compartment was brightly illuminated, and most visible to an observer from outside.

"Now, the sequence of events as I reconstruct them would be after this fashion. This young man with the abnormal number of watches was alone in the carriage of the slow train. His ticket, with his papers and gloves and other things, was, we will suppose, on the seat beside him. He was probably an American, and also probably a man of weak intellect. The excessive wearing of jewellery is an early symptom in some forms of mania.

"As he sat watching the carriages of the express which were (on account of the state of the line) going at the same pace as himself, he suddenly saw some people in it whom he knew. We will suppose for the sake of our theory that these people were a woman whom he loved and man whom he hated—and who in return hated him. This young man was excitable and impulsive. He opened the door of his carriage, stepped from the footboard of the local train to the footboard of the express, opened the other door, and made his way into the presence of these two people. The feat (on the supposition that the trains were going at the same pace) is by no means so perilous as it might appear.

"Having now got our young man without his ticket into the carriage in which the elder man and the young woman are travelling, it is not difficult to imagine that a violent scene ensued. It is possible that the pair were also Americans, which is the more probable as the man carried a weapon—an unusual thing in England. If our supposition of incipient mania is correct, the young man is likely to have assaulted the other. As the upshot of the quarrel the elder man shot the intruder, and then made his escape from the carriage, taking the young lady with him. We will suppose that all this happened very rapidly, and that the train was still going at so slow a pace that it was not difficult for them to leave it. A woman might leave a train going at eight miles an hour. As a matter of fact, we know that this woman *did* do so.

"And now we have to fit in the man in the smoking carriage. Presuming that we have, up to this point, reconstructed the tragedy correctly, we shall find nothing in this other man to cause us to reconsider our conclusions. According to my theory, this man saw the young fellow cross from one train to the other, saw him open the door, heard the pistol-shot, saw the two fugitives spring out on to the line, realized that murder had been done, and sprang out himself in pursuit. Why he has never been heard of since—whether he met his own death in the pursuit, or whether, as is more likely, he was made to realize that it was not a case for his interference—is a detail which we have at present no means of explaining. I acknowledge that there are some difficulties in the way. At first sight, it might seem improbable that at such a moment, a murderer would burden himself in his flight with a brown leather bag. My answer is that he was well aware that if the bag were found his identity would be established. It was absolutely necessary for him to take it with him. My theory stands or falls upon one point, and I call upon the railway company to make strict inquiry as to whether a ticket was found unclaimed in the local train through Harrow and King's Langley upon the 18th of March. If such a ticket were found my case is proved. If not, my theory may still be the correct one, for it is conceivable either that he travelled without a ticket or that his ticket was lost."

To this elaborate and plausible hypothesis the answer of the police and of the company was, first, that no such ticket was found; secondly, that the slow train would never run parallel to the express; and, thirdly, that the local train had been stationary in King's Langley Station when the express, going at fifty miles an hour, had flashed past it. So perished the only satisfying explanation, and five years have elapsed without supplying a new one. Now, at last, there comes a statement which covers all the facts, and which must be regarded as authentic. It took the shape of a letter dated from New York, and addressed to the same criminal investigator whose theory I have quoted. It is given here in extenso, with the exception of the two opening paragraphs, which are personal in their nature: —

"You'll excuse me if I am not very free with names. There's less reason now than there was five years ago when mother was still living. But for all that, I had rather cover up our tracks all I can. But I owe you an explanation, for if your idea of it was wrong, it was a mighty ingenious one all the same. I'll have to go back a little so as you may understand all about it.

"My people came from Bucks, England, and emigrated to the States in the early fifties. They settled in Rochester, in the State of New York, where my father ran a large dry goods store. There were only two sons: myself, James, and my brother Edward. I was ten years older than my brother, and after my father died I sort of took the place of a father to him, as an elder brother would. He was a bright, spirited boy, and just one of the most beautiful creatures that ever lived. But there was always a soft spot in him, and it was like mold in cheese, for it spread and spread, and nothing that you could do would stop it. Mother saw it just as clearly as I did, but she went on spoiling him all the same, for he had such a way with him that you could refuse him nothing. I did all I could to hold him in, and he hated me for my pains.

"At last he fairly got his head, and nothing that we could do would stop him. He got off into New York, and went rapidly from bad to worse. At first he was only fast, and then he was criminal; and then, at the end of a year or two, he was one of the most notorious young crooks in the city. He had formed a friendship with Sparrow MacCoy, who was at the head of his profession as a bunco-steerer, green goodsman, and general rascal. They took to card-sharping, and frequented some of the best hotels in New York. My brother was an excellent actor (he might have made an honest name for himself if he had chosen), and he would take the parts of a young Englishman of title, of a simple lad from the West, or of a college undergraduate, whichever suited Sparrow

MacCoy's purpose. And then one day he dressed himself as a girl, and he carried it off so well, and made himself such a valuable decoy, that it was their favorite game afterwards. They had made it right with Tammany and with the police, so it seemed as if nothing could ever stop them, for those were in the days before the Lexow Commission, and if you only had a pull, you could do pretty nearly anything you wanted.

"And nothing would have stopped them if they had only stuck to cards and New York, but they must needs come up Rochester way, and forge a name upon a check. It was my brother that did it, though everyone knew that it was under the influence of Sparrow MacCoy. I bought up that check, and a pretty sum it cost me. Then I went to my brother, laid it before him on the table, and swore to him that I would prosecute if he did not clear out of the country. At first he simply laughed. I could not prosecute, he said, without breaking our mother's heart, and he knew that I would not do that. I made him understand, however, that our mother's heart was being broken in any case, and that I had set firm on the point that I would rather see him in a Rochester gaol than in a New York hotel. So at last he gave in, and he made me a solemn promise that he would see Sparrow MacCoy no more, that he would go to Europe, and that he would turn his hand to any honest trade that I helped him to get. I took him down right away to an old family friend, Joe Willson, who is an exporter of American watches and clocks, and I got him to give Edward an agency in London, with a small salary and a 5 per cent. commission on all business. His manner and appearance were so good that he won the old man over at once, and within a week he was sent off to London with a case full of samples.

"It seemed to me that this business of the check had really given my brother a fright, and that there was some chance of his settling down into an honest line of life. My mother had spoken with him, and what she said had touched him, for she had always been the best of mothers to him, and he had been the great sorrow of her life. But I knew that this man Sparrow MacCoy had a great influence over Edward, and my chance of keeping the lad straight lay in breaking the connection between them. I had a friend in the New York detective force, and through him I kept a watch upon MacCoy. When within a fortnight of my brother's sailing I heard that MacCoy had taken a berth in the *Etruria,* I was as certain as if he had told me that he was going over to England for the purpose of coaxing Edward back again into the ways that he had left. In an instant I had resolved to go also, and to put my influence against MacCoy's. I knew it was a losing fight, but I thought, and my mother thought, that it was my duty. We passed the last night together in prayer for my success, and she gave me her own Testament that my father had given her on the day of their marriage in the Old Country, so that I might always wear it next my heart.

"I was a fellow-traveller, on the steamship, with Sparrow MacCoy, and at least I had the satisfaction of spoiling his little game for the voyage. The very first night I went into the smoking-room, and found him at the head of a card table, with half-a-dozen young fellows who were carrying their full purses and their empty skulls over to Europe. He was settling down for his harvest, and a rich one it would have been. But I soon changed all that.

" 'Gentlemen,' said I, 'are you aware whom you are playing with?'

" 'What's that to you? You mind your own business!' said he, with an oath.

" 'Who is it, anyway?' asked one of the dudes.

" 'He's Sparrow MacCoy, the most notorious card-sharper in the States.'

"Up he jumped with a bottle in his hand, but he remembered that he was under the flag of the effete Old Country, where law and order run, and Tammany has no pull. Gaol and the gallows wait for violence and murder, and there's no slipping out by the back door on board an ocean liner.

" 'Prove your words, you —— !' said he.

" 'I will!' said I. 'If you will turn up your right shirt-sleeve to the shoulder, I will either prove my words or I will eat them.'

"He turned white and said not a word. You see, I knew something of his ways, and I was aware that part of the mechanism which he and all such sharpers use consists of an elastic down the arm with a clip just above the wrist. It is by means of this clip that they withdraw from their hands the cards which they do not want, while they substitute other cards from another hiding-place. I reckoned on it being there, and it was. He cursed me, slunk out of the saloon, and was hardly seen again during the voyage. For once, at any rate, I got level with Mister Sparrow MacCoy.

"But he soon had his revenge upon me, for when it came to influencing my brother he outweighed me every time. Edward had kept himself straight in London for the first few weeks, and had done some business with his American watches, until this villain came across his path once more. I did my best, but the best was little enough. The next thing I heard there had been a scandal at one of the Northumberland Avenue hotels: a traveller had been fleeced of a large sum by two confederate card-sharpers, and the matter was in the hands of Scotland Yard. The first I learned of it was in the evening paper, and I was at once certain that my brother and MacCoy were back at their old games. I hurried at once to Edward's lodgings. They told me that he and a tall gentleman (whom I recognised as MacCoy) had gone off together, and that he had left the lodgings and taken his things with him. The landlady had heard them give several directions to the cabman, ending with Euston Station, and she had accidentally overheard the tall gentleman saying something about Manchester. She believed that that was their destination.

"A glance at the time-table showed me that the most likely train was at five, though there was another at 4.35 which they might have caught. I had only time to get the later one, but found no sign of them either at the depôt or in the train. They must have gone on by the earlier one, so I determined to follow them to Manchester and search for them in the hotels there. One last appeal to my brother by all that he owed to my mother might even now be the salvation of him. My nerves were overstrung, and I lit a cigar to steady them. At that moment, just as the train was moving off, the door of my compartment was flung open, and there were MacCoy and my brother on the platform.

"They were both disguised, and with good reason, for they knew that the London police were after them. MacCoy had a great astrakhan collar drawn up, so that only his eyes and nose were showing. My brother was dressed like a woman, with a black veil half down his face, but of course it did not deceive me for an instant, nor would it have done so even if I had not known that he had often used such a dress before. I started up, and as I did so MacCoy recognised me. He said something, the conductor slammed the door, and they were shown into the next compartment. I tried to stop the train so as to follow them, but the wheels were already moving, and it was too late.

"When we stopped at Willesden, I instantly changed my carriage. It appears that I was not seen to do so, which is not surprising, as the station was crowded with people. MacCoy, of course, was expecting me, and he had spent the time between Euston and Willesden in saying all he could to harden my brother's heart and set him against me. That is what I fancy, for I had never found him so impossible to soften or to move. I tried this way and I tried that; I pictured his future in an English gaol; I described the sorrow of his mother when I came back with the news; I said everything to touch his heart, but all to no purpose. He sat there with a fixed sneer upon his handsome face, while every now and then Sparrow MacCoy would throw in a taunt at me, or some word of encouragement to hold my brother to his resolutions.

" 'Why don't you run a Sunday-school?' he would say to me, and then, in the same breath: 'He thinks you have no will of your own. He thinks you are just the baby brother and that he can lead you where he likes. He's only just finding out that you are a man as well as he.'

"It was those words of his which set me talking bitterly. We had left Willesden, you understand, for all this took some time. My temper got the better of me, and for the first time in my life I let my brother see the rough side of me. Perhaps it would have been better had I done so earlier and more often.

" 'A man!' said I. 'Well, I'm glad to have your friend's assurance of it, for no one would suspect it to see you like a boarding-school missy. I don't suppose in all this country there is a more contemptible-looking creature than you are as you sit there with that Dolly pinafore upon you.' He coloured up at that, for he was a vain man, and he winced from ridicule.

" 'It's only a dust-cloak,' said he, and he slipped it off. 'One has to throw the coppers off one's scent, and I had no other way to do it.' He took his toque off with the veil attached, and he put both it and the cloak into his brown bag. 'Anyway, I don't need to wear it until the conductor comes round,' said he.

" 'Nor then either,' said I, and taking the bag I slung it with all my force out of the window. 'Now,' said I, 'you'll never make a Mary Jane of yourself while I can help it. If nothing but that disguise stands between you and a gaol, then to gaol you shall go.'

"That was the way to manage him. I felt my advantage at once. His supple nature was one which yielded to roughness far more readily than to entreaty. He flushed with shame, and his eyes filled with tears. But MacCoy saw my advantage also, and was determined that I should not pursue it.

" 'He's my pard, and you shall not bully him,' he cried.

" 'He's my brother, and you shall not ruin him,' said I. 'I believe a spell of prison is the very best way of keeping you apart, and you shall have it, or it will be no fault of mine.'

" 'Oh, you would squeal, would you?' he cried, and in an instant he whipped out his revolver. I sprang for his hand, but saw that I was too late, and jumped aside. At the same instant he fired, and the bullet which would have struck me passed through the heart of my unfortunate brother.

"He dropped without a groan upon the floor of the compartment, and MacCoy and I, equally horrified, knelt at each side of him, trying to bring back some signs of life. MacCoy still held the loaded revolver in his hand, but his anger against me and my resentment towards him had both for the moment been swallowed up in this sudden tragedy. It was he who first realized the situation. The train was for some reason going very slowly at the moment, and he saw his opportunity for escape. In an instant he had the door open, but I was as quick as he, and jumping upon him the two of us fell off the foot-board and rolled in each other's arms down a steep embankment. At the bottom I struck my head against a stone, and I remembered nothing more. When I came to myself I was lying among some low bushes, not far from the railroad track, and somebody was bathing my head with a wet handkerchief. It was Sparrow MacCoy.

" 'I guess I couldn't leave you,' said he. 'I didn't want to have the blood of two of you on my hands in one day. You loved your brother, I've no doubt; but you didn't love him a cent more than I loved him, though you'll say that I took a queer way to show it. Anyhow, it seems a mighty empty world now that he is gone, and I don't care a continental whether you give me over to the hangman or not.'

"He had turned his ankle in the fall, and there we sat, he with his useless foot, and I with my throbbing head, and we talked and talked until gradually my bitterness began to soften and to turn into something like sympathy. What was the use of revenging his death upon a man who was as much stricken by that death as I was? And then, as my wits gradually returned, I began to realize also that I could do nothing against MacCoy which would not recoil upon my mother and myself. How could we convict him without a full account of my brother's career being made public — the very thing which of all others we had to avoid? It was really as much our interest as his to cover the matter up, and from being an avenger of crime I found myself changed to a conspirator against Justice. The place in which we found ourselves was one of those pheasant preserves which are so common in the Old Country, and as we groped our way through it I found myself consulting the slayer of my brother as to how far it would be possible to hush it up.

"I soon realized from what he said that unless there were some papers of which we knew nothing in my brother's pockets, there was really no possible means by which the police could identify him or learn how he had got there. His ticket was in MacCoy's pocket, and so was the ticket for some baggage which they had left at the depôt. Like most Americans, he had found it cheaper and easier to buy an outfit in London than to bring one from New York, so that all his linen and clothes were new and unmarked. The bag, containing the dust cloak, which I had thrown out of the window, may have fallen among some bramble patch where it is still concealed, or may have been carried off by some tramp, or may have come into the possession of the police, who kept the incident to themselves. Anyhow, I have seen nothing about it in the London papers. As to the watches, they were a selection from those which had been intrusted to him for business purposes. It may have been for the same business purposes that he was taking them to Manchester, but — well, it's too late to enter into that.

"I don't blame the police for being at fault. I don't see how it could have been otherwise. There was just one little clew that they might have followed up, but it was a small one. I mean that small circular mirror which was found in my brother's pocket. It isn't a very common thing for a young man to carry about with him, is it? But a gambler might have told you what such a mirror may mean to a card-sharper. If you sit back a little from the table, and lay the mirror, face upwards, upon your lap, you can see, as you deal, every card that you give to your adversary. It is not hard to say whether you see a man or raise him when you know his cards as well as your own. It was as much a part of a sharper's outfit as the elastic clip upon Sparrow MacCoy's arm. Taking that, in connection with the recent frauds at the hotels, the police might have got hold of one end of the string.

"I don't think there is much more for me to explain. We got to a village called Amersham that night in the character of two gentlemen upon a walking tour, and afterwards we made our way quietly to London, whence MacCoy went on to Cairo and I returned to New York. My mother died six months afterwards, and I am glad to say that to the day of her death she never knew what had happened. She was always under the delusion that Edward was earning an honest living in London, and I never had the heart to tell her the truth. He never wrote; but, then, he never did write at any time, so that made no difference. His name was the last upon her lips.

"There's just one other thing that I have to ask you, sir, and I should take it as a kind return for all this explanation, if you could do it for me. You remember that Testament that was picked up. I always carried it in my inside pocket, and it must have come out in my fall. I value it very highly, for it was the family book with my birth and my brother's marked by my father in the beginning of it. I wish you would apply at the proper place and have it sent to me. It can be of no possible value to anyone else. If you address it to X, Bassano's Library, Broadway, New York, it is sure to come to hand."

The Lost Special

The confession of Herbert de Lernac, now lying under sentence of death at Marseilles, has thrown a light upon one of the most inexplicable crimes of the century—an incident which is, I believe, absolutely unprecedented in the criminal annals of any country. Although there is a reluctance to discuss the matter in official circles, and little information has been given to the Press, there are still indications that the statement of this arch-criminal is corroborated by the facts, and that we have at last found a solution for a most astounding business. As the matter is eight years old, and as its importance was somewhat obscured by a political crisis which was engaging the public attention at the time, it may be as well to state the facts as far as we have been able to ascertain them. They are collated from the Liverpool papers of that date, from the proceedings at the inquest upon John Slater, the engine-driver, and from the records of the London and West Coast Railway Company, which have been courteously put at my disposal. Briefly, they are as follows.

On the 3rd of June, 1890, a gentleman, who gave his name as Monsieur Louis Caratal, desired an interview with Mr. James Bland, the superintendent of the Central London and West Coast Station in Liverpool. He was a small man, middle-aged and dark, with a stoop which was so marked that it suggested some deformity of the spine. He was accompanied by a friend, a man of imposing physique, whose deferential manner and constant attention was one of dependence. This friend or companion, whose name did not transpire, was certainly a foreigner, and probably, from his swarthy complexion, either a Spaniard or a South American. One peculiarity was observed in him. He carried in his left hand a small black leather despatch-box, and it was noticed by a sharp-eyed clerk in the Central office that this box was fastened to his wrist by a strap. No importance was attached

35

to the fact at the time, but subsequent events endowed it with some significance. Monsieur Caratal was shown up to Mr. Bland's office, while his companion remained outside.

Monsieur Caratal's business was quickly dispatched. He had arrived that afternoon from Central America. Affairs of the utmost importance demanded that he should be in Paris without the loss of an unnecessary hour. He had missed the London express. A special must be provided. Money was of no importance. Time was everything. If the company would speed him on his way, they might make their own terms.

Mr. Bland struck the electric bell, summoned Mr. Potter Hood, the traffic manager, and had the matter arranged in five minutes. The train would start in three-quarters of an hour. It would take that time to insure that the line should be clear. The powerful engine called Rochdale (No. 247 on the company's register) was attached to two carriages, with a guard's van behind. The first carriage was solely for the purpose of decreasing the inconvenience arising from the oscillation. The second was divided, as usual, into four compartments, a first-class, a first-class smoking, a second-class, and a second-class smoking. The first compartment, which was the nearest to the engine, was the one allotted to the travellers. The other three were empty. The guard of the special train was James McPherson, who had been some years in the service of the company. The stoker, William Smith, was a new hand.

Monsieur Caratal, upon leaving the superintendent's office, rejoined his companion, and both of them manifested extreme impatience to be off. Having paid the money asked, which amounted to fifty pounds five shillings, at the usual special rate of five shillings a mile, they demanded to be shown the carriage, and at once took their seats in it, although they were assured that the better part of an hour must elapse before the line could be cleared. In the meantime a singular coincidence has occurred in the office which Monsieur Caratal had just quitted.

A request for a special is not a very uncommon circumstance in a rich commercial centre, but that two should be required upon the same afternoon was most unusual. It so happened, however, that Mr. Bland had hardly dismissed the first traveller before a second entered with a similar request. This was a Mr. Horace Moore, a gentlemanly man of military appearance, who alleged that the sudden serious illness of his wife in London made it absolutely imperative that he should not lose an instant in starting upon the journey. His distress and anxiety were so evident that Mr. Bland did all that was possible to meet his wishes. A second special was out of the question, as the ordinary local service was already somewhat deranged by the first. There was the alternative, however, that Mr. Moore should share the expense of Monsieur Caratal's train, and should travel in the other empty first-class compartment, if Monsieur Caratal objected to having him in the one which he occupied. It was difficult to see any objection to such an arrangement, and yet Monsieur Caratal, upon the suggestion being made to him by Mr. Potter Hood, absolutely refused to consider it for an instant. The train was his, he said, and he would insist upon the exclusive use of it. All argument failed to overcome his ungracious objections, and finally the plan had to be abandoned. Mr. Horace Moore left the station in great distress, after learning that his only course was to take the ordinary slow train which leaves Liverpool at six o'clock. At four thirty-one exactly by the station clock the special train, containing the crippled Monsieur Caratal and his gigantic companion, steamed out of the Liverpool station. The line was at that time clear, and there should have been no stoppage before Manchester.

The trains of the London and West Coast Railway run over the lines of another company as far as this town, which should have been reached by the special rather before six o'clock. At a quarter after six considerable surprise and some consternation were caused amongst the officials at Liverpool by the receipt of a telegram from Manchester to say that it had not yet arrived. An inquiry directed to St. Helens, which is a third of the way between the two cities, eliciting the following reply: —

"To James Bland, Superintendent, Central L. & W. C., Liverpool. — Special passed here at 4.52, well up to time. — Dowser, St. Helena."

This telegram was received at 6.40. At 6.50 a second message was received from Manchester: —

"No sign of special as advised by you."

And then ten minutes later a third, more bewildering: —

"Presume some mistake as to proposed running of special. Local train from St. Helens timed to follow it has just arrived and has seen nothing of it. Kindly wire advices. — Manchester."

The matter was assuming a most amazing aspect, although in some respects the last telegram was a relief to the authorities at Liverpool. If an accident had occurred to the special, it seemed hardly possible that the local train could have passed down the same line without observing it. And yet, what was alternative? Where could the train be? Had it possibly been side-tracked for some reason in order to allow the slower train to go past? Such an explanation was possible if some small repair had to be effected. A telegram was dispatched to each of the stations between St. Helens and Manchester, and the superintendent and traffic manager waited in the utmost suspense at the instrument for the series of replies which would enable them to say for certain what had become of the missing train. The answers came back in the order of questions, which was the order of the stations beginning at the St. Helens end: —

"Special passed here five o'clock. — Collins Green."

"Special passed here six past five. — Earlestown."

"Special passed here 5.10. — Kenyon Junction."

"No special train has passed here. — Barton Moss."

The two officials stared at each other in amazement.

"This is unique in my thirty years of experience," said Mr. Bland.

"Absolutely unprecedented and inexplicable, sir. The special has gone wrong between Kenyon Junction and Barton Moss."

"And yet there is no siding, as far as my memory serves me, between the two stations. The special must have run off the metals."

"But how could the four-fifty parliamentary pass over the same line without observing it?"

"There's no alternative, Mr. Hood. It *must* be so. Possibly the local train may have observed something which may throw some light upon the matter. We will wire to Manchester for more information, and to Kenyon Junction with instructions that the line be examined instantly as far as Barton Moss."

The answer from Manchester came within a few minutes.

"No news of missing special. Driver and guard of slow train positive that no accident between Kenyon Junction and Barton Moss. Line quite clear, and no sign of anything unusual. — Manchester."

"That driver and guard will have to go," said Mr. Bland, grimly. "There has been a wreck and they have missed it. The special has obviously run off the metals without disturbing the line — how it could have done so passes my comprehension — but so it must be, and we shall have a wire from Kenyon or Barton Moss presently so say that they have found her at the bottom of an embankment."

But Mr. Bland's prophecy was not destined to be fulfilled. A half-hour passed, and then there arrived the following message from the station-master of Kenyon Junction: —

"There are no traces of the missing special. It is quite certain that she passed here, and that she did not arrive at Barton Moss. We have detached engine from goods train, and I have myself ridden down the line, but all is clear, and there is no sign of any accident."

Mr. Bland tore his hair in his perplexity.

"This is rank lunacy, Hood!" he cried. "Does a train vanish into thin air in England in broad daylight? The thing is preposterous. An engine, a tender, two carriages, a van, five human beings — and all lost on a straight line of railway! Unless we get something positive within the next hour I'll take Inspector Collins, and go down myself."

And then at last something positive did occur. It took the shape of another telegram from Kenyon Junction.

"Regret to report that the dead body of John Slater, driver of the special train, has just been found among the gorse bushes at a point two and a quarter miles from the Junction. Had fallen from his engine, pitched down the embankment, and rolled among bushes. Injuries to his head, from the fall, appear to be cause of death. Ground has now been carefully examined, and there is no trace of the missing train."

The country was, as has already been stated, in the throes of a political crisis, and the attention of the public was further distracted by the important and sensational developments in Paris, where a huge scandal threatened to destroy the Government and to wreck the reputations of many of the leading men in France. The papers were full of these events, and the singular disappearance of the special train attracted less attention than would have been the case in more peaceful times. The grotesque nature of the event helped to detract from its importance, for the papers were disinclined to believe the facts as reported to them. More than one of the London journals treated the matter as an ingenious hoax, until the coroner's inquest upon the unfortunate driver (an inquest which elicited nothing of importance) convinced them of the tragedy of the incident.

Mr. Bland, accompanied by Inspector Collins, the senior detective officer in the service of the company, went down to Kenyon Junction the same evening, and their research lasted throughout the following day, but was attended with purely negative results. Not only was no trace found of the missing train, but no conjecture could be put forward which could possibly explain the facts. At the same time, Inspector Collins's official report (which lies before me as I write) served to show that the possibilities were more numerous than might have been expected.

"In the stretch of railway between these two points," said he, "the country is dotted with ironworks and collieries. Of these, some are being worked and some have been abandoned. There are no fewer than twelve which have small guage lines which run trolly-cars down to the main line. These can, of course, be disregarded. Besides these, however, there are seven which have or have had proper lines running down and connecting with points to the main line, so as to convey their produce from the mouth of the mine to the great centres of distribution. In every case these lines are only a few miles in length. Out of the seven, four belong to collieries which are worked out, or at least to shafts which are no longer used. These are the Redgauntlet, Hero, Slough of Despond, and Heartsease mines, the latter having ten years ago been one of the principal mines in Lancashire. These four side lines may be eliminated from our inquiry, for, to prevent possible accidents, the rails nearest to the main line have been taken up and there is no longer any connection. There remain three other lines leading

(a) to the Carnstock Iron Works;
(b) to the Big Ben Colliery;
(c) to the Perserverence Colliery.

Of these the Big Ben line is not more than a quarter of a mile long, and ends at a dead wall of coal waiting removal from the mouth of the mine. Nothing had been seen or heard there of any special. The Carnstock Iron Works line was blocked all day upon the 3rd of June by sixteen truckloads of hematite. It is a single line, and nothing could have passed. As to the Perserverance line, it is a large double line, which does a considerable traffic, for the output of the mine is very large. On the 3rd of June this traffic proceeded as usual; hundreds of men, including a gang of railway platelayers, were working along the two miles and a quarter which constitute the total length of the line, and it is inconceivable that an unexpected train could have come down there without attracting universal attention. It may be remarked in conclusion that this branch line is nearer to St. Helens than the point at which the engine-driver was discovered, so that we have every reason to believe that the train was past that point before misfortune overtook her.

"As to John Slater, there is no clue to be gathered from his appearance or injuries. We can only say that, as far as we can see, he met his end by falling off his engine, though why he fell, or what became of the engine after his fall, is a question upon which I do not feel qualified to offer an opinion." In conclusion, the inspector offered his resignation to the Board, being much nettled by an accusation of incompetence in the London papers.

A month elapsed, during which both the police and the company prosecuted their inquiries without the slightest success. A reward was offered and a pardon promised in case of crime, but they were both unclaimed. Every day the public opened their papers with the conviction that so grotesque a mystery would at last be solved, but week after week passed by, and a solution remained as far off as ever. In broad daylight, upon a June afternoon in the most thickly inhabited portion of England, a train with its occupants had disappeared as completely as if some master of subtle chemistry had volatilized it into gas. Indeed, among the various conjectures which were put forward in the public Press there were some which seriously asserted that supernatural, or, at least, preternatural, agencies had been at work, and that the deformed Monsieur Caratal was probably a person who was better known under a less polite name. Others fixed upon his swarthy companion as being the author of the mischief, but what it was exactly which he had done could never be clearly formulated in words.

Amongst the many suggestions put forward by various news-papers or private individuals, there were one or two which were feasible enough to attract the attention of the public. One which appeared in the *Times,* over the signature of an amateur reasoner of some celebrity at that date, attempted to deal with the matter in a critical and semi-scientific manner. An extract must suffice, although the curious can see the whole letter in the issue of the 3rd of July.

"It is one of the elementary principals of practical reasoning," he remarked, "that when the impossible has been eliminated the residuum, *however improbable,* must contain the truth. It is certain that the train left Kenyon Junction. It is certain that it did not reach Barton Moss. It is in the highest degree unlikely, but still possible, that it may have taken one of the seven available side lines. It is obviously impossible for a train to run where there are no rails, and, therefore, we may reduce our improbables to the three open lines, namely, the Carnstock Iron Works, the Big Ben, and the Perserverence. Is there a secret society of colliers, an English *camorra,* which is capable of destroying both train and passengers? It is improbable, but it is not impossible. I confess that I am unable to suggest any other solution. I should certainly advise the company to direct all their energies towards the observation of those three lines, and of the workmen at the end of them. A careful supervision of the pawnbrokers' shops of the district might possibly bring some suggestive facts to light."

The suggestion coming from a recognised authority upon such matters created considerable interest, and a fierce opposition from those who considered such a statement to be a preposterous libel upon an honest and deserving set of men. The only answer to this criticism was a challenge to the objectors to lay any more feasible explanation before the public. In reply to this two others were forthcoming (*Times,* July 7th and 9th). The first suggested that the train might have run off the metals and be lying submerged in the Lancashire and Staffordshire Canal, which runs parallel to the railway for some hundreds of yards. This suggestion was thrown out of court by the published depth of the canal, which was entirely insufficient to conceal so large an object. The second correspondent wrote calling attention to the bag which appeared to be the sole luggage which the travellers had brought with them, and suggesting that some novel explosive of immense and pulverizing power might have been concealed in it. The obvious absurdity, however, of supposing that the whole train might be blown to dust while the metals remained uninjured reduced any such explanation to a farce. The investigation had drifted into this hopeless position when a new and most unexpected incident occurred, which raised hopes never destined to be fulfilled.

This was nothing less than the receipt by Mrs. McPherson of a letter from her husband, James McPherson, who had been the guard of the missing train. The letter, which was dated July 5th, 1890, was dispatched from New York, and came to hand upon July 14th. Some doubts were expressed as to its genuine character, but Mrs. McPherson was positive as to the writing, and the fact that it contained a remittance of a hundred dollars in five-dollar notes was enough in itself to discount the idea of a hoax. No address was given in the letter, which ran in this way: —

"MY DEAR WIFE, —

"I have been thinking a great deal, and I find it very hard to give you up. The same with Lizzie. I try to fight against it, but it will always come back to me. I send you some money which will change into twenty English pounds. This should be enough to bring both Lizzie and you across the Atlantic, and you will find the Hamburg boats which stop at Southampton very good boats, and cheaper than Liverpool. If you could come here and stop at the Johnston House I would try and send word how to meet, but things are very difficult with me at present, and I am not very happy, finding it hard to give you both up. So no more at present from your loving husband,   "JAMES .McPHERSON."

For a time it was confidently anticipated that this letter would lead to the clearing up of the whole matter, the more so as it was ascertained that a passenger who bore a close resemblance to the missing guard had travelled from Southampton under the name of Summers in the Hamburg and New York liner *Vistula,* which started upon the 7th of June. Mrs. McPherson and her sister Lizzie Dolton went across to New York as directed, and stayed for three weeks at the Johnston House, without hearing anything from the missing man. It is probable that some injudicious comments in the Press may have warned him that the police were using them as

a bait. However this may be, it is certain that he neither wrote nor
came, and the women were eventually compelled to return to
Liverpool.

And so the matter stood, and has continued to stand up to the
present year of 1898. Incredible as it may seem, nothing has
transpired during these eight years which has shed the least light
upon the extraordinary disappearance of the special train which
contained Monsieur Caratal and his companion. Careful inquiries
into the antecedents of the two travellers have only established the
fact that Monsieur Caratal was well known as a financier and
political agent in Central America, and that during his voyage to
Europe he had betrayed extraordinary anxiety to reach Paris. His
companion, whose name was entered upon the passenger lists as
Eduardo Gomez, was a man whose record was a violent one, and
whose reputation was that of a bravo and a bully. There was
evidence to show, however, that he was honestly devoted to the
interests of Monsieur Caratal, and that the latter, being a man of
puny physique, employed the other as a guard and protector. It
may be added that no information came from Paris as to what the
objects of Monsieur Caratal's hurried journey may have been.
This comprises all the facts of the case up to the publication in the
Marseilles papers of the recent confession of Herbert de Lernac,
now under sentence of death for the murder of a merchant named
Bonvalot. This statement may be literally translated as follows: —

"It is not out of mere pride or boasting that I give this
information, for, if that were my object, I could tell a dozen
actions of mine which are quite as splendid; but I do it in order
that certain gentlemen in Paris may understand that I, who am
able here to tell about the fate of Monsieur Caratal, can also tell
in whose interest and at whose request the deed was done, unless
the reprieve which I am awaiting comes to me very quickly. Take
warning, messieurs, before it is too late! You know Herbert de
Lernac, and you are aware that his deeds are as ready as his
words. Hasten then, or you are lost!

"At present I shall mention no names—if you only heard the
names, what would you not think!—but I shall merely tell you how
cleverly I did it. I was true to my employers then, and no doubt
they will be true to me now. I hope so, and until I am convinced
that they have betrayed me, these names, which would convulse

Europe, shall not be divulged. But on that day. . .well, I say no more!

"In a word, then, there was a famous trial in Paris, in the year 1890, in connection with a monstrous scandal in politics and finance. How monstrous that scandal was can never be known save by such confidential agents as myself. The honour and careers of many of the chief men in France were at stake. You have seen a group of nine-pins standing, all so rigid, and prim, and unbending. Then there comes the ball from far away and pop, pop, pop—there are your nine-pins on the floor. Well, imagine some of the greatest men in France as these nine-pins, and then this Monsieur Caratal was the ball which could be seen coming from far away. If he arrived, then it was pop, pop, pop for all of them. It was determined that he should not arrive.

"I do not accuse them all of being conscious of what was to happen. There were, as I have said, great financial as well as political interests at stake, and a syndicate was formed to manage the business. Some subscribed to the syndicate who hardly understood what were its objects. But others understood very well, and they can rely upon it that I have not forgotten their names. They had ample warning that Monsieur Caratal was coming long before he left South America, and they knew that the evidence which he held would certainly mean ruin to all of them. The syndicate had the command of an unlimited amount of money— absolutely unlimited, you understand. They looked round for an agent who was capable of wielding this gigantic power. The man chosen must be inventive, resolute, adaptive—a man in a million. They chose Herbert de Lernac, and I admit that they were right.

"My duties were to choose my subordinates, to use freely the power which money gives, and to make certain that Monsieur Caratal should never arrive in Paris. With characteristic energy I set about my commision within an hour of receiving my instructions, and the steps which I took were the very best for the purposes which could possibly be devised.

"A man whom I could trust was dispatched instantly to South America to travel home with Monsieur Caratal. Had he arrived in time the ship would never have reached Liverpool; but, alas, it had already started before my agent could reach it. I fitted out a small armed brig to intercept it, but again I was unfortunate. Like all great organizers I was, however, prepared for failure, and had a series of alternatives prepared, one or the other of which must succeed. You must not underrate the difficulties of my undertaking, or imagine that a mere commonplace assassination would meet the case. We must destroy not only Monsieur Caratal, but Monsieur Caratal's documents, and Monsieur Caratal's companions also, if we had reason to believe that he had communicated his secrets to them. And you must remember that they were on the alert, and keenly suspicious of any such attempt. It was a task which was in every way worthy of me, for I am always most masterful where another would be appalled.

"I was all ready for Monsieur Caratal's reception in Liverpool, and I was the more eager because I had reason to believe that he had made arrangements by which he would have a considerable guard from the moment that he arrived in London. Anything which was to be done must be done between the moment of his setting foot upon the Liverpool quay and that of his arrival at the London and West Coast terminus in London. We prepared six plans, each more elaborate than the last; which plan would be used would depend upon his own movements. Do what he would, we were ready for him. If he had stayed in Liverpool, we were ready. If he took an ordinary train, an express, or a special, all was ready. Everything had been foreseen and provided for.

"You may imagine that I could not do all this myself. What could I know of the English railway lines? But money can procure willing agents all the world over, and I soon had one of the acutest brains in England to assist me. I will mention no names, but it would be unjust to claim all the credit for myself. My English ally was worthy of such an alliance. He knew the London and West Coast line thoroughly, and he had the command of a band of workers who were trustworthy and intelligent. The idea was his, and my own judgment was only required in the details. We bought over several officials, amongst whom the most important was James McPherson, whom we had ascertained to be the guard most likely to be employed upon a special train. Smith, the stoker, was also in our employ. John Slater, the engine-driver, had been approached, but had been found to be obstinate and dangerous, so we desisted. We had no certainty that Monsieur Caratal would take a special, but we thought it very probable, for it was of the utmost importance to him that he should reach Paris without delay. It was for this contingency, therefore, that we made special preparations — preparations which were complete down to the last detail long before his steamer had sighted the shores of England. You will be amused to learn that there was one of my agents in the pilot-boat which brought that steamer to its moorings.

"The moment that Caratal arrived in Liverpool we knew that he suspected danger and was on his guard. He had brought with him as an escort a dangerous fellow, named Gomez, a man who carried weapons, and was prepared to use them. This fellow carried Caratal's confidential papers for him, and was ready to protect either them or his master. The probability was that Caratal had taken him into his counsels, and that to remove Caratal without removing Gomez would be a mere waste of energy. It was necessary that they should be involved in a common fate, and our plans to that end were much facilitated by their request for a special train. On that special train you will understand that two out of the three servants of the company were really in our employ, at a price which would make them independent for a lifetime. I do not go so far as to say that the English are more honest than any other nation, but I have found them more expensive to buy.

"I have already spoken of my English agent — who is a man with a considerable future before him, unless some complaint of the throat carries him off before his time. He had charge of all arrangements at Liverpool, whilst I was stationed at the inn at Kenyon, where I awaited a cipher signal to act. When the special was arranged for, my agent instantly telegraphed to me and warned me how soon I should have everything ready. He himself under the name of Horace Moore applied immediately for a special also, in the hope that he would be sent down with Monsieur Caratal, which might under certain circumstances have been helpful to us. If, for example, our great *coup* had failed, it would then have become the duty of my agent to have shot them both and destroyed their papers. Caratal was on his guard, however, and refused to admit any other traveller. My agent then left the station, returned by another entrance, entered the guard's van on the side farthest from the platform, and travelled down with McPherson, the guard.

"In the meantime you will be interested to know what my own movements were. Everything had been prepared for days before, and only the finishing touches were needed. The side line which we had chosen had once joined the main line, but it had been disconnected. We had only to replace a few rails to connect it once more. These rails had been laid down as far as could be done without danger of attracting attention, and now it was merely a case of completing a juncture with the line, and arranging the points as they had been before. The sleepers had never been removed, and the rails, fish-plates, and rivets were all ready, for we had taken them from a siding on the abandoned portion of the line. With my small but competent band of workers, we had everything ready long before the special arrived. When it did arrive, it ran off upon the small side line so easily that the jolting of the points appears to have been entirely unnoticed by the two travellers.

"Our plan had been that Smith the stoker should chloroform John Slater the driver, and so that he should vanish with the others. In this respect, and in this respect only, our plans miscarried — I except the criminal folly of McPherson in writing home to his wife. Our stoker did his business so clumsily that Slater in his struggles fell off the engine, and though fortune was with us so far that he broke his neck in the fall, still he remained as a blot upon that which would otherwise have been one of those complete masterpieces which are only to be contemplated in silent admiration. The criminal expert will find in John Slater the one flaw in all our admirable combinations. A man who has had as many triumphs as I can afford to be frank, and I therefore lay my finger upon John Slater, and I proclaim him to be a flaw.

"But now I have got our special train upon the small line two kilomètres, or rather more than one mile in length, which leads, or rather used to lead, to the abandoned Heartsease mine, once one of the largest coal mines in England. You will ask how it is that no one saw the train upon this unused line. I answer that along its entire length it runs through a deep cutting, and that, unless someone had been on the edge of that cutting, he could not have seen it. There *was* someone on the edge of that cutting. I was there. And now I will tell you what I saw.

"My assistant had remained at the points in order that he might superintend the switching off of the train. He had four armed men with him, so that if the train ran off the line — we thought it probable, because the points were very rusty — we might still have resources to fall back upon. Having once seen it safely on the side line, he handed over the responsibility to me. I was waiting at a point which overlooks the mouth of the mine, and I was also armed, as were my two companions. Come what might, you see, I was always ready.

"The moment that the train was fairly on the side line, Smith, the stoker, slowed-down the engine, and then, having turned it on to the fullest speed again, he and McPherson, with my English lieutenant, sprang off before it was too late. It may be that it was this slowing-down which first attracted the attention of the travellers, but the train was running at full speed again before their heads appeared at the open window. It makes me smile to think how bewildered they must have been. Picture to yourself your own feelings if, on looking out of your luxurious carriage, you suddenly perceived that the lines upon which you ran were rusted and corroded, red and yellow with disuse and decay! What a catch must have come in their breath as in a second it flashed upon them that it was not Manchester but Death which was waiting for them at the end of that sinister line. But the train was running with frantic speed, rolling and rocking over the rotten line, while the wheels made a frightful screaming sound upon the rusted surface. I was close to them, and could see their faces. Caratal was praying, I think—there was something like a rosary dangling out of his hand. The other roared like a bull who smells the blood of the slaughter-house. He saw us standing on the bank, and he beckoned to us like a madman. Then he tore at his wrist and threw his despatch-box out of the window in our direction. Of course, his meaning was obvious. Here was the evidence, and they would promise to be silent if their lives were spared. It would have been very agreeable if we could have done so, but business is business. Besides, the train was now as much beyond our control as theirs.

"He ceased howling when the train rattled round the curve and they saw the black mouth of the mine yawning before them. We had removed the boards which had covered it, and we had cleared the square entrance. The rails had formerly run very close to the shaft for the convenience of loading the coal, and we had only to add two or three lengths of rail in order to lead to the very brink of the shaft. In fact, as the lengths would not quite fit, our line projected about three feet over the edge. We saw the two heads at the window: Caratal below, Gomez above; but they had both been struck silent by what they saw. And yet they could not withdraw their heads. The sight seemed to have paralyzed them.

"I had wondered how the train running at a great speed would take the pit into which I had guided it, and I was much interested in watching it. One of my colleagues thought that it would actually jump it, and indeed it was not very far from doing so. Fortunately, however, it fell short, and the buffers of the engine struck the other lip of the shaft with a tremendous crash. The funnel flew off into the air. The tender, carriages, and van were all smashed into one jumble, which, with the remains of the engine, choked for a minute or so the mouth of the pit. Then something gave way in the middle, and the whole mass of green iron, smoking coals, brass fittings, wheels, woodwork, and cushions all crumbled together and crashed down into the mine. We heard the rattle, rattle, rattle, as the *débris* struck against the walls, and then quite a long time afterwards there came a deep roar as the remains of the train struck the bottom. The boiler may have burst, for a sharp crash came after the roar, and then a dense cloud of steam and smoke swirled up out of the black depths, falling in a spray as thick as rain all round us. Then the vapour shredded off into thin wisps, which floated away in the summer sunshine, and all was quiet again in the Heartsease mine.

"And now, having carried out our plans so successfully, it only remained to leave no trace behind us. Our little band of workers at the other end had already ripped up the rails and disconnected the side line, replacing everything as it had been before. The funnel and other fragments were thrown in, the shaft was planked over as it used to be, and the lines which led to it were torn up and taken away. Then, without flurry, but without delay, we all made our way out of the country, most of us to Paris, my English colleague to Manchester, and McPherson to Southampton, whence he emigrated to America. Let the English papers of that date tell how thoroughly we had thrown the cleverest of their detectives off our track.

"You will remember that Gomez threw his bag of papers out of the window, and I need not say that I secured that bag and brought them to my employers. It may interest my employers now, however, to learn that out of that bag I took one or two little papers as a souvenir of the occasion. I have no wish to publish these papers; but, still, it is every man for himself in this world, and what else can I do if my friends will not come to my aid when I want them? Messieurs, you may believe that Herbert de Lernac is quite as formidable when he is against you as when he is with you, and that he is not a man to go to the guillotine until he has seen that every one of you is *en route* for New Caledonia. For your own sake, if not for mine, make haste, Monsieur de ——, and General ——, and Baron —— (you can fill up the blanks for yourselves as you read this). I promise you that in the next edition there will be no blanks to fill.

"P.S. — As I look over my statement there is only one omission which I can see. It concerns the unfortunate man McPherson, who was foolish enough to write to his wife and to make an appointment with her in New York. It can be imagined that when interests like ours were at stake, we could not leave them to the chance of whether a man in that class of life would or would not give away his secrets to a woman. Having once broken his oath by writing to his wife, we could not trust him any more. We took steps therefore to insure that he should not see his wife. I have sometimes thought that it would be a kindness to write to her and to assure her that there is no impediment to her marrying again."

William Gillette
as Sherlock Holmes

Then came William Gillette, and Sherlock Holmes has never been the same.

There is some uncertainty about the sequence of events leading to Gillette's writing SHERLOCK HOLMES. *The first initiative would appear to have been taken by Charles Frohman, the successful Broadway producer and theatrical agent, early in the 1890s. Someone had mentioned to Frohman the idea of a Sherlock Holmes play, and while he did not think the stories then running in the* STRAND *lent themselves to dramatization, he nonetheless allowed himself to be persuaded "to secure the title of 'Sherlock Holmes' for dramatic use, and on this suggestion Mr. Frohman negotiated with [Conan Doyle] on a royalty basis for the use of the name, regardless of what it might be put to in the future," according to an article by Harold J. Shepstone which appeared in the* STRAND *for December 1901.*

The second initiative, taken some years later, apparently was Doyle's. He wrote a five-act play of his own about Holmes. His agent, A. P. Watt, supervised a revision, and it was sent off to Frohman in New York. Frohman did not think the piece good enough as it stood and set sail for London to tell Doyle so in person —and to recommend William Gillette as the man to rewrite it as well as to play Sherlock Holmes in the final version. Doyle, who had seen Gillette in his Civil War drama SECRET SERVICE *during its recent London engagement, agreed to both suggestions.*

"Temperamentally, Gillette was ideal for the part," Charles Higham has written in THE ADVENTURES OF CONAN DOYLE. *"He did not have to pretend to be taciturn, cold, reserved, and sardonically logical. His humour was acrid and mocking. The opposite sex was no longer of interest to him [since] the death of his wife. . . He was as eccentric as Holmes. He was a night owl." He was physically right as well—fortyish, slim, an inch over six*

feet in height. He had grown up near Hartford, Connecticut, where his father had been a retired U.S. Senator, a distant relative of Henry Ward Beecher, and a great friend of Mark Twain. He first went on the stage in 1875, at the age of eighteen. As early as 1881 he was acting in his own plays.

By the standards of his day, Gillette was an extreme proponent of "realistic" plays and unaffected acting. He was "one of the first American actors to speak rather than declaim his rôles," Doris E. Cook has written in SHERLOCK HOLMES AND MUCH MORE—OR SOME OF THE FACTS ABOUT WILLIAM GILLETTE. *That is undoubtedly one reason he turned to playwrighting, to give himself parts suited to his style. "The idea is that we are not reciting literature—not reciting anything that has ever been written or said before," he told a* NEW YORK TIMES *reporter in 1914; "we are talking, saying the first things that come into our heads, thinking them out as we say them, hesitating and wandering and sometimes blundering over it all." His romantic melodramas, which seem so corny today, were then wonders of realism. His approach made him the obvious choice to adapt and portray such a "modern" character as Sherlock Holmes.*

He set to work in characteristic style. First he read all the Sherlock Holmes stories Doyle had written so far—which he had never read before. Then he took four weeks off from the American tour of SECRET SERVICE *and wrote* SHERLOCK HOLMES. *As John Dickson Carr has said in* THE LIFE OF SIR ARTHUR CONAN DOYLE, *the Doyle effort "got itself so thoroughly re-written into another play that nobody knows what the original play was about."*

At one point "in the throes of composition" he sent an urgent telegram to Doyle in England: "MAY I MARRY HOLMES?"

"YOU MAY MARRY OR MURDER OR DO WHAT YOU LIKE WITH HIM," *was Doyle's now-classic reply.*

The play written, Gillette rejoined the company of SECRET SERVICE *in San Francisco—where the manuscript was destroyed in the Baldwin Hotel fire of 23 November 1898, which took many lives. All the costumes, properties, and scenery for* SECRET SERVICE *were lost as well, for the show was then appearing at the Baldwin Theatre within the hotel. Doyle's manuscript may have burned at the same time, if it were still in Gillette's possession. At any rate, it had disappeared by now and was not seen again.*

Undaunted, Gillette wrote the play again—and this time changed the ending. "In this version," Higham writes, "Holmes puts a plaster bust of himself in a window. Moriarty shoots it with an air gun, goes in to inspect the body, and is seized." He was persuaded to restore the original climax, but this alternative ending was used in the Paris production of SHERLOCK HOLMES *and was later appropriated by Doyle for "The Adventure of the Empty House."*

It still remained for playwright and author to meet face to face. In May 1899, Gillette took ship for England. Doyle went to meet the train at the South Norwood station—and stared in wonder as Sherlock Holmes himself stepped from the carriage, dressed in an ulster and deerstalker cap and carrying a silver-headed stick. He strode up to Doyle, whipped out a huge magnifying glass, and looked the Englishman up and down. "Unquestionably an author," he pronounced.

Doyle roared with laughter, and the two were fast friends immediately. Holmes's creator even relented in his disapproval of the great detective falling in love at the end of the play. SHERLOCK HOLMES *went into production.*

It débuted "out of town" in Buffalo on 23 October 1899 and opened at the Garrick Theatre in New York on 6 November. It was, in a word, a smash.

Never before or since was there such a perfect fusion of actor and character. In a very real sense, Gillette was *Sherlock Holmes. They shared so many traits, and Gillette superimposed so many of his own characteristics upon the detective, that the popular Holmes image of today owes every bit as much to William Gillette as to Conan Doyle.*

While it had been Sidney Paget, the illustrator for the STRAND, *who first gave Holmes the deerstalker cap and caped travelling-cloak, it was Gillette who really made them his trademark by wearing them in over 1300 performances spanning more than thirty years. It was Gillette too who introduced the curved meerschaum, or calabash, pipe. When he found he could not hold a straight pipe clenched in his teeth, speak his lines, and at the same time keep his hands free for other business, he adopted the balanced meerschaum as a balm to his jaw muscles. The American magazine artist Frederic Dorr Steele, when he began illustrating Holmes for* COLLIER'S WEEKLY *in 1903, based his drawings on Gillette, and the cap, the cloak, the curved pipe, and the silver-headed walking-stick became stereotyped symbols of Sherlock Holmes for millions of people who had never seen the play. Along with the magnifying lens, the violin, and the cocaine syringe, they made nearly complete the modern Holmes image. All that remained was the catch-phrase: "Elementary, my dear Watson!" That would not come until Basil Rathbone and the talkies.*

Like Holmes, Gillette was a chronic smoker. "Indeed," as Harold Shepstone remarked in the STRAND, *"he seldom takes a part in a play where he cannot smoke," and in* SHERLOCK HOLMES *he wrote in several excuses for lighting up his pipe as well as cigarettes and a cigar. All served to further the plot. Holmes's penchant for reclining on cushions before the fireplace was another of Gillette's own traits grafted onto the play, but one which did not attain permanence.*

And like Holmes, Gillette lived in a "world of effect." SHERLOCK HOLMES *demonstrated his love of taciturn heroes, spectacular lighting and sound effects, fast-moving, unrelenting action punctuated by long, meaningful pauses, and the gratuitous introduction of romantic interests. It was a very "modern" play, a very "American" play—in contrast, for example, to Doyle's own* THE SPECKLED BAND *of 1910. It made use of lighting effects which could be accomplished only by electricity, controlled through a specially-made switchboard which the company carried with them even on tour. The transition between the first and second scenes of Act II was accomplished as a "dark change," without lowering the curtain, during which the setting and every stick of furniture for Professor Moriarty's headquarters was removed and Sherlock Holmes's apartment revealed in the space of thirty-five seconds—a technical feat which was invariably greeted with a burst of admiring applause.*

In September 1901, SHERLOCK HOLMES *was brought to the Lyceum in London for a seven-months' engagement—followed by a brief tour of the provinces, in which a twelve-year-old actor named Charles Chaplin played Billy the page. It was every bit the triumph it had been in the States, and on 1 February 1902 the King and Queen attended the performance. Despite Gillette's "bloodless" portrayal and the insertion of the love interest, Conan Doyle was delighted with the production and invited the Americans in the company to spend Christmas with him at his house in the South London suburbs. Gillette had generously given Doyle top billing as the play's author, and Sir Arthur was receiving a royalty on every performance as well. "I was charmed both with the play, the acting and the pecuniary result," he joked in* MEMORIES AND ADVENTURES. *He had, indeed, little to complain of.*

No other actor in history spent more time in a single rôle. Gillette wrote many other plays, but none was ever the success that SHERLOCK HOLMES *continued to be. It got so that he could not even take his plays on tour unless he promised at least one performance of* SHERLOCK HOLMES *at each stopping-place. During the next thirty-five years he played Holmes 1300 times and grossed more than $1,500,000 on the one drama alone.*

In 1910, "so grim and grave, so worn and repressed," in the words of one Boston reviewer, Gillette effectively retired, though he continued for the next twenty years in a series of revivals and "farewell tours." He performed in a silent film adaptation of SHERLOCK HOLMES *in 1916, but it was not a success. He lived to see the formation of the Baker Street Irregulars and was guest of honour at their dinner of January 1935. Later that year, at the age of 82, he played Sherlock Holmes for the last time in a one-hour radio version of his play on WABC in New York. He died in Hartford on 29 April 1937.*

Gillette and Doyle revised SHERLOCK HOLMES *for one of the actor's many "farewell tours" in 1922, and the version given here is based on that text. It was edited again by Gillette and Sherlockian expert Vincent Starrett for publication by Doubleday, Doran in 1935. It was revised yet again for the 1974 revival by the British Royal Shakespeare Company, which starred John Wood as Holmes, and this "updated" text is also available from Doubleday, though in a very inferior edition.*

As Doyle had done before him, as Basil Rathbone was to do in later years, William Gillette eventually tired of his constant identification with Sherlock Holmes. The public simply did not want him to do other things. Even some reviewers could not resist invidious comparisons. In the spring of 1905, though, Gillette was able to take good-natured revenge on both the character and the critics.

Just back from originating the title rôle in J. M. Barrie's THE
ADMIRABLE CRICHTON *in London, he was appearing in one of the
innumerable New York revivals of* SHERLOCK HOLMES *when he
was invited to participate in a benefit for a down-on-his-luck
character actor named Joseph Jefferson Holland. Gillette and a
young actress, Ethel Barrymore, intended to do an old two-
character comedy sketch called "The Silent System," but for some
reason it could not be gotten together in time. Virtually at the last
moment, Gillette wrote* THE PAINFUL PREDICAMENT OF SHERLOCK
HOLMES. *He and Miss Barrymore rehearsed for a total of twenty
minutes—and the piece, "A Fantasy in about One-Tenth of an
Act," went on the evening of 24 March 1905.*

The NEW YORK TRIBUNE *found it a "delicious travesty and
thrillingly funny." In it, Gillette took the opportunity to lampoon
his own play, and the critics too, by turning some clever variations
on those elements which had come in for special comment during
the last five years—the cluttered Baker Street sitting-room,
Holmes's smoking on stage, the cocaine business, Madge
Larrabee's gushing society lady, Billy's frenzied entrances, the
eerie lighting, the three melodramatic knocks against the floor-
boards.*

But mainly THE PAINFUL PREDICAMENT *spoofed his own
reserved acting style. His contemporaries often chided him over
his "halting, staccato" delivery as Holmes—the same which Basil
Rathbone copied and clichéd in the movies—as well as the many
pauses built into the Sherlock Holmes play, in which Gillette
would stroll, smoke, reflect, and otherwise demonstrate Holmes's
imperturbability, sometimes at agonizing length.*

*He had the laugh on them all by a very simple device. In all the
pandemonious action of* THE PAINFUL PREDICAMENT, *he uttered
not one sound. Miss Barrymore had virtually every line (bracketed
by Billy's at beginning and end), and Gillette spent the whole time
going through the pantomimic business to which his audiences
had become accustomed—only this time it was because his
Holmes could get no word in as his client kept up an uninterrupted
stream of dialogue.*

*The parody was a great success, and Gillette appeared in it
again for another charity performance three weeks later, this time
for the benefit fund of the Actors Society of America on 14 April.*

On this occasion it was called THE HARROWING PREDICAMENT OF SHERLOCK HOLMES.

In September of the same year, Gillette débuted his new comedy CLARICE, *his first play since* SHERLOCK HOLMES, *in London, where he had been so well received in* THE ADMIRABLE CRICHTON. *The less than enthusiastic response prompted him to add* THE PAINFUL PREDICAMENT *to the bill as a curtain-raiser, with young Charlie Chaplin once again cast as Billy. It didn't help.* CLARICE *closed, and Gillette was compelled to finish the engagement with a substitute play—yet another revival of* SHERLOCK HOLMES.

Sherlock Holmes

A Drama in Four Acts

by Sir Arthur Conan Doyle and William Gillette

Cast of Characters

In the order of their appearance

MADGE LARRABEE

JOHN FORMAN

JAMES LARRABEE

TÉRÈSE

MRS. FAULKNER

SIDNEY PRINCE

ALICE FAULKNER

SHERLOCK HOLMES

PROFESSOR MORIARTY

JOHN

ALFRED BASSICK

BILLY

DOCTOR WATSON

JIM CRAIGIN

THOMAS LEARY

"LIGHTFOOT" MCTAGUE

MRS. SMEEDLEY

PARSONS

COUNT VON STALBURG

SIR EDWARD LEIGHTON

ACT I

Drawing-room at the LARRABEES. *Evening.*

ACT II

Scene 1

PROFESSOR MORIARTY'S *Underground Office. Morning.*

Scene 2

SHERLOCK HOLMES'S *Apartments in Baker Street. Evening.*

ACT III

The Stepney Gas Chamber. Midnight.

ACT IV

DOCTOR WATSON'S *Consulting Room, Kensington.*
The following evening.

The place is London.

ACT I

The scene represents the drawing-room at Edelweiss Lodge, an old house, gloomy and decayed, situated in a lonely district in a little-frequented part of London.

The furniture is old and decayed, with the exception of the piano—a baby-grand. The desk is very solid. The ceiling is heavily beamed. Many places out of repair in the walls and ceilings. Carvings broken here and there.

The music stops an instant before rise of curtain. A short pause after curtain is up. Curtain rises in darkness—lights come up. MADGE LARRABEE *is discovered anxiously waiting. A strikingly handsome woman, but with a somewhat hard face. Black hair. Richly dressed.*

Enter FORMAN *with evening paper. He is a quiet, perfectly trained servant. He is met by* MADGE, *who takes the paper from him quickly.*

FORMAN *(speaks always very quietly)*: Pardon, ma'am, but one of the maids wishes to speak with you.

*(*MADGE *is scanning the paper eagerly and sinks on to seat at the foot of the piano.)*

MADGE *(not looking from paper)*: I can't spare the time now.
FORMAN: Very well, ma'am. *(Turns to go.)*
MADGE *(without looking up from paper)*: Which maid was it?
FORMAN *(turning towards* MADGE *again)*: Térèse, ma'am.
MADGE *(looking up. Very slight surprise in her tone)*: Térèse!
FORMAN: Yes, ma'am.
MADGE: Have you any idea what she wants?
FORMAN: Not the least, ma'am.
MADGE: She must tell you. I'm very busy, and can't see her unless I know.
FORMAN: I'll say so, ma'am.

(Turns and goes out, carefully and quietly closing the door after him—immediately coming in again and watching MADGE,

65

*who is busy with paper. Finds what she has been looking for
and starts eagerly to read it. As if not seeing the print well, she
leans near light and resumes reading with the greatest avidity.*
FORMAN *quietly shuts door. He stands at the door looking at*
MADGE *as she reads the paper. This is prolonged somewhat, so
that it may be seen that he is not waiting for her to finish from
mere politeness. His eyes are upon her sharply and intensely, yet
he does not assume any expression otherwise. She finishes and
angrily rises, casting the paper violently down on the piano. She
turns and goes near the large heavy desk. Pauses there. Then
turns away angrily. Sees* FORMAN, *calms herself at once. Just as*
MADGE *turns,* FORMAN *seems to be coming into room.)*

I could get nothing from her, ma'am. She insists that she must
speak to you herself.

MADGE: Tell her to wait till to-morrow.

FORMAN: I asked her to do that, ma'am, and she said that she
would not be here to-morrow.

(MADGE *turns toward* FORMAN *with some surprise.)*

MADGE: What does she mean by that?

FORMAN: Pardon me for mentioning it, ma'am, but she is a bit
singular, as I take it.

MADGE: Tell her to come here —

(FORMAN *bows and turns to go.* MADGE *goes toward the piano,
near where the paper lies. She sees it. Stops with hand on piano.)*

Oh — Judson!

(FORMAN *stops and comes down. Everything quiet, subdued,
cat-like in his methods.)*

How did you happen to imagine that I would be interested in this
marriage announcement? *(Takes up paper and sits in seat below
the piano.)*

FORMAN: I could 'ardly help it, ma'am.

(MADGE *turns and looks hard at him an instant.* FORMAN *stands
deferentially.)*

MADGE: I suppose you have overheard certain references to the
matter — between myself and my brother?

FORMAN: I 'ave, ma'am, but I would never have referred to it in the least if I did not think it might be of some importance to you, ma'am, to know it.

MADGE: Oh no — of no special importance! We know the parties concerned, and are naturally interested in the event. Of course, you do not imagine there is anything more. *(She does not look at him as she says this.)*

FORMAN *(not looking at* MADGE—*eyes front)*: Certainly not, ma'am. Anyway, if I did imagine there was something more, I'm sure you'd find it to your interest, ma'am, to remember my faithful services in helpin' to keep it quiet.

MADGE *(after slight pause, during which she looks steadily in front)*: Judson, what sort of a fool are you?

(FORMAN *turns to her with feigned astonishment.)*

(Speaks with sharp, caustic utterances, almost between her teeth. Turns to him.) Do you imagine I would take a house, and bring this girl and her mother here, and keep up the establishment for nearly two years without protecting myself against the chance of petty blackmail by my own servants?

FORMAN *(protestingly)*: Ah — ma'am — you misunderstand me — I —

MADGE *(rising—throws paper on to the piano)*: I understand you too well! And now I beg you to understand me. I have had a trifle of experience in the selection of my servants, and can recognize certain things when I see them! It was quite evident from your behaviour you had been in something yourself, and it didn't take me long to get it out of you. You are a self-confessed forger.

FORMAN *(quick movement of apprehension)*: No! *(Apprehensive look around.)* Don't speak out like that! *(Recovers a little.)* It was — it was in confidence — I told you in confidence, ma'am.

MADGE: Well, I'm telling you in confidence that at the first sign of any underhand conduct on *your* part this little episode of yours will —

FORMAN *(hurriedly—to prevent her from speaking it)*: Yes, yes! I will — bear it in mind, ma'am. I will bear it in mind!

MADGE *(after a sharp look at him as if satisfying herself that he is now reduced to proper condition)*: Very well. . . . Now, as to the maid — Térèse —

(FORMAN inclines head for instruction.)

Do you think of anything which might explain her assertion that she will not be here to-morrow?

FORMAN *(his eyes turned away from* MADGE. *Speaking in low tones, and behaviour subdued as if completely humiliated)*: It has occurred to me, ma'am, since you first asked me regarding the matter, that she may have taken exceptions to some occurrences which she thinks she 'as seen going on in this 'ouse.

MADGE: I'll raise her wages if I find it necessary; tell her so. If it isn't money that she wants — I'll see her myself.

FORMAN: Very well, ma'am. *(He turns and goes out quietly.)*

(MADGE *stands motionless a moment. There is a sound of a heavy door opening and closing.* MADGE *gives a quick motion of listening. Hurries to look off. Enter* JIM LARRABEE, *through archway, in some excitement. He is a tall, heavily-built man, with a hard face. Full of determination and a strong character. He is well dressed, and attractive is some respects. A fine looking man. Dark hair and eyes, but the hard sinister look of a criminal.)*

MADGE: Didn't you find him?

LARRABEE: No. *(Goes to the heavy desk and throws open the wooden doors of lower part, showing the iron and combination lock of a safe or strong-box. Gives knob a turn or two nervously, and works at it.)*

(MADGE *follows, watching him.)*

He wasn't there! *(Rises from desk.)* We'll have to get a lock-smith in.

MADGE *(quickly)*: No, no! We can't do that! It isn't safe!

LARRABEE: We've got to do something, haven't we? *(Stoops down quickly before door of safe again, and nervously tries it.)* I wish to God I knew a bit about these things. *(Business at safe.)* There's no time to waste, either! They've put Holmes on the case!

MADGE: Sherlock Holmes?

LARRABEE: Yes. *(At safe, trying knob.)*

MADGE: How do you know?

LARRABEE: I heard it at Leary's. They keep track of him down there, and every time he's put on something they give notice round.

MADGE: What could he do?

LARRABEE *(rises and faces her)*: I don't know—but he'll make some move—he never waits long! It may be any minute! *(Moves about restlessly but stops when* MADGE *speaks.)*

MADGE: Can't you think of someone else—as we can't find Sid?

LARRABEE: He may turn up yet. I left word with Billy Rounds, and he's on the hunt for him. *(Between his teeth.)* Oh! it's damnable. After holding on for two good years just for this and now the time comes and she's blocked us! *(Goes to and looks off and up stairway. Look at* MADGE. *Goes to her.)* Look here! I'll just get at her for a minute. *(Starting to go out.)* I have an idea I can change her mind.

MADGE *(quickly)*: Yes—but wait, Jim.

(LARRABEE *stops and turns to her.*)

(She goes near him.) What's the use of hurting the girl? We've tried all that!

LARRABEE: Well, I'll try something else! *(Turns and goes to archway.)*

MADGE *(quick, half whisper)*: Jim! (LARRABEE *turns,* MADGE *approaches him.)* Remember—nothing that'll show! No marks! We might get into trouble.

LARRABEE *(going doggedly)*: I'll look out for that.

(LARRABEE *goes out, running upstairs in haste. As* MADGE *looks after him with a trifle of anxiety standing in archway, enter* TÉRÈSE. *She is a quiet-looking French maid with a pleasant face. She stands near the door.* MADGE *turns into the room and sees her. Stands an instant. She seats herself in the arm-chair.)*

MADGE: Come here.

(TÉRÈSE *comes down a little way—with slight hesitation.)*

What is it?

TÉRÈSE: Meester Judson said I vas to come.

MADGE: I told Judson to arrange with you himself.

TÉRÈSE: He could not, madame. I do not veesh longer to re-main.

MADGE: What is it? You must give me some reason!

TÉRÈSE: It is zat I wish to go.

MADGE: You've been here months, and have made no complaint.

TÉRÈSE: Ah, madame — it is not so before! It is now beginning zat I do not like.

MADGE *(rising)*: What? What is it you do not like?

. TÉRÈSE *(with some little spirit but low voice)*: I do not like eet, madame — eet — here — zis place — what you do — ze young lady you have up zere! I cannot remain to see! *(Indicating above.)* Eet ees not well! I cannot remain to see!

MADGE: You know nothing about it! The young lady is ill. She is not right here — *(Touching forehead.)* She is a great trouble to us, but we take every care of her, and treat her with the utmost kindness and —

(A piercing scream, as if muffled by something, heard in distant part of house above.)

(Music on scream. Very pianissimo. Agitato.)

(Pause. Both motionless. TÉRÈSE does not assume a horrified expression; she simply stands motionless. After quite a pause, MRS. FAULKNER *comes down stairway rapidly, a white-haired lady, dressed in an old black gown.)*

MRS. FAULKNER: My child! my child! They're hurting my child!

(MRS. FAULKNER *stands just within archway, looking vacantly, helplessly, at* MADGE. MADGE *turns, sees her and goes quickly to her.)*

MADGE *(between her teeth)*: What are you doing here? Didn't I tell you never to come down!

(The old lady simply stares vacantly, but a vague expression of trouble is upon her face.)

Come with me! *(Taking* MRS. FAULKNER *by the arm and drawing her towards stairs.)*

(The old lady hangs back in a frightened way.)

Come, I say! *(The scream again—more muffled—from above. Sudden change. Tenderly.)* Don't be alarmed, dear, your poor daughter's head is bad to-day. She'll be better soon! *(Turns to* TÉRÈSE.) Térèse — come to me in the morning. *(To old lady.)* Come along, dear. *(Then angrily in low threatening voice.)* Do you hear me? Come!

(Takes MRS. FAULKNER *off with some force up the stairs.* TÉRÈSE *stands looking after them. Enter* FORMAN *quietly. He looks a moment toward where* MADGE *has just taken the old lady off.* TÉRÈSE *is looking also the same way.* FORMAN *goes down to* TÉRÈSE. *They look at one another at instant in silence. Then he speaks to her in a low voice. Just before* FORMAN *speaks the music stops.)*

FORMAN: She's made it quite satisfactory, I suppose.

(TÉRÈSE *looks at* FORMAN.)

You will not leave her — now?

TÉRÈSE: Leave her now? More zan evaire before! Do you hear zee young lady? What is eet they make to her?

FORMAN *(low voice)*: It may be she is ill.

TÉRÈSE: Indeed, I think it is so zat zey make her eel! I weel not remain to see! *(Turning a little.)* I can find another place; eet eez not so difficult.

FORMAN: Not so difficult if you know where to go!

TÉRÈSE: Ah — zhat eez it!

FORMAN: I have one address —

TÉRÈSE *(turns to him quickly)*: Bien — you know one?

(FORMAN *nods.)*

Est-ce serieux? What you call re-li-ah-ble?

FORMAN *(moves to her)*: Here — on this card — *(Quickly takes card from pocket and pushes it into her hands.)* Go to that address! Don't let anyone see it!

TÉRÈSE *(quickly looking at card while* FORMAN *looks away — begins slowly to read)*: Meester — Sheer — lock —

FORMAN *(with a quick warning exclamation and sudden turn, seizes her, covering her mouth with one hand; they stand a moment, he looks slowly round)*: Some one might hear you! Go to that address in the morning.

(The front door bell rings. FORMAN *motions her off with quick, short motion. She goes out.* FORMAN *goes out to open the house door — quickly. Sound of house door opening — a solid, heavy sound — not sharp. Enter* SID PRINCE, *walking in quickly. He is a short, stoutish, dapper little fellow. He carries a small black*

*satchel, wears overcoat and hat, gloves, etc., and is well dressed
and jaunty. He wears diamond scarf pin, rings, etc., is quick in
movements and always on the alert.* FORMAN *follows him on,
standing near archway.)*

PRINCE *(going across towards piano)*: Don't waste toime, you
fool; tell 'em I'm 'ere, can't yer?

FORMAN: Did you wish to see Mr. Chetwood, sir, or was it Miss
Chetwood?

FORMAN *(stopping and turning to* FORMAN): Well, I'll be
blowed! You act as if I'd never been 'ere before! 'Ow do you know
but I was born in this 'ere 'ouse? Go on and tell 'em as it's Mr.
Sidney Prince, Esq. *(He puts satchel, which is apparently heavy,
on seat at foot of piano.)*

FORMAN: Oh yes, sir—I beg your pardon! I'll announce you
immediate, sir. *(Goes out upstairs.)*

(PRINCE *takes off hat, gloves, etc., laying them so as to cover the
satchel. Looks about room. Walks over to the heavy desk and
glances at it. Swings door of the desk open in easy business-like
way.)*

PRINCE: Ah! *(As if he had found what he was looking for. Not
an exclamation of surprise. Drops on one knee and gives the lock a
turn. Rises and goes over to his satchel—which he uncovers and
opens. Feels about for something.)*

(MADGE *and* LARRABEE *come downstairs and enter.* PRINCE *sees
them, but does not stop what he is doing.)*

MADGE *(going across to* PRINCE): Oh, is that you, Sid? I'm so
glad you've come.

LARRABEE: Hallo, Sid! . . . Did you get my note?

PRINCE *(going right on with what he is doing)*: Well, I'm 'ere,
ain't I? *(Business at satchel.)* . . . That's what it is, I take it?
(Motion of head towards desk.)

MADGE: Yes. . . We're awfully glad you turned up, Sid. We
might have had to get in some stranger to do it. *(Going across to
below piano in front of* PRINCE.)

PRINCE *(standing up and looking at* LARRABEE *and* MADGE):
That would be nice now, wouldn't it? If your game 'appens to be
anything off colour—!!!

LARRABEE: Oh—it isn't so specially dark.

PRINCE: That different. *(Goes across to desk with tools from satchel.)* I say, Larrabee—

(Quick "Sh!" from MADGE *just behind him.)*

LARRABEE *(at same time)*: Shut up!

(They look round. PRINCE *looks up surprised.)*

For Heaven's sake, Sid, remember—*my* name is Chetwood here.

PRINCE: Beg your pardon. My mistake. Old times when we was learnin' the trade together—eh!

LARRABEE: Yes, yes!

PRINCE: I 'ardly expected you'd be doin' the 'igh tone thing over 'ere, wen I first come up with you workin' the Sound Steamer Line out o' New York.

LARRABEE: Come! Don't let's go into that now.

PRINCE: Well, you needn't get so 'uffy about it! You wouldn't a' been over 'ere at all, if it 'adn't been for me. . . An' youd a' never met Madge 'ere neither—and a devil of a life of it you might a' been leadin'.

LARRABEE: Yes, yes.

MADGE: We know all that, Sid—but can't you open that box for us now? We've no time to lose.

PRINCE: Open it! I should say I could! It's one o' those things that'll fall open if you let it alone long enough! I'd really like to know where you picked up such a relic as this 'ere box! It's an old timer and no mistake! *(About to try some tools on lock, looks about.)* All clear, you say, no danger lurking?

LARRABEE *(shaking head)*: Not the least!

*(*MADGE *moves away a little, glancing cautiously about.* PRINCE *tries tools.* LARRABEE *remains near piano. Both watch him as he tries tools in the lock.)*

PRINCE *(at lock)*: You're not robbing *yourselves,* I trust?

LARRABEE *(near* PRINCE*)*: It does look a little like it!

PRINCE: I knew you was on some rum lay—squatting down in this place for over a year; but I never could seem to—*(business)* —get a line on you. *(He works a moment, then crosses to get a tool out of satchel, and goes near light on piano and begins to adjust it. This must bring him where he commands stage. Stopping and looking sharply at* MADGE *and* LARRABEE.) What do we get here? Oof, I trust?

LARRABEE: Sorry to disappoint you, but it isn't.

PRINCE: That's too bad!

MADGE *(shakes head)*: Only a bundle of papers, Sid.

(PRINCE *works at tool an instant before speaking.)*

PRINCE: Pipers!

LARRABEE: Um! *(Grunt of assent.)*

PRINCE: Realize, I trust?

MADGE: We can't tell—it may be something—it may be nothing.

PRINCE: Well, if it's something, I'm in it, I hope.

MADGE: Why, of course, Sid—whatever you think is due for opening the box.

PRINCE: Fair enough. *(As if it was all settled to go on.)* Now 'ere. *(Glances round quickly.)* Before we starts 'er goin' what's the general surroundin's?

LARRABEE: What's the good of wasting time on— *(Going near* PRINCE.)

PRINCE *(up to him)*: If I'm in this, I'm in it, ain't I? An' I want to know *wot* I'm in.

MADGE: Why don't you tell him, Jimmie?

PRINCE: If anything 'appened, 'ow'd I let the office know 'oo to look out for?

LARRABEE: Well—I'm willing to give him an idea of what it is but I won't give the name of the— *(Hesitates.)*

(MADGE *goes up to arch.)*

PRINCE: That's all I ask—*wot it is.* I don't want no names.

LARRABEE *(nearer* PRINCE *and speaking lower)*: You know we've been working the Continent. Pleasure places and all that.

PRINCE: So I've 'eard.

(MADGE *motions them to wait. Looking off quietly. Nods them to proceed.)*

LARRABEE: It was over there—Homburg was the place. We ran across a young girl who'd been havin' trouble. Sister just died. Mother seemed wrong here. *(Touches forehead.)*

PRINCE: Well — you run across 'er.

LARRABEE: Madge took hold and found that this sister of hers had been having some kind of love affair with a — well — with a foreign gentleman of exceedingly high rank — or at least — expectations that way.

PRINCE: A foreign gentleman?

LARRABEE: That's what I said.

PRINCE: I don't so much care about that, yer know. My lay's 'ere at home.

LARRABEE: Well, this is good enough for me.

PRINCE: 'Ow much was there to it?

LARRABEE: Promise of marriage.

PRINCE: Broke it, of course.

LARRABEE: Yes — and her heart with it. I don't know what more she expected — anyway, she *did* expect more. She and her child died together.

PRINCE: Oh — dead!

LARRABEE: Yes, but the case isn't; there are evidences — letters, photographs, jewellery with inscriptions that he gave her. The sister's been keeping them. . . . *(A glance about.)* We've been keeping the sister. . . . You see?

PRINCE *(whistles)*: Oh, it's the sister you've got 'ere? An' what's 'er little game?

LARRABEE: To get even.

PRINCE: Ah! To get back on 'im for the way 'e treated 'er sister?

LARRABEE: Precisely.

PRINCE: She don't want money?

LARRABEE: No.

PRINCE: An' your little game?

LARRABEE *(shrug of shoulders)*: Whatever there is in it.

PRINCE: These papers an' things ought to be worth a little something!

LARRABEE: I tell you it wouldn't be safe for him to marry until he gets them out of the way! He knows it very well. But what's more, the *family* knows it!

PRINCE: Oh — family! . . . Rich, I take it.

LARRABEE: Rich isn't quite the word. They're something else.

PRINCE: You don't mean —

(LARRABEE *moves nearer* PRINCE *and whispers a name in his ear.*)

My Gawd! Which of 'em?

LARRABEE *(shakes head)*: I don't tell you that.

PRINCE: Well, we *are* a-movin' among the swells now, ain't we? But this 'ere girl—the sister o' the one that died—'ow did you manage to get 'er into it?

MADGE: I picked her up, of course, and sympathized and consoled. I invited her to stay with me at my house in London. Jimmy came over and took this place—and when I brought her along a week later it was all ready—and a private desk safe for the letters and jewellery.

LARRABEE *(turning)*: Yes—combination lock and all. . . Everything worked smooth until a couple of weeks ago, when we began to hear from a firm of London solicitors, some veiled proposals were made—which showed that the time was coming. They wanted the things out of the way. Suddenly all negotiations on their side stopped. The next thing for me to do was to threaten. I wanted the letters for this, but when I went to get them—I found that in some way the girl had managed to change the lock on us. The numbers were wrong—and we couldn't frighten or starve her into opening the thing.

PRINCE: Oh—I see it now. You've got the stuff in there! *(Indicating safe.)*

LARRABEE: That's what I'm telling you! It's in there, and we can't get it out! She's juggled the lock.

PRINCE *(going at once to safe)*: Oh, well, it won't take long to rectify that triflin' error. *(Stops.)* But wot gets *me* is the w'y they broke off with their offers that way—can you make head or tail of that?

LARRABEE: Yes. *(Goes nearer to* PRINCE.) It's simple enough.

(PRINCE *turns to him for explanation.*)

They've given it up themselves, and have got in Sherlock Holmes on the case.

PRINCE *(suddenly starting)*: Wot's that! *(Pause.)* Is 'Olmes in this?

LARRABEE: That's what they told me!

MADGE: But what can he *do,* Sid? We haven't—

PRINCE: 'Ere, don't stand talking about that—I'll get the box open. *(Goes to piano in front of* LARRABEE.) You send a telegram, that's all I want! *(Tears page out of his note-book and writes hurriedly. The other two watch him,* LARRABEE *a little suspiciously. Silence for a few moments while he writes.)* Where's your nearest telegraph office?

MADGE: Round the corner. *(Going to above piano.)*

PRINCE *(down to* LARRABEE *and giving him the telegram he has written)*: Run for it! Mind what I say—*run for it.*

(LARRABEE *is looking at him hard.)*

That's to Alf Bassick. He's Professor Moriarty's confidential man. Moriarty is king of 'em all in London. He runs everything that's shady—an' 'Olmes 'as been settin' lines all round 'im for months—and he didn't know it—an' now he's beginnin' to find out that 'Olmes is trackin' 'im down—and there's the devil to pay. 'E wants any cases 'Olmes is on—it's a dead fight between 'em! 'E'll take the case just to get at 'Olmes! 'E'll kill 'im before 'e's finished with 'im, you can lay all you've got on it.

LARRABEE: What are you telling him?

PRINCE: Nothing whatever, except I've got a job on as I wants to see 'im about in the mornin'. . . . Read it yourself.

(LARRABEE *looks at what* PRINCE *has written.)*

But don't take all night over it! You cawn't tell wot might 'appen. *(Crosses to safe.)*

MADGE: Go on, Jim!

(LARRABEE *crosses,* MADGE *following him.)*

LARRABEE *(to* MADGE *near archway)*: Keep your eyes open.
MADGE *(to* LARRABEE): Don't you worry!

(LARRABEE *goes out.)*

(MADGE *is looking after him. Quick sound of door closing.* PRINCE *drops down to work—real work now—at desk. Short pause.* MADGE *stands watching* PRINCE *a moment. She moves over to near piano and picks up a book carelessly, which she glances at with perfect nonchalance. After a time she speaks without taking eyes from book.)*

I've heard of this Professor Moriarty.

PRINCE: If you 'aven't you must've been out *in the woods.*

MADGE: You say he's king of them all.

PRINCE *(working)*: Bloomin' Hemperor — that's wot I call 'im.

MADGE: He must be a good many different things.

PRINCE: You might see it that way if you looked around an' didn't breathe too 'ard!

MADGE: What does he do?

PRINCE: I'll tell you one thing he does! *(Turns to her and rests a moment from work.)* He sits at 'ome — quiet and easy — an' runs nearly every big operation that's on. All the clever boys are under him one way or another — an' he 'olds them in 'is 'and without moving a muscle! An' if there's a slip and the police get wind of it, there ain't never any 'old on 'im. They can't touch him. And wot's more, they wouldn't want to if they could.

MADGE: Why not?

PRINCE: Because they've tried it — that's w'y — an' the men as did try it was found shortly after a-floatin' in the river — that is, if they was found at all! The moment a man's marked there ain't a street that's safe for 'im! No — nor yet an alley. *(Resumes drilling.)*

MADGE *(after pause)*: What's the idea of telling him about this? He might not want —

PRINCE *(turning to her)*: I tell yer, 'e'll come into anything that gives 'im a chance at 'Olmes — he wants ter trap 'im — that's wot it is an' just what he'll do. *(Resumes work.)*

(PRINCE *works rapidly, drill going in suddenly as if he had one hole sunk. He tries a few tools in it and quickly starts another hole with drills.* MADGE *starts forward at business of drill.)*

MADGE *(recovering to careless)*: Have you got it, Sid?

PRINCE: Not yet — but I'll be there soon. *(Works.)* I know where I am now.

(Sound of door closing outside. Enter LARRABEE *hurriedly. He is breathless from running.)*

LARRABEE: Well, Sid. How goes it?

PRINCE *(working)*: So-so.

LARRABEE: Now about this Professor Moriarty? *(Gets chair from near piano and sits behind* PRINCE.*)*

PRINCE *(working)*: Ask 'er.

MADGE: It's all right, Jim. It was the proper thing to do.

(Music. Melodramatic, very pp. Hardly audible.)

(MADGE *and* LARRABEE *move near* PRINCE, *looking over him eagerly. He quickly introduces small punch and hammers rapidly; sound of bolts, etc., falling inside lock as if loosened. Eagerness of all three increases with final sound of loose iron work inside lock, and* PRINCE *at once pulls open the iron doors. All three give a quick look within.* MADGE *and* LARRABEE *start back with subdued exclamation.* PRINCE *looks in more carefully, then turns to them. Pause.* LARRABEE *in moving back pushes chair along with him. Pause. Music stops.)*

MADGE *(turning to* LARRABEE): Gone!

LARRABEE *(to* MADGE): She's taken 'em out.

PRINCE *(rising to his feet)*: What do you mean?

LARRABEE: The girl!

(MADGE *stops and goes quickly to safe in front of* PRINCE *and dropping down feels carefully about inside. Others watch her closely.* PRINCE *gives back a little for her.)*

(NOTE. — *Their dialogue since opening of safe has dropped to low excited tones, almost whispers, as they would if it were a robbery. Force of habit in their intense excitement.)*

MADGE *(rises and turns to* LARRABEE): She's got them!

PRINCE: 'Ow can you tell as she 'asn't done the trick already?

LARRABEE *(quick turn on* PRINCE): What's that?

PRINCE: She wants to get even, you say.

MADGE: Yes! yes!

PRINCE: Well, then, if she's got the thing out of the box there — ain't it quite likely she's sent 'em along to the girl as 'e wants to marry. *(Brief pause.)*

MADGE: No! She hasn't had the chance.

LARRABEE: She couldn't get them out of this room. We've watched her too close for that.

MADGE: Wait! *(Turns and looks rapidly about piano, etc.)*

(LARRABEE *hurriedly looks about under cushions.)*

LARRABEE: Here! *(Strides towards archway.)* I'll get her down! She'll tell us where they are or strangle for it! *(Turns hurriedly.)* Wait here! When I get her in, don't give her time to think!

(LARRABEE *goes out.* PRINCE *comes to the end of the piano, looking off after* LARRABEE.)

(Music. Very pp.)

(Brief pause. MADGE *glances nervously.)*

PRINCE: Wot's he goin' to do?

MADGE: There's only one thing, Sid. We've got to get it out of her or the whole two years' work is wasted.

(Muffled cry of pain from ALICE *in distance. Pause.)*

PRINCE *(glances off anxiously)*: Look 'ere, I don't so much fancy this sort of thing. *(Goes to safe and collects tools.)*

MADGE: Don't you worry, we'll attend to it!

(Sound of LARRABEE *approaching outside and speaking angrily. Nearer and nearer. Footsteps heard just before entrance.* LARRABEE *drags* ALICE FAULKNER *on, jerking her across him.)*

LARRABEE *(as he brings* ALICE *on)*: Now, we'll see whether you will or not! *(Pause for an instant.)*

(NOTE. — *This scene should be played well up stage.)*

(Music stops.)

(Coming down.) Now tell her what we want.

ALICE *(low voice—slight shake of head)*: You needn't tell me, I know well enough.

MADGE *(drawing nearer to* ALICE *with quiet cat-like glide. Smiling)*: Oh no, dear, you don't know. It isn't anything about locks, or keys, or numbers this time. *(Points slowly to the open safe.)* We want to know what you've done with them!

(Pause. ALICE *looks at* MADGE *calmly. No defiance or suffering in her expression.)*

(Comes closer and speaks with set teeth.) Do you hear! We want to know what you've done with them.

ALICE *(low voice—but clear and distinct)*: You will not know from me.

LARRABEE *(sudden violence, yet subdued, as if not wishing servants to overhear)*: We will know from you—and we'll know before— *(As if to cross* MADGE *to* ALICE.*)*

MADGE *(motioning him)*: Wait, Jim! *(Moves down with him a little.)*

LARRABEE *(to* MADGE, *violently)*: I tell you, they're in this room —she couldn't have got them out—and I'm going to make her— *(As if to seize* ALICE.*)*

MADGE *(detaining him)*: No! Let me speak to her first!

(LARRABEE, *after an instant's sullen pause, turns and walks up stage. Watches from above sullenly.* MADGE *turns to* ALICE *again.)*

Don't you think, dear, it's about time to remember that you owe us a little consideration? Wasn't it something, just a little something, that we found you friendless and ill in Homburg and befriended you?

ALICE: It was only to rob me.

MADGE: Wasn't it something that we brought you and your mother across to England with us—that we kept you here—in our own home—and supported and cared for you—

ALICE: So that you could rob me.

MADGE: My dear child—you have nothing of value. That package of letters wouldn't bring you sixpence.

ALICE: Then why do you want it? Why do you persecute me and starve me to get it? *(Pause—*MADGE *looking at her cruelly.)* All your friendship to me and my mother was a pretence—a *sham.* It was only to get what you wanted away from me when the time came.

MADGE: Why, we have no idea of such a thing!

ALICE *(turning slightly on* MADGE): I don't believe you.

LARRABEE *(who has controlled himself with difficulty)*: Well, believe *me,* then.

(ALICE *turns to him, frightened but calm. No forced expressions of pain and despair anywhere in the scene.)*

(Moves towards her.) You're going to tell us what you've done with that package before you leave this room to-night!

(MADGE *backs away a step or two.*)

ALICE: Not if you kill me.

LARRABEE *(seizing* ALICE *violently by the arms or wrists at back of her)*: It isn't killing that's going to do it — it's something else.

(Music melodramatic and pathetic.)

(LARRABEE *gets* ALICE'S *arms behind her, and holds her as if wrenching or twisting them from behind. She gives slight cry of pain.* MADGE *comes to her.* PRINCE *looks away during following—appearing not to like the scene but not moving.)*

MADGE *(sharp hard voice)*: Tell us where it is! Tell us and he'll stop.

LARRABEE *(a little behind—business of gripping as if wrenching her arms)*: Out with it!

ALICE *(suppressed cry or moan)*: Oh!

(NOTE. — ALICE *has little expression of pain on her face. The idea is to be game.)*

MADGE: *Where is it?*

LARRABEE: Speak quick now! I'll give you a turn next time that'll take it out of you.

MADGE *(low voice)*: Be careful, Jimmie!

LARRABEE *(angry)*: Is this any time to be careful? I tell you, we've got to get it out of her — and we'll do it too! *(Business.)* Will you tell? *(Business.)* Will you tell? *(Business.)* Will you —

(Loud ringing of door bell in distant part of house.)

(NOTE. — *This must on no account be close at hand.)*

(After bell music stops.)

PRINCE *(quick turn on ring. Short sharp whisper as he starts up)*: Look out!

(All stand listening an instant. ALICE, *however, heard nothing, as the pain has made her faint, though not unconscious.* LARRABEE *pushes* ALICE *into chair facing fire-place. He then hides her.* MADGE *goes quickly and cautiously draws picture from a small concealed window.* LARRABEE *stands near* ALICE *close up to her.*

Steps heard outside. LARRABEE *turns quickly, hearing steps. Make these steps distinct—slow—not loud.)*

LARRABEE *(speaking off)*: Here!

(Enter FORMAN. *He stands waiting.)*

Don't go to that door; see who it is.

(FORMAN *simply waits—no surprise on his face.* MADGE *turning and speaking in low but clear voice.* LARRABEE *stands so that* FORMAN *will not see* ALICE.)

MADGE *(standing on ottoman)*: Tall, slim man in a long coat — soft hat — smooth face — carries . . . an ebony cane —

(Short, quick exclamation from PRINCE.)

PRINCE *(breaks in with quick exclamation under breath.* MADGE *stopped by* PRINCE'S *exclamation)*: Sherlock 'Olmes! He's 'ere!

(Pause. PRINCE *quickly conceals his satchel above safe—also closing door of safe. Music melodramatic, very pp.)*

LARRABEE *(moving towards piano, turns out lamp)*: We won't answer the bell.

PRINCE *(turning from tools, etc., and stopping him quickly)*: Now that won't do, ye know! Looks crooked at the start!

LARRABEE: You're right! We'll have him in — and come the easy innocent. *(He turns up the lamp again.)*

MADGE: There's the girl!

PRINCE *(at piano)*: Get her away — *quick!*

(ALICE *is beginning to notice what goes on in a dreamy way.)*

LARRABEE: Take her up the back stairway!

(MADGE *takes* ALICE *quickly and forces her to door as they speak.)*

MADGE *(stopping to speak to* LARRABEE *and speaking out very distinctly)*: She's in poor health and can't see anyone — *you understand.*

LARRABEE: Yes! yes! Lock her in the room — and stay by the door.

(MADGE *and* ALICE *quickly go out.* LARRABEE *closes door at once and stands an instant, uncertain. Then he goes to and opens lid of box on wall seat, and gets a loaded club—an ugly looking weapon —and shoves it into* PRINCE'S *hand.)*

You get out there! *(Indicating.)* Keep quiet there till he gets in the house—then come round to the front.

PRINCE: I come round to the front after 'e's in the 'ouse—that's plain.

LARRABEE: Be ready for 'im when he comes out! If he's got the things in spite of us, I'll give you two sharp whistles! If you don't hear it, let him pass.

PRINCE: But if I *do* 'ear the two whistles—?

LARRABEE: Then let 'im have it.

(PRINCE *gets off at window, which he closes at once.* LARRABEE *moves rapidly, kicking door of desk shut as he passes. Stands at piano, leaning on it carelessly. Turns to* FORMAN.)

Go on, answer the bell.

(FORMAN *bows slightly and goes.* LARRABEE *strolls about trying to get into an assumption of coolness. Picks up book off piano. Sound of heavy door closing outside. Brief pause. Enter* SHERLOCK HOLMES, *hat and stick in hand—wearing a long coat, or ulster, and gloves. He lingers in the archway, apparently seeing nothing in particular, and slowly drawing off gloves. Then moves to the wall seat close at hand and sits.)*

(Music stops.)

(After quite a time LARRABEE *turns, throws book on piano, and saunters towards* HOLMES *in rather an ostentatious manner.)*

Mr. Holmes, I believe.

HOLMES *(rises and turning to* LARRABEE *as if mildly surprised)*: Yes, sir.

LARRABEE: Who did you wish to see, Mr. Holmes?

HOLMES *(looking steadily at* LARRABEE *an instant. Speaks very quietly)*: Thank you so much—I sent my card—by the butler.

LARRABEE *(stands motionless an instant—after an instant's pause)*: Oh—very well.

(Long pause. Enter FORMAN *down stairs.* LARRABEE *moves up near piano and turns to hear what* FORMAN *says.)*

FORMAN *(to* HOLMES): Miss Faulkner begs Mr. Holmes to excuse her. She is not well enough to see anyone this evening.

(HOLMES *takes out note-book and pencil and writes a word or two on a card or leaf of the book. Tears it out of book. Pulls out watch and glances at it. Hands the card to* FORMAN, *taking off coat first.)*

HOLMES: Hand Miss Faulkner this — and say that I have —

LARRABEE: I beg your pardon, Mr. Holmes, but it's quite useless — really.

HOLMES: Oh — I'm so sorry to hear it.

(HOLMES *turns quietly to* LARRABEE *and looks at him.* LARRABEE *is a trifle affected by* HOLMES'S *quiet scrutiny.)*

LARRABEE: Yes — Miss Faulkner is — I regret to say — quite an invalid. She is unable to see anyone — her health is so poor.

HOLMES: Did it ever occur to you that she might be confined to the house too much?

(An instant's pause.)

LARRABEE *(suddenly in low threatening tone, but not too violent)*: How does that concern you?

HOLMES *(easily)*: It doesn't. . . . I simply made the suggestion.

(The two look at one another an instant. HOLMES *turns quietly to* FORMAN.)

That's all. *(Motions him slightly.)* Go on. Take it up.

(FORMAN *goes out up stairway. After a moment* LARRABEE *turns, breaking into hearty laughter.)*

LARRABEE: Ha! ha! This is really too good. *(Strolling about laughing.)* Why, of *course* he can take up your card — or your note — or whatever it is, if you wish it so much; I was only trying to save you the trouble.

HOLMES *(who has been watching him through foregoing speech)*: Thanks — hardly any trouble at all to send a card. *(Seats himself in an easy languid way — picks up* Punch.)

LARRABEE *(endeavours to be easy, careless and patronizing)*: Do you know, Mr. Holmes, you interest me very much.

HOLMES *(easily)*: Ah!

LARRABEE: Upon my word, yes! We've all heard of your wonderful methods. *(Coming towards* HOLMES.) Your marvellous insight—your ingenuity in picking up and following clues—and the astonishing manner in which you gain information from the most trifling details. . . . Now, I dare say—in this brief moment or two you've discovered any number of things about me.

HOLMES: Nothing of consequence, Mr. Chetwood—I have scarcely more than asked myself why you rushed off and sent that telegram in such a frightened hurry—what possible excuse you could have had for gulping down that tumbler of raw brandy at the "Lion's Head" on the way back—why your friend with the auburn hair left so suddenly by the terrace window—and what there can possibly be about the safe in the lower part of that desk to cause you such painful anxiety.

(Pause. LARRABEE *standing motionless looking at* HOLMES. HOLMES *picks up paper and reads.)*

LARRABEE: Ha! ha! very good! Very good indeed! If those things were only true now, I'd be wonderfully impressed. It would be absolutely—

(He breaks off as FORMAN *enters—coming down stairs. He quietly crosses to* LARRABEE, *who is watching him, and extends salver with a note upon it.* HOLMES *is looking over paper languidly.* LARRABEE *takes note.* FORMAN *retires.)*

You'll excuse me, I trust.

(HOLMES *remains silent, glancing over paper and looking quietly at* FORMAN. LARRABEE *reads the note hastily.)*

(First a second's thought after reading, as he sees that HOLMES *is not observing him—then speaking.)* Ah—it's from—er—Miss Faulkner! Well really! She begs to be allowed to see—Mr. Holmes. She absolutely *implores it!* (HOLMES *looks slowly up as though scarcely interested.)* Well, I suppose I shall have to give way. *(Turns to* FORMAN.) Judson!

FORMAN: Sir.

LARRABEE *(emphasizing words in italics)*: *Ask Miss Faulkner* to come down to the drawing-room. Say that Mr. Holmes is waiting to see her.

FORMAN: Yes, sir. *(Bows and goes out upstairs.)*

LARRABEE *(trying to get on the free and easy style again)*: It's quite remarkable, upon my soul! May I ask—*(turns toward* HOLMES*)*—if it's not an impertinent question, what message you sent up that could have so aroused Miss Faulkner's desire to come down?

HOLMES *(looking up at* LARRABEE *innocently)*: Merely that if she wasn't down here in five minutes I'd go up.

LARRABEE *(slightly knocked)*: Oh, that was it!

HOLMES: Quite so. *(Rises and takes his watch out.)* And unless I am greatly mistaken I hear the young lady on the stairs. In which case she has a minute and a half to spare. *(Moving by piano— taking opportunity to look at keys, music, etc.)*

(Enter MADGE LARRABEE *downstairs as if not quite strong. She has made her face pale, and steadies herself a little by columns, side of arch, furniture, etc., as she comes on, but not overdoing this. She gives the impression of a person a little weak, but endeavouring not to let it be seen.)*

LARRABEE *(advancing to* MADGE*)*: Alice—or—that is, Miss Faulkner, let me introduce Mr. Sherlock Holmes.

*(*HOLMES *is near piano.* MADGE *goes a step to him with extended hand.* HOLMES *meets* MADGE *and takes her hand in the utmost confidence.)*

MADGE: Mr. Holmes! *(Coming toward him with extended hand.)*

HOLMES *(meeting* MADGE*)*: Miss Faulkner!

MADGE: I'm really most charmed to meet you—although it does look as if you had made me come down in spite of myself, doesn't it? But it isn't so at all, Mr. Holmes. I was more than anxious to come, only the doctor has forbidden me seeing anyone —but when Cousin Freddie said I might come, of course that fixed the responsibility on him, so I have a perfectly clear conscience.

HOLMES: I thank you very much for consenting to see me, Miss Faulkner, but regret that you were put to the trouble of making such a very rapid change of dress.

(MADGE *slightest possible start, and recover at once.*)

MADGE: Ye—yes! I did hurry a trifle, I confess. *(Crosses toward* LARRABEE.) Mr. Holmes is quite living up to his reputation, isn't he, Freddie?

LARRABEE: Yes. . . . But he didn't quite live up to it a moment ago.

MADGE: Oh, didn't he! I'm so sorry. *(Sits on seat at foot of piano.)*

LARRABEE: No. He's been telling me the most astonishing things.

MADGE: And they weren't true?

LARRABEE: Well hardly! (HOLMES *sits in arm-chair.)* He wanted to know what there was about the safe in the lower part of that desk that caused me such horrible anxiety! Ha! ha! ha!

MADGE *(above* LARRABEE'S *laugh—to* HOLMES): Why, there isn't anything. *(To* LARRABEE.) Is there?

LARRABEE: That's just it! Ha! ha! ha! *(With a quick motion swings back the doors.)* There's a *safe* there, but nothing in it.

(MADGE *joins him in laughter.)*

MADGE *(as she laughs)*: Really Mr. Holmes, that's too grotesque, ha! ha!

(HOLMES, *seated in arm-chair among the cushions, regards* MADGE *and* LARRABEE *with a peculiar whimsical look.)*

LARRABEE *(laughing)*: Perhaps you'll do better next time! *(Closes safe door.)*

MADGE: Yes, next time— (HOLMES *is looking at them.)* You might try on me, Mr. Holmes. *(Looking playfully at* HOLMES, *as if greatly enjoying the lark.)*

LARRABEE: Yes, what do you think of her?

HOLMES: It is very easy to discern one thing about Miss Faulkner—and that is, that she is particularly fond of the piano— that her touch is exquisite, her expression wonderful, and her technique extraordinary. While she likes light music very well, she is extremely fond of some of the great masters, among whom are Chopin, Liszt. She plays a great deal indeed; I see it is her chief diversion — which makes it all the more remarkable *that she has not touched the piano for three days.*

(Pause.)

MADGE *(turning to* LARRABEE—*a trifle disconcerted by* HOLMES'S *last words, but nearly hiding it with success)*: Why that's quite surprising, isn't it?

LARRABEE: Certainly better than he did for me.

HOLMES *(rising)*: I am glad to somewhat repair my shattered reputation, and as a reward, will Miss Faulkner be so good as to play me something of which I am particularly fond?

MADGE: I shall be delighted — if I *can. (Looks questioningly at* HOLMES.)

HOLMES: If you can! Something tells me that Chopin's Prelude Number Fifteen is at your finger ends.

MADGE: Oh yes! *(Rising and forgetting her illness, and going to keyboard—crossing in front of piano)*: I can give you *that.*

HOLMES: It will please me so much.

MADGE *(stopping suddenly as she is about to sit at piano)*: But tell me, Mr. Holmes, how did you know so much about my playing — my expression — technique?

HOLMES: Your hands.

MADGE: And my preference for the composers you mentioned?

HOLMES: Your music-rack.

MADGE: How simple! But you said I hadn't played for three days. How did —

HOLMES: The keys.

MADGE: The keys?

HOLMES: A light layer of dust.

MADGE: Dust! Oh dear! *(Quick business with handkerchief on keyboard.)* I never knew Térèse to forget before. *(To* HOLMES.) You must think us very untidy, I'm sure.

HOLMES: Quite the reverse. I see from many things that you are not untidy in the least, and therefore I am compelled to conclude that the failure of Térèse is due to something else.

MADGE *(a little under breath—and hesitatingly—yet compelled by* HOLMES'S *pointed statement to ask)*: Wh—what?

HOLMES: To some unusual excitement or disturbance that has recently taken place in this house.

MADGE *(after an instant's pause)*: You're doing very well, Mr. Holmes, and you deserve your Chopin. *(Sits, makes preparations to play rather hurriedly in order to change the subject.)*

HOLMES: Thanks.

(LARRABEE *looks toward safe, far from easy in his mind, and leans on piano, giving* HOLMES *a glance as he turns to* MADGE. MADGE *strikes a few preliminary chords during above business and soon begins to play the composition spoken of. Shortly after the music begins, and while* LARRABEE *is looking to front or elsewhere,* HOLMES *reaches quietly back and pulls the bell crank. No sound of bell heard, the music supposed to make it inaudible. He then sinks into seat just at bell. After a short time* FORMAN *enters and stands waiting just in the archway.* LARRABEE *does not see* FORMAN *at first, but happening to turn discovers him standing there and speaks a warning word to* MADGE *under his breath.* MADGE, *hearing* LARRABEE *speak, looks up and sees* FORMAN. *She stops playing in the midst of a bar—a hesitating stop. Looks at* FORMAN *a moment.)*

MADGE: What are you doing here, Judson?

(Brief pause because FORMAN *seems surprised.)*

FORMAN: I came to see what was wanted, ma'am.

(Brief pause.)

MADGE: What was wanted?

(Brief pause.)

LARRABEE: Nobody asked you to come here.

FORMAN: I beg pardon, sir. I answered the bell.

LARRABEE *(becoming savage)*: What bell?

FORMAN: The drawing-room bell, sir.

LARRABEE *(threateningly)*: What do you mean, you blockhead?

FORMAN: I'm quite sure it rung, sir.

LARRABEE *(loud voice)*: Well, I tell you it did *not* ring!

(Pause. The LARRABEES *look angrily at* FORMAN.)*

HOLMES *(quietly—after slight pause—clear incisive voice)*: Your butler is right, Mr. Chetwood—the bell *did* ring.

(Brief pause. LARRABEE *and* MADGE *looking at* HOLMES.)

LARRABEE: How do you know?
HOLMES: I rang it.

(MADGE *rises.)*

LARRABEE *(roughly)*: What do you want?

(HOLMES *rises, takes card from case or pocket.)*

HOLMES: I want to send my card to Miss Faulkner. *(Gives card to* FORMAN.)

(FORMAN *stands apparently paralysed.)*

LARRABEE *(angrily—approaching* HOLMES): What right have you to ring for servants and give orders in my house?
HOLMES *(turning on* LARRABEE): What right have you to prevent my cards from reaching their destination—and how does it happen that you and this woman are resorting to trickery and deceit to prevent me from seeing Alice Faulkner? *(The situation is held an instant and then he turns quietly to* FORMAN.) Through some trifling oversight, Judson, neither of the cards I handed you have been delivered. See that this *error—* does not occur again.

(FORMAN *stands, apparently uncertain what to do.)*

FORMAN: My orders, sir—
HOLMES *(quick—sharp)*: Ah! you have orders! *(A sudden sharp glance at* LARRABEE *and back in an instant.)*
FORMAN: I can't say, sir, as I—
HOLMES *(quickly breaking in)*: You were told *not to deliver my card!*
LARRABEE *(step or two up)*: What business is this of yours, I'd like to know?
HOLMES: I shall satisfy your curiosity on that point in a *very short time.*
LARRABEE: Yes—and you'll find out in a very short time that it isn't safe to meddle with me! It wouldn't be any trouble at all for me to throw you out into the street.
HOLMES *(sauntering easily towards him—shaking finger ominously)*: Possibly not—but trouble would swiftly follow such an experiment on your part.

LARRABEE: It's a cursed lucky thing for you I'm not armed.

HOLMES: Yes — well, when Miss Faulkner comes down you can go and arm yourself.

LARRABEE: Arm myself! I'll call the police! And what's more, I'll do it now.

(HOLMES *steps down and faces* LARRABEE.)

HOLMES: You will not do it now. You will remain where you are until the lady I came here to see has entered this room.

LARRABEE: What makes you so sure of that?

HOLMES *(in his face)*: Because you will infinitely prefer to avoid an investigation of your very suspicious conduct, Mr. James Larrabee —

(A sharp start from both LARRABEE *and* MADGE *on hearing* HOLMES *address the former by his proper name.)*

— an investigation that shall certainly take place if you or your wife presume further to interfere with my business. *(Turns to* FORMAN.) As for you, my man — it gives me great pleasure to recall the features of an old acquaintance. Your recent connexion with the signing of another man's name to a small piece of paper has made your presence at Bow Street much desired. You will either deliver that card to Miss Faulkner at once — or you sleep in the police station to-night. It is a matter of small consequence to me which you do. *(Turns and strolls near fire, picking book up from mantelpiece — and sits.)*

(FORMAN *stands motionless, but torn with conflicting fears.)*

FORMAN *(finally in a low painful voice — whispers hoarsely)*: Shall I go, sir?

(MADGE *moves to near* LARRABEE, *at piano.)*

LARRABEE: Go on. Take up the card — it makes no difference to me.

MADGE *(quick sharp aside to* LARRABEE): If she comes down can't he get them away from her?

LARRABEE *(to* MADGE): If he does Sid Prince is waiting for him outside.

(FORMAN, *appearing to be greatly relieved, turns and goes out up stairs with* HOLMES'S *card.*)

(Pathetic music, very pp.)

(A pause—no one moves.)

(Enter ALICE FAULKNER. *She comes down a little—very weak—looking at* LARRABEE, *then seeing* HOLMES *for first time.*)

(Stop music.)

HOLMES *(on seeing* ALICE, *rises and puts book on mantel. After a brief pause, turns and comes down to* LARRABEE): A short time since you displayed an acute anxiety to leave the room. Pray do not let me detain you or your wife — any longer.

(The LARRABEES *do not move. After brief pause,* HOLMES *shrugs shoulders slightly and goes over to* ALICE. HOLMES *and* ALICE *regard each other a moment.*)

ALICE: This is Mr. Holmes?

HOLMES: Yes.

ALICE: You wished to see me?

HOLMES: Very much indeed, Miss Faulkner, but I am sorry to see— *(placing chair near her)* —you are far from well.

ALICE *(a step.* LARRABEE *gives a quick glance across at her, threateningly, and a gesture of warning, but keeping it down)*: Oh no— *(Stops as she catches* LARRABEE'S *angry glance.)*

HOLMES *(pausing as he is about to place chair, and looking at her)*: No? *(Lets go of his chair.)* I beg your pardon—but— *(Goes to her and takes her hand delicately—looks at red marks on her wrist. Looking up at her.)* What does this mean?

ALICE *(shrinking a little. Sees* LARRABEE'S *cruel glance)*: Oh—nothing.

*(HOLMES *looks steadily at her an instant.*)*

HOLMES: Nothing?

ALICE *(shaking head)*: No!

HOLMES: And the— *(pointing lightly)* —mark here on your neck plainly showing the clutch of a man's fingers? *(Indicating a place on her neck where more marks appear.)* Does that mean nothing also?

(Pause. ALICE *turns slightly away without answering.)*

(Looking straight before him to front.) It occurs to me that I would like to have an explanation of this. . . . Possibly — *(turns slowly towards* LARRABEE) — you can furnish one, Mr. Larrabee?

(Pause.)

LARRABEE *(doggedly)*: How should I know?

HOLMES: It seems to have occurred in your house.

LARRABEE *(advancing a little, becoming violently angry)*: What if it did? You'd better understand that it isn't healthy for you or anyone else to interfere with my business.

HOLMES *(quickly — incisively)*: Ah! Then it is your business. We have that much at least.

(LARRABEE *stops suddenly and holds himself in.)*

(Turning to ALICE.) Pray be seated, Miss Faulkner. *(Placing chair as if not near enough.)*

(ALICE *hesitates an instant — then decides to remain standing for the present.* LARRABEE *stands watching and listening to interview between* HOLMES *and* ALICE.)

ALICE: I don't know who you are, Mr. Holmes, or why you are here.

HOLMES: I shall be very glad to explain. So far as the question of my identity is concerned, you have my name and address as well as the announcement of my profession upon the card, which I observe you still hold clasped tightly in the fingers of your left hand.

(ALICE *at once looks at the card in her hand.)*

ALICE *(a look at him)*: A — detective! *(Sits on ottoman, looking at* HOLMES.)

HOLMES *(draws near her and sits)*: Quite so. And my business is this. I have been consulted as to the possibility of obtaining from you certain letters and other things which are supposed to be in your possession, and which — I need not tell you — are the source of the greatest anxiety.

ALICE *(her manner changing and no longer timid and shrinking)*: It is quite true I have such letters, Mr. Holmes, but it will be impossible to get them from me; others — have tried — and failed.

HOLMES: What others have or have not done, while possibly instructive in certain directions, can in no way affect my conduct, Miss Faulkner. I have come to you frankly and directly, to beg you to pity and forgive.

ALICE: There are some things, Mr. Holmes, beyond pity — beyond forgiveness.

HOLMES: But there are other things that are not. (ALICE *looks at him.*) I am able to assure you of the sincere penitence — the deep regret — of the one who inflicted the injury, and of his earnest desire to make — any reparation in his power.

ALICE: How can reparation be made to the dead?

HOLMES: How indeed! And for that very reason, whatever injury you yourself may be able to inflict by means of these things can be no reparation — no satisfaction — no indemnity to the one no longer here. You will be acting for the *living* — not the dead. For your own satisfaction, Miss Faulkner, your own gratification, your own revenge!

(ALICE *starts slightly at the idea suggested and rises. Pause.* HOLMES *rises, moves his chair back a little, standing with his hand on it.*)

ALICE *(stands a moment, very quiet low voice)*: I know — from this and from other things that have happened — that a — a marriage is — contemplated.

HOLMES: It is quite true.

ALICE: I *cannot* give up what I intend to do, Mr. Holmes. There are other things beside revenge — there is punishment. If I am not able to communicate with the family — to which this man proposes to ally himself — in time to prevent such a thing — the punishment will come later — but you may be perfectly sure it will come. (HOLMES *is about to speak. She motions him not to speak.*) There is nothing more to say!

(HOLMES *gives a signal.*)

(She looks at HOLMES *an instant.)* Good night, Mr. Holmes. *(She turns and starts to go.)*

HOLMES: But my dear Miss Faulkner, before you —

(A confused noise of shouting and terrified screams from below, followed by sounds of people running up a stairway and through the halls.)

HOLMES: *What's that?*

(All stop and listen. Noise louder. Enter FORMAN, *breathless and white. At same time smoke pours in through archway.)*

FORMAN *(gasping)*: Mr. Chetwood! Mr. Chetwood!
MADGE *and* LARRABEE: What is it?

(HOLMES *keeps his eyes sharply on* ALICE. ALICE *stands back alarmed.)*

FORMAN: The lamp—in the kitchen, sir! It fell off the table—an' everything down there is blazin', sir.
MADGE: The house—is on fire! *(She gives a glance towards safe, forgetting that the package is gone—but instantly recovers.)*

(LARRABEE *hurriedly goes out,* MADGE *after him.* FORMAN *disappears. Noise of people running downstairs, etc.* ALICE, *on cue "Blazin', sir," gives a scream and looks quickly at chair, at the same time making an involuntary start toward it. She stops upon seeing* HOLMES *and stands. Noises grow less and die away outside and below.)*

HOLMES: Don't alarm yourself, Miss Faulkner—*(slight shake of head)*—there is no fire.
ALICE *(shows by tone that she fears something)*: No fire! *(Stands dreading what may come.)*
HOLMES: The smoke was all arranged for by me. *(Slight pause.)*
ALICE: Arranged for? *(Looks at* HOLMES.)

(HOLMES *quickly moves to large upholstered chair which* ALICE *glanced at and made start towards a moment since.)*

What does it mean, Mr. Holmes?

(HOLMES *feels rapidly over chair. Rips away upholstery.* ALICE *attempts to stop him—but is too late, and backs to piano almost in a fainting condition.* HOLMES *stands erect with a package in his hand.)*

HOLMES: That I wanted this package of letters, Miss Faulkner—

(ALICE *stands looking at* HOLMES *speechless—motionless—meets* HOLMES'S *gaze for a moment, and then covers her face with her hands, and very slight motion of convulsive sob or two.* HOLMES *with a quick motion steps quickly in a business-like way to the seat where his coat, hat and cane are, and picks up coat, throwing it over his arm as if to go at once. As he is about to take his hat, he catches sight of* ALICE'S *face and stops dead where he is.)*

(Music. Very pp. Scarcely audible.)

(HOLMES *stands looking at her, motionless. She soon looks up at him again, brushing hand across face as if to clear away any sign of crying. The tableau of the two looking at one another is held a moment or two.* HOLMES'S *eyes leave her face and he looks down an instant. After a moment he lays his coat, hat and cane back on seat. Pauses an instant. Turns toward her.)*

HOLMES *(low voice. Brief pause)*: I won't take them, Miss Faulkner. *(He looks down an instant. Her eyes are upon his face steadily.)* As you—*(still looking down)*—as you—very likely conjecture, the alarm of fire was only to make you betray their hiding-place—which you did. . .and I—availed myself of that betrayal—as you see. But now that I witness your great distress—I find that I cannot keep them—unless—*(looking up at her)*—you can possibly—change your mind and let me have them—of your own free will. . . . *(He looks at her a moment. She shakes her head very slightly.)* I hardly supposed you could. *(Looks down a moment. Looks up.)* I will therefore—return it to you. *(Very slight pause, and he is about to start toward her as if to hand her the package.)*

(Sound of quick footsteps outside. Enter LARRABEE, *with a revolver in his hand, followed by* MADGE.)

(Stop music.)

LARRABEE: So! You've got them, have you? And now, I suppose we're going to see you walk out of the house with them. *(Handles revolver with meaning.)*

(HOLMES *looks quietly at* LARRABEE *an instant.)*

HOLMES: On the contrary, you're going to see me return them to their rightful owner.

LARRABEE *(with revolver)*: Yes—I think that'll be the safest
thing for Mr. Sherlock Holmes to do.

(HOLMES *stops dead and looks at* LARRABEE *and walks quietly
down facing him.)*

HOLMES: You flatter yourself, Mr. Larrabee. The reason I do
not leave the house with this package of papers is not because of
you, or what you may do—or say—or think—or feel! It is on
account of this young lady! I care that for your cheap bravado!
(Looks at revolver and smiles.) Really! *(He looks quietly in*
LARRABEE'S *eyes an instant, then turns and goes to* ALICE.)
Miss Faulkner, permit me to place this in your hands. *(Gives her
the package.)*

(ALICE *takes the package with sudden eagerness—then turns and
keeps her eyes steadily on* HOLMES.)

Should you ever change your mind and be so generous, so
forgiving, as to wish to return these letters to the one who wrote
them, you have my address. In any event, rest assured there will
be no more cruelty, no more persecution in this house. You are
perfectly safe with your property now—for I shall so arrange it
that your faintest cry of distress will be heard! And if that cry is
heard—it will be a very unfortunate thing for those who are
responsible. Good night, Miss Faulkner. *(Pause—turns to*
LARRABEE *and* MADGE. *Coming to them.)* As for you, sir, and
you, madam, I beg you to understand that you continue your
persecution of that young lady *at your peril.*

(ALICE *looks at* HOLMES *an instant, uncertain what to do. He
makes a slight motion indicating her to go.* ALICE, *after slight
pause, crosses in front of* HOLMES *and goes out.* LARRABEE *makes
slight move towards* ALICE, *but is checked by a look from*
HOLMES. HOLMES *waits, motionless, eyes on* ALICE, *until her
exit. Then he looks after her for a moment. Then turns and
takes his coat and hat. Looks at them an instant.)*

Good evening— *(Walks out, and the sound of heavy door closing
is heard outside.)*

(Pause. LARRABEE *and* MADGE *stand where* HOLMES *left them.
Sound of window opening.* SID PRINCE *hurries in at window.)*

PRINCE (*sharp but subdued*): Well! 'E didn't get it, did 'e?

(LARRABEE *shakes head.* PRINCE *looks at him, puzzled, and then turns towards* MADGE.)

Well—wot is it? Wot's the pay if 'e didn't?
MADGE: He gave it to *her.*
PRINCE: What!—'e found it?

(MADGE *indicates* "Yes" *by slight movement.*)

An' gave it to the girl?

(MADGE *repeats slight affirmative motion.*)

Well 'ere—I say! Wot are you waiting for? Now's the chance—before she 'ides it again! (*Starting as if to go.*)
MADGE (*stopping* PRINCE): No! Wait! (*Glances round nervously.*)
PRINCE: Wot's the matter! (*Going to* LARRABEE.) Do you want to lose it?
LARRABEE: No! you're right! It's all a cursed bluff! (*Starting as if to go.*)
MADGE (*meeting them, as if to stop them*): No, no, Jim!
LARRABEE: I tell you we will! Now's our chance to get a hold of it! (*Pushing her aside.*)
PRINCE: Well, I should say so!

(*Three knocks are heard just as* PRINCE *and* LARRABEE *reach archway. A distant sound of three heavy blows, as if struck from underneath up against the floor, reverberates through the house. All stop motionless.*)

(*Pause.*)

(*Music, melodramatic agitato, very pp. till Curtain.*)

LARRABEE (*in a low voice*): What's that?
MADGE: Someone at the door.
LARRABEE (*low voice*): No—it was on that side!

(PRINCE *glances round alarmed.* MADGE *rings bell. Enter* FORMAN. *All stand easily as if nothing out of the usual.*)

MADGE: I think someone knocked, Judson.

(FORMAN *at once goes out quietly but quickly. Sound of door outside closing again.* FORMAN *re-enters.)*

FORMAN: I beg pardon, ma'am, there's no one at the door.

MADGE: That's all.

(FORMAN *goes.)*

PRINCE *(speaks almost in a whisper from above the piano):* 'E's got us watched! Wot we want to do is to leave it alone an' let the Hemperor 'ave it!

MADGE *(low voice—taking a step or two toward* PRINCE): Do you mean — Professor Moriarty?

PRINCE: That's 'oo I mean. Once let 'im get at it and 'e'll settle it with 'Olmes pretty quick. *(Turns to* LARRABEE.) Meet me at Leary's—nine sharp—in the morning. Don't you worry a minute! I tell you the Professor'll get at 'im before to-morrow night! 'E don't wait long either! An' w'en he strikes—it means *death. (He goes out at window.)*

(Brief pause. After PRINCE *goes,* MADGE *looks after him.* LARRABEE, *with a despairing look on his face, leans on chair— looks round puzzled. His eyes meet* MADGE'S *as lights fade away.)*

CURTAIN.

ACT II

SCENE I. — *This scene is built inside the Second.* PROFESSOR MORIARTY'S *underground office. A large vault-like room, with rough masonry walls and vaulted ceiling. The general idea of this place is that it has been converted from a cellar room of a warehouse into a fairly comfortable office or head-quarters. There are no windows.*

The colour or tone of this set must not be similar to the third Act set, which is a gloomy and dark bluish-brown. The effect in this set should be of masonry that has long ago been whitewashed and is now old, stained and grimy. Maps on wall of England, France, Germany, Russia, etc. Also a marked map of London— heavy spots upon certain localities. Many charts of buildings, plans of floors—possible tunnellings, etc. Many books about—on impoverished shelves, etc.

PROFESSOR ROBERT MORIARTY *is seated at a large circular desk facing the front. He is looking over letters, telegrams, papers, etc., as if morning mail. He is a middle-aged man, with massive head and grey hair, and a face full of character, overhanging brow, heavy jaw. A man of great intellectual force, extremely tall and thin. His forehead domes out in a white curve, and his two eyes are deeply sunken in his head. Clean-shaven, pale, ascetic-looking. Shoulders rounded, and face protruding forward, and for ever oscillating from side to side in a curiously reptilian fashion. Deep hollow voice.*

The room is dark, with light showing on his face, as if from lamp. Pause. MORIARTY *rings a gong at desk, which has a peculiar sound. In a second, buzzer outside door replies twice. He picks up a speaking tube and puts it to his mouth.*

MORIARTY *(speaking into tube in a low voice)*: Number. *(He places tube to his ear and listens, then speaks into it again.)* Correct. *(Drops tube. He moves a lever up against wall and the bolt of the door slides back with a solid heavy sound.)*

101

(Enter JOHN *noiselessly. No sound of steps. He stands just within the door in the half darkness.)*

Has any report come in from Chibley?

JOHN: Nothing yet, sir.

MORIARTY: All the others are heard from?

JOHN: Yes, sir.

MORIARTY: I was afraid we'd have trouble there. If anything happened we lose Hickson — one of our best men. Send Bassick.

*(*JOHN *goes out. Bolt slides back. Buzzer outside door rings twice.* MORIARTY *picks up tube and speaks into it.)*

(Speaking into tube.) Number. *(Listens. Speaks into tube again.)* Correct. *(He slides back bolt of door.)*

(Enter BASSICK *noiselessly. Bolt of door slides back.* BASSICK *goes to* MORIARTY'S *desk at once and stands.* MORIARTY *motions him to sit. He does so.)*

Before we go into anything else, I want to refer to Davidson.

BASSICK: I've made a note of him myself, sir; he's holding back money.

MORIARTY: Something like six hundred short on that last haul, isn't it?

BASSICK: Certainly, as much as that.

MORIARTY: Have him attended to. Craigin is the one to do it. (BASSICK *writes a memo, quickly.)* And see that his disappearance is noticed. Have it spoken of. That finishes Davidson. . . . Now as to this Blaisdell matter — did you learn anything more?

BASSICK: The whole thing was a trap.

MORIARTY: What do you mean?

BASSICK: Set and baited by an expert.

MORIARTY: But those letters and papers of instructions — you brought them back, or destroyed them, I trust?

BASSICK: I could not do it, sir— Manning has disappeared and the papers are gone!

(Music melodramatic. Cue, as MORIARTY *looks at* BASSICK.)*

MORIARTY: Gone! Sherlock Holmes again. That's bad for the Underwood trial.

BASSICK: I thought Shackleford was going to get a post-ponement.

MORIARTY: He tried to — and found he was blocked.

BASSICK: Who could have done it?

(MORIARTY *turns and looks at* BASSICK *almost hypnotically—his head vibrating from side to side as if making him speak the name.*)

Sherlock Holmes?

MORIARTY: Sherlock Holmes again. *(His eyes still on* BASSICK. BASSICK *as if fascinated by* MORIARTY. *Slight affirmative motion.)* He's got hold of between twenty and thirty papers and instructions in as many different jobs, and some as to putting a man or two out of the way — and he's gradually completing chains of evidence which, if we let him go on, will reach to me as sure as the sun will rise. Reach to me! — Ha! *(Sneer.)* He's playing rather a dangerous game! Inspector Wilson tried it seven years ago. Wilson is dead. Two years later Henderson took it up. We haven't heard anything of Henderson lately, eh?

BASSICK *(shaking head)*: Not a thing, sir.

MORIARTY: Ha! *(Sneer.)* This Holmes is rather a talented man. He hopes to drag me in at the Underwood trial, but he doesn't realize what can happen between now and Monday. He doesn't know that there isn't a street in London that'll be safe for him if I whisper his name to Craigin — I might even make him a little call myself — just for the satisfaction of it — *(business of head swaying, etc.)* — just for the satisfaction of it. (BASSICK *watches* MORIARTY *with some anxiety.)* Baker Street, isn't it? His place — Baker Street — eh?

BASSICK: Baker Street, sir.

MORIARTY: We could make it safe. We could make it absolutely secure for three streets each way.

BASSICK: Yes, sir, but —

MORIARTY: We could. We've done it over and over again elsewhere — Police decoyed. Men in every doorway. *(Sudden turn to him.)* Do this to-night — in Baker Street! At nine o'clock call his attendants out on one pretext and another, and keep them out — you understand! I'll see this Sherlock Holmes myself — I'll give him a chance for his life. If he declines to treat with me —

(He takes a savage-looking bulldog revolver from under desk and examines it carefully, slowly placing it in breast pocket. Ring of a telephone bell is heard, but not until the revolver business is finished.)

(The music stops.)

(MORIARTY *gives a nod to* BASSICK, *indicating him to attend to 'phone.* BASSICK *rises and goes to and picks up telephone.* MORIARTY *resumes business of examining papers on his desk.)*

BASSICK *(speaks into receiver and listens as indicated)*: Yes — yes — Bassick — What name did you say? Oh, Prince, yes. He'll have to wait — Yes — I got his telegram last night — Well, tell him to come and speak to me at the 'phone. *(Longer wait.)* Yes — I got your telegram, Prince, but I have an important matter on. You'll have to wait — Who? *(Suddenly becomes very interested.)* What sort of a game is it? — Where is he now? — Wait a moment. *(To* MORIARTY.) Here's something, sir. Sid Prince has come here over some job, and he says he's got Holmes fighting against him.

MORIARTY *(quickly turning to* BASSICK): Eh! Ask him what it is. Ask him what it is. (BASSICK *is about to speak through the telephone. Quickly.)* Wait! (BASSICK *stops.)* Let him come here. (BASSICK *turns in surprise.)*

BASSICK: No one sees you — no one knows you. That has meant safety for years.

MORIARTY: No one sees me now. You talk with him — I'll listen from the next room. (BASSICK *looks at him hesitatingly an instant.)* This is *your office* — you understand — *your office* — I'll be there.

(BASSICK turns to telephone.)

BASSICK *(speaking into telephone)*: Is that you, Prince? — Yes, I find I can't come out — but I'll see you here — What interest have they got? What's the name? *(Listening a moment. Looks round to* MORIARTY.) He says there's two with him — a man and a woman named Larrabee. They won't consent to any interview unless they're present.

MORIARTY: Send them in.

BASSICK *(speaking into telephone)*: Eh, Prince — ask Beads to come to the telephone — Beads — eh — ? *(Lower voice.)* Those people with Prince, do they seem to be all right? Look close —

Yes?—Well—take them out through the warehouse and down by
the circular stairway and then bring them up here by the long
tunnel—Yes, here—Look them over as you go along to see they're
not carrying anything—and watch that no one sees you come
down—Yes— *(Hangs up ear-piece, turns and looks at* MORIARTY.)
I don't like this, sir!

MORIARTY *(rises)*: You don't like this! You don't like this! I tell
you it's certain death unless we can settle with this man Holmes.

(The buzzer rings three times.)

(Moves towards opening.) Your office, you understand—your
office.

(BASSICK *looks at* MORIARTY. MORIARTY *goes out.* BASSICK, *after*
MORIARTY *is well off, goes and takes* MORIARTY'S *place at the
back of the desk. Rings gong at desk. Buzzer replies twice from
outside.)*

BASSICK *(speaking into tube)*: Send John here.

(BASSICK *pushes back bolt. Enter* JOHN *noiselessly. He stands just
within door. Bolt of door slides back when door shuts.)*

There are some people coming in here, you stand over there, and
keep your eye on them from behind. If you see anything
suspicious, drop your handkerchief. If it's the woman pick it up—
if it's the man leave it on the floor.

*(Three knocks are distinctly heard on door from outside. On last
knock* JOHN *goes near wall.)*

(Picks up tube and speaks into it.) Number. *(Listens—speaking
into tube.)* Are the three waiting with you? *(Listens—drops tube
and pushes lever back, and the bolt slides back from the door.
The door slowly swings open.)*

(Enter SID PRINCE, *followed by* MADGE *and* LARRABEE. *The door
closes and the bolts slide back with a clang. At the sound of the
bolts* LARRABEE *looks round at door very sharply, realizing that
they are all locked in.* BASSICK *motions* MADGE *to chair.* MADGE
sits. LARRABEE *is suspicious, and does not like the look of the
place.* PRINCE *remains standing.* BASSICK *sits behind desk.* JOHN

is in the dark, watching LARRABEE *and* MADGE, *with a handkerchief in hand.)*

I understand you to say — through our private telephone — that you've got something with Sherlock Holmes against you.

PRINCE: Yes, sir — we 'ave.

BASSICK: Kindly let me have the particulars.

(LARRABEE *gives* "H'm," *indicating that he wants to hear.)*

PRINCE: Jim and Madge Larrabee here, which you used to know in early days, they have picked up a girl at 'Omburg, where her sister had been havin' a strong affair of the 'eart with a very 'igh young foreign nob who promised to marry 'er — but the family stepped in and threw the whole thing down. 'E be'aved very bad to 'er, an' had let 'imself out, an' written her letters, an' given her rings and tokens, yer see — and there was photographs too. Now, as these various things showed how 'e'd deceived and betrayed 'er, they wouldn't look nice at all considerin' who the young man was, an' wot 'igh titles he was comin' into. So when this girl up and dies of it all, these letters and things all fall into the 'ands of the sister — which is the one my friends 'ere has been nursin' all along — together with 'er mother.

BASSICK *(to* LARRABEE): Where have you had the people?

LARRABEE: We took a house up the Norrington Road.

BASSICK: How long have you been there?

LARRABEE: Two years, the fourteenth of next month.

BASSICK: And those letters and — other evidences of the young man's misconduct — when will they reach their full value?

(LARRABEE *is about to answer, but* PRINCE *jumps in quickly.)*

PRINCE: It's now, don't you see. It's now — There's a marriage comin' on, an' there's been offers, an' the problem is to get the papers in our 'ands.

BASSICK: Where are they?

PRINCE: Why, the girl's got 'old of 'em, sir!

(BASSICK *turns for explanation of this to* LARRABEE.)

LARRABEE: We had a safe for her to keep them in, supposing that when the time came we could open it, but the lock was out of order and we got Prince in to help us. He opened it last night, and the package containing the things was gone — she had taken them out herself.

BASSICK: What did you do when you discovered this?

PRINCE: Do — I 'adn't any more than got the box open, sir, an' given one look at it, when Sherlock Holmes rings the front door bell.

BASSICK *(intent)*: There — at your house?

LARRABEE: At my house.

BASSICK: He *didn't get those letters?*

LARRABEE: Well, he did get them, but he passed them back to the Faulkner girl.

BASSICK *(rises—in surprise)*: Passed them back, eh? What did that mean? *(Goes down a little, thinking.)*

LARRABEE *(slight shrug of shoulders)*: There's another thing that puzzles me. There was an accident below in the kitchen — a lamp fell off the table and scattered burning oil about, the butler came running up, yelling fire. We ran down there, and a few buckets of water put it out.

(MORIARTY *suddenly appears at his desk. Lights on his face.)*

MORIARTY: *I have a suggestion to make. (All turn in surpirse and look at* MORIARTY.) The first thing we must do is to get rid of your butler — not discharge him —*get rid of him. (To* BASSICK.) Craigin for that! To-day! As soon as it's dark. Give him two others to help — Mr. Larrabee will send the man into the cellar for something — they'll be ready for him there. Doulton's van will get the body to the river. (MADGE *shudders slightly.)* It need not inconvenience you at all, Madam, we do these things quietly.

(BASSICK *is writing orders.)*

(To BASSICK.) What's the Seraph doing?

BASSICK: He's on the Reading job to-morrow night.

MORIARTY: Put him with Craigin to-day to help with that butler. But there's something else we want. Have you seen those letters, the photographs, and whatever else there may be? Have you seen them? Do you know what they're like?

MADGE: I have, sir. I've looked them through carefully several times.

MORIARTY: Could you make me a counterfeit set of these things and tie them up so that they will look exactly like the package Sherlock Holmes held in his hand last night?

MADGE: I could manage the letters — but —

MORIARTY: If you manage the letters, I'll send some one who can manage the rest — from your description. Bassick — that old German artist — eh —

BASSICK: Leuftner.

MORIARTY: Pre-cisely! Send Leuftner to Mrs. Larrabee at eleven. *(Looks at watch.)* Quarter past ten — that gives you three-quarters of an hour to reach home. I shall want that counterfeit packet an eleven to-night — twelve hours to make it.

MADGE: It will be ready, sir.

MORIARTY: Good! Bassick — notify the Lascar that I may require the Gas Chamber at Stepney to-night.

BASSICK: The Gas Chamber?

MORIARTY: Yes. The one backing over the river — and have Craigin there a quarter before twelve with two others. Mr. Larrabee — *(turning slightly to him)* — I shall want you to write a letter to Mr. Sherlock Holmes which I shall dictate — and to-night I may require a little assistance from you both. *(Taking in* PRINCE *with his glance.)* Meet me here at eleven.

LARRABEE: This is all very well, sir, but you have said nothing about — the business arrangements. I'm not sure that I —

MORIARTY *(turning front)*: You have no choice.

LARRABEE: No choice. *(Looks fiercely to* MORIARTY.*)*

(MADGE *rises to quiet him.* JOHN *drops handkerchief. Pause.)*

MORIARTY *(looking at him)*: No choice. (PRINCE *aghast.)* I do what I please. It pleases me to take hold of this case.

LARRABEE *(angry — crossing to desk)*: Well, what about pleasing me?

(BASSICK *looks across at* LARRABEE.*)*

MORIARTY *(perfectly quiet — looks at* LARRABEE *an instant)*: I am not so sure but I shall be able to do that as well. I will obtain the original letters from Miss Faulkner and negotiate them for much more than you could possibly obtain. In addition — you will have an opportunity to sell the counterfeit package to Holmes to-night, for a good round sum. And the money obtained from both these sources shall be divided as follows: you will take one hundred per cent. and I — nothing.

(Brief pause of astonishment.)

LARRABEE: Nothing!
MORIARTY: Nothing!

(LARRABEE *moves to* PRINCE.)

BASSICK: But we cannot negotiate those letters until we know who they incriminate. Mr. Larrabee has not yet informed us.

MORIARTY: Mr. Larrabee — (LARRABEE *looks round to* MORIARTY) — is wise in exercising caution. He values the keystone to his arch. But he will consent to let me know.

(LARRABEE *goes to* MADGE.)

MADGE *(going across to* MORIARTY): Professor Moriarty, that information we would like to give — only to you. *(Looking toward* BASSICK).

(MORIARTY *motions* BASSICK *away.* BASSICK *moves a little.* MORIARTY *hands a card and pencil to* MADGE *from desk.* MADGE *writes a name and hands it to* MORIARTY. *He glances at name on card, then looks more closely. Looks up at* MADGE *astonished.)*

MORIARTY: This is an absolute certainty.
LARRABEE: Absolute.
MORIARTY: It means that you have a fortune.

(PRINCE *drinks in every word and look.)*

Had I known this, you should hardly have had such terms.

LARRABEE: Oh well — we don't object to a —

MORIARTY *(interrupting)*: The arrangement is made, Mr. Larrabee — I bid you good morning. *(Bowing with dignity and pulling lever back.)*

(LARRABEE, PRINCE *and* MADGE *move toward door. Bolts, etc., slide back on door.* BASSICK *motions* JOHN, *who stands ready to conduct the party.* BASSICK *crosses to door. All bow a little and go out, followed by* JOHN — *business of door closing, bolts, etc.* BASSICK *turns at door and looks at* MORIARTY.)

Bassick, place your men at nine to-night for Sherlock Holmes's house in Baker Street.

BASSICK: You will go there *yourself,* sir!

MORIARTY: I will go there *myself—myself. (Revolver out.)* I am the one to attend to this.

BASSICK: But this meeting to-night at twelve, to trap Holmes in the Gas Chamber in Swandem Lane.

MORIARTY: If I fail to kill him in Baker Street, we'll trap him to-night in Swandem Lane. Either way I have him, Bassick. I have him. I have him.

(Lights off gradually but not too slow on this act, and leave light on MORIARTY'S *face last.)*

(Music. Swell out forte for change.)

DARK CHANGE.

SCENE II. — *In* SHERLOCK HOLMES'S *rooms in Baker Street — the large drawing-room of his apartments. An open, cheerful room, but not too much decorated. Rather plain. The walls are a plain tint, the ceiling ditto. The furniture is comfortable and good, but not elegant. Books, music, violins, tobacco pouches, pipes, tobacco, etc., are scattered in places about the room with some disorder. Various odd things are hung about. Some very choice pictures and etchings hang on the walls here and there, but the pictures do not have heavy gilt frames. All rather simple. The room gives more an impression of an artist's studio. A wide door up right side to hall (and thus by stairway to street door). Door communicating with bedroom or dining-room. A fireplace with cheerful grate fire burning, throwing a red glow into room. Through a large arch can be seen a laboratory and a table with chemicals and various knick-knacks. The lighting should be arranged so that after the dark change the first thing that becomes visible — even before the rest of the room — is the glow of the fire, the blue flame of the spirit lamp — and* SHERLOCK HOLMES *seated among cushions on the floor before the fire. Light gradually on, but still leaving the effect of only firelight.*

Music stops, just as lights up.

SHERLOCK HOLMES *is discovered on the floor before the fire. He is in a dressing-gown and slippers and has his pipe.* HOLMES *leans against the chesterfield. A violin is upon the chesterfield, and the bow near it, as if recently laid down. Other things scattered about him. He sits smoking awhile in deep thought. Enter* BILLY, *the boy page, or buttons. He comes down to back of table.*

BILLY: Mrs. 'Udson's compliments, sir, an' she wants to know if she can see you?

HOLMES *(without moving, looking into fire thoughtfully)*: Where is Mrs. Hudson?

BILLY: Downstairs in the back kitchen, sir.

HOLMES: My compliments and I don't think she can — from where she is.

BILLY: She'll be very sorry, sir.

HOLMES: Our regret will be mutual.

(BILLY *hesitates.*)

BILLY: She says it was terribly important, sir, as she wants to know what you'll have for your breakfast in the mornin'.

HOLMES: Same.

(Slight pause.)

BILLY: Same as when, sir?

HOLMES: This morning.

BILLY: You didn't 'ave nothing, sir — you wasn't 'ere.

HOLMES: Quite so — I won't be here tomorrow.

BILLY: Yes, sir. Was that all, sir?

HOLMES: Quite so.

BILLY: Thank you, sir.

(BILLY *goes out. After long pause bell rings off. Enter* BILLY.)

It's Doctor Watson, sir. You told me as I could always show 'im up.

HOLMES: Well! I should think so. *(Rises and meets* WATSON.)

BILLY: Yes, sir, thank you, sir. Dr. Watson, sir!

(Enter DR. WATSON. BILLY, *grinning with pleasure as he passes in, goes out at once.)*

HOLMES *(extending left hand to* WATSON): Ah, Watson, my dear fellow.

WATSON *(going to* HOLMES *and taking his hand)*: How are you, Holmes?

HOLMES: I'm delighted to see you, my dear fellow, perfectly delighted, upon my word — but — I'm sorry to observe that your wife has left you in this way.

WATSON *(laughing)*: She has gone on a little visit. *(Puts hat on chair between bookcases.)* But how did you know?

HOLMES *(goes to laboratory table and puts spirit lamp out, then turns up lamp on table. All lights up)*: How do I know? Now, Watson, how absurd for you to me such a question as that. How do I know anything? *(Comes down a little way. Gives a very little sniff an instant, smelling something.)* How do I know that you've opened a consulting room and resumed the practice of medicine without letting me hear a word about it? How do I know that you've been getting yourself very wet lately? That you have an extremely careless servant girl — and that you've moved your dressing-table to the other side of your room?

WATSON *(turning and looking at* HOLMES *in astonishment)*: Holmes, if you'd lived a few centuries ago, they'd have burned you alive. *(Sits.)*

HOLMES: Such a conflagration would have saved no considerable trouble and expense. *(Strolls over to near fire.)*

WATSON: Tell me, how did you know all that?

HOLMES *(pointing)*: Too simple to talk about. *(Pointing at* WATSON'S *shoe.)* Scratches and clumsy cuts — on the side of shoe there just where the fire strikes it, somebody scraped away crusted mud — and did it badly — badly. There's your wet feet and careless servant all on one foot. Face badly shaved on one side — used to be on left — light must have come from other side — couldn't well move your window — must have moved your dressing-table. *(Goes to mantel and gets cocaine, etc.)*

WATSON: Yes, by Jove! But my medical practice — I don't see how you —

HOLMES *(glancing up grieved)*: Now, Watson! How perfectly absurd of you to come marching in here, fairly reeking with the odour of iodoform, and with the black mark of nitrate of silver on the inner side of your right forefinger and ask me how I know —

WATSON *(interrupting with a laugh)*: Ha! ha! of course. But how the deuce did you know my wife was away and —

HOLMES *(breaking in)*: Where the deuce is your second waistcoat button, and what the deuce is yesterday's boutonnière doing in to-day's lapel — and why the deuce do you wear the expression of a —

WATSON *(toying with a cigarette and laughing)*: Ha, ha, ha!

HOLMES: Ho! *(Sneer.)* Elementary! The child's play of deduction!

(HOLMES *has a neat morocco case and a phial in hand, which he brings to the table and lays carefully upon it. As* WATSON *sees* HOLMES *with the open case he looks restless and apparently annoyed at what* HOLMES *is about to do, throwing cigarette on table.* HOLMES *opens the case and takes therefrom a hypodermic syringe, carefully adjusting the needle. Fills from phial. Then rolls back left cuff of shirt a little. Pauses, looks at arm or wrist a moment. Inserts needle. Presses piston home.)*

(Music. A weird bar or two—keeping on a strange pulsation on one note for cocaine business. Begin as HOLMES *fills syringe.)*

(WATSON *has watched him with an expression of deep anxiety, but with effort to restrain himself from speaking.)*

WATSON *(as* HOLMES *puts needle in case again. Finally speaks)*: Which is it to-day? Cocaine or morphine or—

HOLMES: Cocaine, my dear fellow. I'm back to my old love. A seven per cent. solution. *(Offering syringe and phial.)* Would you like to try some?

WATSON *(emphatically—rise)*: Certainly *not.*

HOLMES *(as if surprised)*: Oh! I'm sorry!

WATSON: I have no wish to break *my* system down before its time.

(Pause.)

HOLMES: Quite right, my dear Watson—quite right—but, you see, my time has come. *(Goes to mantel and replaces case thereon. Throws himself languidly into chesterfield and leans back in luxurious enjoyment of the drug.)*

WATSON *(goes to table, resting hand on upper corner, looking at* HOLMES *seriously)*: Holmes, for months I have seen you use these deadly drugs—in ever-increasing doses. When they lay hold of you there is no end. It must go on, and on—until the finish.

HOLMES *(lying back dreamily)*: So must you go on and on, eating your breakfast—until the finish.

WATSON *(approaches* HOLMES): Breakfast is food. These drugs are poisons—slow but certain. They involve tissue changes of a most *serious* nature.

HOLMES: Just what I want. I'm bored to death with my present tissues, and I'm trying to get a brand-new lot.

WATSON *(going near* HOLMES—*putting hand on* HOLMES'S *shoulder)*: Ah, Holmes—I'm trying to save you.

HOLMES *(earnest at once—places right hand on* WATSON'S *arm)*: You can't do it, old fellow—so don't waste your time.

(Music stops.)

(They look at one another an instant. WATSON *sees cigarette on table—picks it up and sits.)*

Watson, to change the subject a little. In the enthusiasm which has prompted you to chronicle and—if you will excuse my saying so, to somewhat embellish—a few of my little—adventures, you have occasionally committed the error—or indiscretion—of giving them a certain tinge of romance which struck me as being a trifle out of place. Something like working an elopement into the fifth proposition of Euclid. I merely refer to this in case you should see fit at some future time—to chronicle the most important and far-reaching case in my career—one upon which I have laboured for nearly fourteen months, and which is now rapidly approaching a singularly diverting climax—the case of Professor Robert Moriarty.

WATSON: Moriarty! I don't remember ever having heard of the fellow.

HOLMES: The Napoleon of crime. The Napoleon! Sitting motionless like an ugly venomous spider in the centre of his web—but that web having a thousand radiations and the spider knowing every quiver of every one of them.

WATSON: Really! This is very interesting. *(Turns chair facing* HOLMES.)

HOLMES: Ah—but the real interest will come when the Professor begins to realize his position—which he cannot fail to do shortly. By ten o'clock to-morrow night the time will be ripe for the arrests. Then the greatest criminal trial of the century. . .the clearing up of over forty mysteries. . .and the rope for every one.

WATSON: Good! What will he do when he sees that you have him?

HOLMES: Do? He will do me the honour, my dear Watson, of turning every resource of his wonderful organization of criminals to the one purpose of my destruction.

WATSON: Why, Holmes, this is a *dangerous* thing. *(Rises.)*

HOLMES: Dear Watson, it's perfectly delightful! It saves me any number of doses of those deadly drugs upon which you occasionally favour me with your medical views! My whole life is spent in a

series of frantic endeavours to escape from the dreary common-
places of existence! For a brief period I escape! You should
congratulate me!

WATSON: But you could escape them without such serious
risks! Your other cases have not been so dangerous, and they were
even more interesting. Now, the one you spoke of — the last time I
saw you — the recovery of those damaging letters and gifts from a
young girl who —

(HOLMES *suddenly rises—stands motionless.* WATSON *looks at
him surprised. Brief pause. Then* WATSON *sits in arm-chair.)*

A most peculiar affair as I remember it. You were going to try the
experiment of making her betray their hiding-place by an alarm
of fire in her own house — and after that —

HOLMES: Precisely — after that.

(Pause.)

WATSON: Didn't the plan succeed?

HOLMES: Yes — as far as I've gone.

WATSON: You got Forman into the house as butler?

HOLMES *(nods)*: Forman was in as butler.

WATSON: And upon your signal he overturned a lamp in the
kitchen —(HOLMES *moves up and down)* — scattered the smoke
balls and gave an alarm of fire?

(HOLMES *nods and mutters* "Yes" *under his breath.)*

And the young lady — did she —

HOLMES *(turning and interrupting)*: Yes, she did, Watson.
(Going down near him as if he had recovered himself.) The young
lady did. It all transpired precisely as planned. I took the packet
of papers from its hiding-place — and as I told you I would, I
handed it back to Miss Faulkner.

WATSON: But you never told me *why* you proposed to hand it
back.

HOLMES: For a very simple reason, my dear Watson. That it
would have been theft for me to take it. The contents of the
packet were the absolute property of the young lady.

WATSON: What did you *gain* by this?

HOLMES: Her confidence, and so far as I was able to secure it,
her regard. As it was impossible for me to take possession of the

letters, photographs and jewellery in that packet without her consent, my only alternative is to obtain that consent — to induce her to give it to me of her own free will. Its return to her after I had laid hands on it was the first move in this direction. The second will depend entirely upon what transpires to-day. I expect Forman here to report in half an hour.

(Light hurried footsteps outside. Short quick knock at door and enter TÉRÈSE *in great haste and excitement.* WATSON *rises and turns and faces her near table.* HOLMES *turns towards fire-place.)*

TÉRÈSE: I beg you to pardon me, sir, ze boy he say to come right up as soon as I come.

HOLMES: Quite right! quite right!

TÉRÈSE: Ah! I fear me zere is trouble — Messieurs — ze butlair — you assesstant — ze one who sent me to you —

HOLMES: Forman? *(Turning to her.)*

TÉRÈSE: Heem! Forman. Zere ees somesing done to heem! I fear to go down to see.

HOLMES: Down where?

(WATSON *watches.)*

TÉRÈSE: Ze down. *(Gesture.)* Ze cellaire of zat house. Eet ees a dreadful place. He deed not come back. He went down — he deed not return. *(Business of anguish.)*

(HOLMES *goes to table—rings bell and takes revolver from drawer and slides it into his hip pocket, at same time unfastening dressing-gown.)*

HOLMES *(during business)*: Who sent him down?

TÉRÈSE: M'sieur of ze house, M'sieur Chetwood.

HOLMES: Larrabee?

TÉRÈSE: Yes.

HOLMES *(during business)*: Has he been down there long?

TÉRÈSE: No — for I soon suspect — ze dreadful noise was heard. Oh — *(covers face)* — ze noise! Ze noise!

HOLMES: What noise? *(Goes to her and seizes her arm.)*

TÉRÈSE: Ze noise!

HOLMES: Try to be calm and answer me. What did it sound like?

TÉRÈSE: Ze dreadful cry of a man who eez struck down by some deadly seeng.

(Enter BILLY.)

HOLMES: Billy! Coat—boots, and order a cab—quick. *(Back again to table, takes a second revolver out.)*
BILLY *(darting off at door)*: Yes, sir.
HOLMES *(to TÉRÈSE)*: Did anyone follow him down?

(BILLY *is back in a second.)*

TÉRÈSE: I did not see.
HOLMES: Don't wait. The cab.

(BILLY *shoots off, having placed coat over chesterfield and boots on floor.)*

Take this, Watson, and come with me. *(Handing WATSON a revolver. WATSON advances a step to meet HOLMES and takes revolver.)*
TÉRÈSE: I had not better go also?
HOLMES: No. . . . Wait here! *(Ready to go. About to take off dressing-gown.)*

(Hurried footsteps heard outside.)

(Pause.) Ha! I hear Forman coming now.

(Enter FORMAN.)

TÉRÈSE *(seeing FORMAN—under her breath)*: Ah! *(Backing a little.)*

(FORMAN *coming rapidly on, is covered with black coal stains, and his clothing otherwise stained. He has a bad bruise on his forehead. But he must not be made to look grotesque. There must be no suspicion of comedy about his entrance. Also he must not be torn, as BILLY is later in the scene. HOLMES just above table stops taking off his dressing-gown, slips it back on his shoulders again.)*

FORMAN *(to HOLMES, in an entirely matter-of-fact tone)*: Nothing more last night, sir. After you left, Prince came in, and they made a start for her room to get the package away, but I gave the three knocks with an axe on the floor beams as you directed, and they didn't go any farther. This morning, a little after nine —

HOLMES: One moment.

FORMAN: Yes, sir?

HOLMES *(quietly turns to* TÉRÈSE): Mademoiselle — step into that room and rest yourself. *(Indicating bedroom door.)*

TÉRÈSE *(who has been deeply interested in* FORMAN'S *report)*: Ah! *(Shaking head.)* I am not tired, Monsieur.

HOLMES: Step in and walk about, then. I'll let you know when you are required.

TÉRÈSE *(after an instant's pause sees it)*: Oui, Monsieur. *(Goes out.)*

(HOLMES *goes over and quickly closes the door after her—he then turns to* WATSON, *but remains at the door with right ear alert to catch any sound from within.)*

HOLMES: Take a look at his head, Watson. *(Listens at door.)*

(WATSON *at once goes to* FORMAN.)

FORMAN: It's nothing at all.

HOLMES: Take a look at his head, Watson.

WATSON: An ugly bruise, but not dangerous. *(Examining head.)*

(WATSON *goes quickly and stands near end of chesterfield facing around to* FORMAN.)

HOLMES: Very well. . . . At a little after nine, you say —

(HOLMES *has attention on door, where* TÉRÈSE *went off, while listening to* FORMAN—*but not in such a marked way as to take the attention off from what he says, and after a few seconds sits on chesterfield.)*

FORMAN: Yes, sir! *(Coming down a little.)* This morning a little after nine, Larrabee and his wife drove away and she returned about eleven without him. A little later, old Leuftner came and the two went to work in the library. I got a look at them from the outside and found they were making up a *counterfeit of the package we're working for!* You'll have to watch for some sharp trick, sir.

HOLMES: *They'll* have to watch for the trick, my dear Forman!
And Larrabee, what of him?

FORMAN: He came back a little after three.

HOLMES: How did he seem?

FORMAN: Under great excitement, sir.

HOLMES: Any marked resentment towards you?

FORMAN: I think there was, sir—though he tried not to show it.

HOLMES: He has consulted some one outside. Was the Larrabee-
woman's behaviour different also?

FORMAN: Now I come to think of it, she gave me an ugly look as
she came in.

HOLMES: Ah, an ugly look. She was present at the consultation.
They were advised to get you out of the way. He sent you into
the cellar on some pretext. You were attacked in the dark by two
men—possibly three—and received a bad blow from a sand club.
You managed to strike down one of your assailants with a stone or
piece of timber, and escaped from the others in the dark, crawling
out through a coal grating.

FORMAN: That's what took place, sir.

HOLMES: They've taken in a partner, and a dangerous one at
that. He not only directed this conspiracy against you, but he
advised the making of the counterfeit package as well. Within a
very short time I shall receive an offer from Larrabee to sell me
the package of letters. He will indicate that Miss Faulkner has
changed her mind, and has concluded to get what she can for
them. He will desire to meet me on the subject—and will then
endeavour to sell me his bogus package for a large sum of money.
After that—

(Enter BILLY *with a letter.)*

BILLY: Letter, sir! Most important letter, sir! *(After giving*
HOLMES *letter, he stands waiting.)*

HOLMES: Unless I am greatly mistaken—the said communication is at hand. *(Lightly waves letter across before face once as if
getting the scent.)* It is. Read it, Watson, there's a good fellow—
my eyes— *(With a motion across eyes. Half smile.)* You know,
cocaine—and all those things you like so much.

*(*BILLY *goes with letter to* WATSON. WATSON *takes letter and goes
up to lamp.)*

WATSON *(opens letter and reads)*: "Dear Sir."

(After WATSON *is at lamp,* FORMAN *waits.)*

HOLMES: Who—thus—addresses me? *(Slides further on to chesterfield, supporting head on pillows.)*

WATSON *(glances at signatûre)*: "James Larrabee."

HOLMES *(whimsically)*: What a surprise! And what has James to say this evening?

WATSON: "Dear Sir."

HOLMES: I hope he won't say that again.

WATSON: "I have the honour to inform you that Miss Faulkner has changed her mind regarding the letters, etc., which you wish to obtain, and has decided to dispose of them for a monetary consideration. She has placed them in my hands for this purpose, and if you are in a position to offer a good round sum, and to pay it down at once in cash, the entire lot is yours. If you wish to negotiate, however, it must be to-night, at the house of a friend of mine, in the city. At eleven o'clock you will be at the Guards' Monument at the foot of Waterloo Place. You will see a cab with wooden shutters to the windows. Enter it and the driver will bring you to my friend's house. If you have the cab followed, or try any other underhand trick, you won't get what you want. Let me know your decision. Yours truly, James Larrabee."

(HOLMES *during the reading of the letter begins to write something in a perfectly leisurely way. The light of the fire is upon him, shining across the room—on his left—as he writes.)*

HOLMES: Now see if I have the points. To-night, eleven o'clock —Guards' Monument—cab with wooden shutters. No one to come with me. No one to follow cab—or I don't get what I want.

WATSON: Quite right.

HOLMES: Ah!

WATSON: But this cab with the wooden shutters. *(Coming down and placing letter on table.)*

HOLMES: A little device to keep me from seeing where I am driven. Billy!

BILLY *(going to* HOLMES *at once)*: Yes, sir.

HOLMES *(reaching out letter to* BILLY *back of him without looking)*: Who brought it?

BILLY: It was a woman, sir.

HOLMES *(slight dead stop as he is handing letter)*: Ah—old or young? *(He does not look round for these questions, but faces as he was, front or nearly so.)*

BILLY: Werry old, sir.

HOLMES: In a cab?

BILLY: Yes, sir.

HOLMES: Seen the driver before?

BILLY: Yes, sir—but I can't think where.

HOLMES *(rising)*: Hand this over to the old lady—apologize for the delay, and look at the driver again.

BILLY *(takes letter)*: Yes, sir. *(Goes out.)*

WATSON: My dear Holmes—you did not say you would go?

HOLMES: Certainly I did.

WATSON: But it is the counterfeit.

HOLMES *(moves towards bedroom door)*: The counterfeit is just what I want.

WATSON: Why so?

HOLMES *(turning to WATSON an instant)*: Because with it I shall obtain the original. *(Turns and speaks off at door.)* Mademoiselle! *(Turns back.)*

WATSON: But this fellow means mischief.

(Enter TÉRÈSE. She comes into and stands a little way inside the room.)

HOLMES *(facing WATSON—touching himself lightly)*: This fellow means the same.

(As HOLMES turns away to TÉRÈSE, WATSON crosses and stands with back to fire.)

(To TÉRÈSE.) Be so good, Mademoiselle, as to listen to every word. To-night at twelve o'clock I meet Mr. Larrabee and purchase from him the false bundle of letters to which you just now heard us refer, as you were listening at the keyhole of that door.

TÉRÈSE *(slightly confused, but staring blankly)*: Oui, Monsieur.

HOLMES: I wish Miss Faulkner to know *at once* that I propose to buy this package to-night.

TÉRÈSE: I will tell her, Monsieur.

HOLMES: That is my wish. But do not tell her that I know this packet and its contents to be counterfeit. She is to suppose that I think I am buying the genuine.

TÉRÈSE: Oui, Monsieur, je comprends. When you purchase you think you have the *real*.

HOLMES: Precisely. *(Motions her up to door and moving towards door with her.)* One thing more. Tomorrow evening I shall want you to accompany her to this place, here. Sir Edward Leighton and Count von Stalburg will be here to receive the package from me. However, you will receive further instructions as to this in the morning.

TÉRÈSE: Oui, Monsieur. *(Turns and goes out at once.)*

HOLMES: Forman.

FORMAN: Yes, sir.

HOLMES: Change to your beggar disguise No. 14 and go through every place in the Riverside District. Don't stop till you get a clue to this new partner of the Larrabees. I must have that. *(Turns away towards* WATSON.) I must have that.

FORMAN: Very well, sir. *(Just about to go.)*

(Enter BILLY.)

BILLY: If you please, sir, there's a man a-waitin' at the street door — and 'e says 'e must speak to Mr. Forman, sir, as quick as 'e can.

(HOLMES—*who was moving—stops suddenly and stands motionless—eyes front. Pause.)*

(Music. Danger. Melodramatic. Very low. Agitato. B String.)

HOLMES *(after a pause)*: We'd better have a look at that man, Billy, show him up.

BILLY: 'E can't come up, sir—'e's a-watchin' a man in the street. 'E says 'e's from Scotland Yard.

FORMAN *(going toward door)*: I'd better see what it is, sir.

HOLMES: No!

(FORMAN *stops. Pause. Music heard throughout this pause, but without swelling forte in the least.* HOLMES *stands motionless a moment.)*

Well — *(a motion indicating* FORMAN *to go)* — take a look at him first. *Be ready for anything.*

> FORMAN: Trust me for that, sir. *(Goes out.)*
> HOLMES: Billy, see what he does.
> BILLY: Yes, sir.

(HOLMES *stands an instant thinking.)*

WATSON: This is becoming interesting.

(HOLMES *does not reply. He goes up to near door and listens, then moves to window and glances down to street, then turns and goes down to table.)*

Look here, Holmes, you've been so kind as to give me a half-way look into this case —

> HOLMES *(looking up at him)*: What case?
> WATSON: This strange case of — Miss —
> HOLMES: Quite so. One moment, my dear fellow. *(Rings bell.)*

(After slight wait enter BILLY.)

Mr. Forman — is he there still?

> BILLY: No, sir — 'e's gone. *(Second's pause.)*
> HOLMES: That's all.
> BILLY: Yes, sir. Thank you, sir. *(Goes out.)*

(Music stops.)

HOLMES: As you were saying, Watson. *(Eyes front.)* This strange case — of — *(Stops, but does not change position. As if listening or thinking.)*

WATSON: Of Miss Faulkner.

HOLMES *(abandoning further anxiety and giving attention to* WATSON)*: Precisely. This strange case of Miss Faulkner. *(Eyes down an instant as he recalls it.)*

WATSON: You've given me some idea of it. Now don't you think it would be only fair to let me have the rest?

(HOLMES *looks at him.)*

HOLMES: What shall I tell you?

WATSON: Tell me what you propose to do with that counterfeit package — which you are going *to risk your life to obtain.*

(HOLMES *looks at* WATSON *an instant before speaking.*)

HOLMES: I intend, with the aid of the counterfeit, to make her willingly hand me the genuine. I shall accomplish this by a piece of trickery and deceit of which I am heartily ashamed — and which I would never have undertaken if I — if I had known her — as I do now — *(Looks to the front absently.)* It's too bad. She's — she's rather a nice girl, Watson. *(Goes over to mantel and gets a pipe.)*

WATSON *(following* HOLMES *with his eyes)*: Nice girl, is she?

(HOLMES *nods "Yes" to* WATSON. *Brief pause. He turns with pipe in hands and glances towards* WATSON, *then down.*)

Then you think that possibly —

(Enter BILLY *quickly.)*

BILLY: I beg pardon, sir, Mr. Forman's just sent over from the chemist's on the corner to say 'is 'ead is a-painin' 'im a bit, an' would Dr. Watson — (WATSON, *on hearing his name, turns and looks in direction of* BILLY) — kindly step over and get 'im something to put on it.

WATSON *(moving at once towards door)*: Yes — certainly — I'll go at once. *(Picking up hat off chair.)* That's singular. *(Stands puzzled.)* It didn't look like anything serious. *(At door.)* I'll be back in a minute, Holmes. *(Goes out.)*

(HOLMES *says nothing.*)

HOLMES: Billy.
BILLY: Yes, sir.
HOLMES: Who brought that message from Forman?
BILLY: Boy from the chemist's, sir.
HOLMES: Yes, of course, but which boy?
BILLY: Must-a-bin a new one, sir — I ain't never seen 'im before.

(Music. Danger. Melodramatic. Very low. Agitato.)

HOLMES: Quick, Billy, run down and look after the doctor. If the boy's gone and there's a man with him it means mischief. Let me know, quick. Don't stop to come up, ring the door bell. I'll hear it. Ring it loud. Quick now.

BILLY: Yes, sir. *(Goes out quickly.)*

(HOLMES *waits motionless a moment, listening.*)

(*Music heard very faintly.*)

(HOLMES *moves quickly towards door. When half-way to the door he stops suddenly, listening; then begins to glide backward toward table, stops and listens—eyes to the front; turns towards door, listening. Pipe in left hand—waits—sees pipe in hand—picks up match—lights pipe, listening, and suddenly shouts of warning from* BILLY—*turns—at the same time picking up revolver from off table and puts in pocket of dressing-gown, with his hand still clasping it.* HOLMES *at once assumes easy attitude, but keeping eyes on door. Enter* MORIARTY. *He walks in at door very quietly and deliberately. Stops just within doorway, and looks fixedly at* HOLMES, *then moves forward a little way. His right hand is behind his back. As* MORIARTY *moves forward,* HOLMES *makes slight motion for the purpose of keeping him covered with a revolver in his pocket.* MORIARTY, *seeing what* HOLMES *is doing, stops.*)

MORIARTY *(very quiet low voice)*: It is a dangerous habit to finger loaded firearms in the pocket of one's dressing-gown.

HOLMES: You'll be taken from here to the hospital if you keep that hand behind you.

(*After slight pause* MORIARTY *slowly takes his hand from behind his back and holds it with the other in front of him.*)

In that case, the table will do quite as well. (*Places his revolver on the table.*)

MORIARTY: You evidently don't know me.

HOLMES *(takes pipe out of mouth, holding it. With very slight motion toward revolver)*: I think it quite evident that I do. Pray take a chair, Professor. (*Indicating arm-chair.*) I can spare you five minutes — if you have anything to say.

(*Very slight pause—then* MORIARTY *moves his right hand as if to take something from inside his coat. Stops instantly on* HOLMES *covering him with revolver, keeping hand exactly where it was stopping.*)

What were you about to do?

MORIARTY: Look at my watch.

HOLMES: I'll tell you when the five minutes is up.

(Slight pause. MORIARTY *comes slowly forward. He advances to back of arm-chair. Stands motionless there an instant, his eyes on* HOLMES. *He then takes off his hat, and stoops slowly, putting it on floor, eyeing* HOLMES *the while. He then moves down a little to right of chair, by its side.* HOLMES *now places revolver on table, but before he has quite let go of it,* MORIARTY *raises his right hand, whereupon* HOLMES *quietly takes the revolver back and holds it at his side.* MORIARTY *has stopped with right hand near his throat, seeing* HOLMES'S *business with revolver. He now slowly pulls away a woollen muffler from his throat and stands again with hands down before him.* HOLMES'S *forefinger motionless on table.* MORIARTY *moves a little in front of chair. This movement is only a step or two. As he makes it* HOLMES *moves simultaneously on the other side of the table so that he keeps the revolver between them on the table. That is the object of this business.)*

MORIARTY: All that I have to say has already crossed your mind.

HOLMES: My answer thereto has already crossed *yours.*

MORIARTY: It is your intention to pursue this case against me?

HOLMES: That is my intention to the very end.

MORIARTY: I regret this — not so much on my own account — but on yours.

HOLMES: I share your regrets, Professor, but solely because of the rather uncomfortable position it will cause you to occupy.

MORIARTY: May I inquire to what position you are pleased to allude, Mr. Holmes?

*(*HOLMES *motions a man being hanged with his left hand—slight pause. A tremor of passion.* MORIARTY *slowly advances towards* HOLMES. *He stops instantly as* HOLMES'S *hand goes to his revolver, having only approached him a step or two.)*

And have you the faintest idea that you would be permitted to live to see the day?

HOLMES: As to that, I do not particularly care, so that I might bring you to see it.

*(*MORIARTY *makes a sudden impulsive start towards* HOLMES, *but stops on being covered with revolver. He has now come close to the table on the other side of* HOLMES. *This tableau is held briefly.)*

MORIARTY *(passionately but in a low tone)*: You will never bring me to see it. You will find — *(He stops, recollecting himself as* HOLMES *looks at him—changes to quieter tone.)* Ah! you are a bold man, Mr. Holmes, to insinuate such a thing to my face — *(turning towards front)* — but it is the boldness born of ignorance. *(Turning still further away from* HOLMES *in order to get his back to him, and after doing so, suddenly raising his right hand to breast; he is again stopped with hand close to pocket by hearing the noise of* HOLMES'S *revolver behind him. He holds that position for a moment, then passes the matter off by feeling muffler as if adjusting it. He mutters to himself.)* You'll never bring me to see it, you'll never bring me to see it. *(Then begins to move in front of table, still keeping his back towards* HOLMES. *Business as he moves forward of stopping suddenly on hearing the noise of revolver sliding along table, then when in front of table slowly turns so that he brings his hands into view of* HOLMES, *then a slight salute with hand and bow and back slowly with dignity into chair.)*

(Business of HOLMES *seating himself on stool opposite* MORIARTY, *revolver business, and coming motionless.)*

(After HOLMES'S *business.)* I tell you it is the boldness born of ignorance. Do you think that I would be here if I had not made the streets *quite safe in every respect?*

HOLMES *(shaking head)*: Oh no! I could never so grossly overestimate your courage as that.

MORIARTY: Do you imagine that your friend, the doctor, and your man, *Forman,* will soon return?

HOLMES: Possibly not.

MORIARTY: So it leaves us quite alone — doesn't it, Mr. Holmes — quite alone — so that we can talk the matter over quietly and not be disturbed. In the first place, I wish to call your attention to a few memoranda which I have jotted down — *(suddenly putting both hands to breast pocket)* — which you will find —

HOLMES: Look out! Take your hands away.

(Music. Danger pp.)

*(*MORIARTY *again stopped with his hands at breast pocket.)*

Get your hands down.

(MORIARTY *does not lower his hands at first request.*)

A little further away from the memorandum book you are talking about.

MORIARTY *(lowers hands to his lap. Slight pause, raising hands again slowly as he speaks)*: Why, I was merely about to—

HOLMES: Well, merely don't do it.

MORIARTY *(remonstratingly—his hands still up near breast)*: But I would like to show you a—

HOLMES: I don't want to see it.

MORIARTY: But if you will allow me—

HOLMES: I don't care for it at all. I don't require any notebooks. If you want it so badly we'll have someone get it for you.

(MORIARTY *slowly lowers hands again.*)

(Rings bell on table with left hand.) I always like to save my guests unnecessary trouble.

MORIARTY *(after quite a pause)*: I observe that your boy does not answer the bell.

HOLMES: No. But I have an idea that he will before long.

MORIARTY *(leaning towards* HOLMES *and speaking with subdued rage and significance)*: It may possibly be longer than you think, Mr. Holmes.

HOLMES *(intensely)*: What! That boy!

MORIARTY *(hissing at* HOLMES*)*: Yes, your boy.

(Hold the tableau for a moment, the two men scowling at each other. HOLMES *slowly reaching left hand out to ring bell again.* MORIARTY *begins to raise right hand slowly towards breast pocket, keeping it concealed beneath his muffler as far as possible. On slight motion of* HOLMES'S *left hand, he lowers it again, giving up the attempt this time.)*

HOLMES: At least we will try the bell once more, Professor. *(Rings bell.)*

(Short wait.)

MORIARTY *(after pause)*: Doesn't it occur to you that he may possibly have been detained, Mr. Holmes?

HOLMES: It does. But I also observe that *you are in very much the same predicament. (Pause.)*

(HOLMES *rings bell for the third time. Noise on stairway outside. Enter* BILLY *with part of his coat, and with sleeves of shirt and waistcoat badly torn.)*

(Music stops.)

BILLY *(up near door)*: I beg pardon, sir—someone tried to 'old me, sir! *(Panting for breath.)*

HOLMES: It's quite evident, however, that he failed to do so.

BILLY: Yes, sir—'e's got my coat, sir, but 'e 'asn't got *me!*

HOLMES: Billy!

BILLY *(cheerfully)*: Yes, sir. *(Still out of breath.)*

HOLMES: The gentleman I am pointing out to you with this sixshooter desires to have us get something out of his left-hand coat pocket.

(MORIARTY *gives a very slight start or movement of right hand to breast pocket, getting it almost to his pocket, then recollecting himself, seeing that* HOLMES *has got him covered.)*

Ah, I thought so. Left-hand coat pocket. As he is not feeling quite himself to-day, and the exertion might prove injurious, suppose you attend to it.

BILLY: Yes, sir. *(He goes quickly to* MORIARTY, *puts hand in his pocket and draws out a bull-dog revolver.)* Is this it, sir?

HOLMES: It has the general outline of being it. Quite so. Put it on the table.

(MORIARTY *makes a grab for it.)*

Not there, Billy. Look out. Push it a little further this way.

(BILLY *does so, placing it so that it is within easy reach of* HOLMES.)

HOLMES: That's more like it.

BILLY: Shall I see if he's got another, sir?

HOLMES: Why, Billy, you surprise me, after the gentleman has taken the trouble to inform you that he hasn't.

BILLY: When, sir?

HOLMES: When he made a snatch for this one. Now that we have your little memorandum book, Professor, do you think of anything else you'd like before Billy goes?

(MORIARTY *does not reply.*)

Any little thing that you've got, that you want? No! Ah, I am sorry that's all, Billy.

(Pause. MORIARTY *motionless, eyes on* HOLMES. HOLMES *puts his own revolver in his pocket quietly.* MORIARTY *remains motionless, his eyes on* HOLMES, *waiting for a chance.)*

BILLY: Thank you, sir. *(Goes out.)*

(HOLMES *carelessly picks up* MORIARTY'S *weapon, turns it over in his hands a little below table for a moment, then tosses it back on table again—during which business* MORIARTY *looks front savagely.)*

HOLMES *(tapping revolver with pipe)*: Rather a rash project of yours, Moriarty—even though you have made the street quite safe in every respect—to make use of that thing—so early in the evening and in this part of the town.

MORIARTY: Listen to me. On the 4th of January you crossed my path—on the 23rd you incommoded me. And now, at the close of April, I find myself placed in such a position through your continual interference that I am in positive danger of losing my liberty.

HOLMES: Have you any suggestion to make?

MORIARTY *(head swaying from side to side)*: No! *(Pause and look fiercely at* HOLMES.) I have no suggestion to make. I have a fact to state. If you do not drop it at once your life is not worth that. *(Snap of finger.)*

HOLMES: I shall be pleased to drop it—at ten o'clock to-morrow night.

MORIARTY: Why then?

HOLMES: Because at that hour, Moriarty. . .*your* life will not be worth that. *(A snap of finger.)* You will be under arrest.

MORIARTY: At that hour, Sherlock Holmes, your eyes will be closed in death.

(Both look at one another motionless an instant.)

HOLMES *(rising as if rather bored)*: I am afraid, Professor, that in the pleasure of this conversation I am neglecting more important business. *(Turns away to mantel and business of looking for match, etc.)*

(MORIARTY *rises slowly, picks up hat, keeping his eyes on* HOLMES. *Suddenly catches sight of revolver on table—pause—and putting hat on table.)*

MORIARTY *(nearing* HOLMES *and looking towards door)*: I came here this evening to see if peace could not be arranged between us.

HOLMES: Ah, yes. *(Smiling pleasantly and pressing tobacco in pipe.)* I saw that. That's rather good.

MORIARTY *(passionately)*: You have seen fit not only to reject my proposals, but to make insulting references coupled with threats of arrest.

HOLMES: Quite so! Quite so! *(Lights match and holds it to pipe.)*

MORIARTY *(moving a little so as to be nearer table)*: Well— *(slyly picking up revolver)* — you have been warned of your danger —you do not heed that warning—perhaps you will heed this! *(Making a sudden plunge and aiming at* HOLMES'S *head he rapidly snaps the revolver in quick attempt to fire.)*

(HOLMES *turns quietly toward him, still holding match to pipe so that the last snap of hammer is directly in his face. Very slight pause on* MORIARTY *being unable to fire—and back up, at same time boiling with rage.)*

HOLMES: Oh! ha!—here! *(As if recollecting something. Tosses away match, and feeling quickly in left pocket of dressing-gown brings out some cartridges and tosses them carelessly on table towards* MORIARTY.) I didn't suppose you'd want to use that thing again, so I took all your cartridges out and put them in my pocket. You'll find them all there, Professor. *(Reaches over and rings bell on table with right hand.)*

(Enter BILLY.)

Billy!
BILLY: Yes, sir!
HOLMES: Show this gentleman nicely to the door.
BILLY: Yes, sir! This way, sir! *(Standing within door.)*

(PROFESSOR MORIARTY *looks at* HOLMES *a moment, then flings revolver down and across the table, clenches fist in* HOLMES'S *face, turns boiling with rage, picks hat up, and exits quickly at door, muttering aloud as he goes.*)

HOLMES *(after exit of* MORIARTY): Billy! Come here!

BILLY: Yes, sir! (BILLY *comes quickly down.*)

HOLMES: Billy! You're a good boy!

BILLY: Yes, sir! Thank you, sir! *(Stands grinning up at* HOLMES.)

(The lights go out suddenly.)

(No music at end of this Act.)

CURTAIN.

ACT III

SCENE. — *The Gas Chamber at Stepney. A large, dark, grimy room on an upper floor of an old building backing on wharves, etc. Plaster cracking off, masonry piers or chimney showing. As uncanny and gruesome appearance as possible. Heavy beams and timbers showing. Door leads to the landing and then to the entrance. Another door leads to a small cupboard. The walls of the cupboard can be seen when the door is opened. Large window, closed. Grimy and dirty glass so nothing can be seen through it. The window is nailed with spike nails securely shut. Black backing—no light behind. Strong bars outside back of windows, to show when window is broken. These bars must not be seen through the glass. Trash all over the room. The only light in the room on the rise of the curtain is from a dim lantern—carried on by* MCTAGUE.

Characteristic Music for Curtain.

CRAIGIN *and* LEARY *are discovered.* CRAIGIN *is sitting on a box. He sits glum and motionless, waiting.* LEARY *is sitting on table, his feet on the chair in front of it.*

MCTAGUE *enters with safety lamp. He stops just within a moment, glancing around in the dimness. Soon moves up near a masonry pier, a little above the door, and leans against it, waiting.* CRAIGIN, LEARY *and* MCTAGUE *are dressed in dark clothes and wear felt-soled shoes.*

LEARY: What's McTague doing 'ere?
MCTAGUE: I was sent 'ere.

(All dialogue in this part of Act in low tones, but distinct, to give a weird effect, echoing through the large grimy room among the deep shadows.)

LEARY: I thought the Seraph was with us in this job.
CRAIGIN: 'E ain't.
LEARY: Who was the last you put the gas on?

(Pause.)

134

CRAIGIN: I didn't 'ear 'is name. *(Pause.)* 'E'd been 'oldin' back money on a 'aul out some railway place.

(Pause.)

McTAGUE: What's this 'ere job he wants done? *(Sits on box, placing lamp on floor by his side.)*

(Pause.)

CRAIGIN: I ain't been told.

(Pause.)

LEARY: As long as it's 'ere we know what it's likely to be.

(Door opens slowly and hesitatingly. Enter SID PRINCE. *He stands just within door, and looks about a little suspiciously as if uncertain what to do. Pause. He notices that the door is slowly closing behind him and quietly holds it back. But he must not burlesque this movement with funny business.* McTAGUE *holds lantern up to see who it is, at the same time rising and coming down near* PRINCE.)

PRINCE: Does any one of you blokes know if this is the place where I meet Alf Bassick?

(Pause. Neither of the other men take notice of PRINCE. McTAGUE *goes back to where he was sitting before* PRINCE'S *entrance.)*

(After waiting a moment.) From wot you say, I take it you don't.

CRAIGIN: We ain't knowin' no such man. 'E may be 'ere and 'e. may not.

PRINCE: Oh! *(Comes a little farther into room and lets the door close.)* It's quite right then, thank you. *(Pause. No one speaks.)* Nice old place to find, this 'ere is. *(No one answers him.)* And when you do find it — *(looks about)* — I can't say it's any too cheerful. *(He thereupon pulls out a cigarette-case, puts a cigarette in his mouth, and feels in pocket for matches. Finds one. About to light it. Has moved a few steps during this.)*

CRAIGIN: Here! . . . .

*(*PRINCE *stops.)*

Don't light that! . . . It ain't safe!

(PRINCE *stops motionless, where above speech caught him, for an instant. Pause.* PRINCE *begins to turn his head slowly and only a little way, glances carefully about, as if expecting to see tins of nitro-glycerine. He sees nothing on either side, and finally turns towards* CRAIGIN.)

PRINCE: If it ain't askin' too much, wot's the matter with the place? It looks all roight to me.

CRAIGIN: Well don't light no matches, and it'll stay lookin' the same.

(Pause. Door opens, and BASSICK *enters hurriedly. He looks quickly about.)*

BASSICK: Oh, Prince, you're here. I was looking for you outside.

PRINCE: You told me to be 'ere, sir. That was 'ow the last arrangement stood.

BASSICK: Very well! *(Going across* PRINCE *and glancing about to see that the other men are present.)* You've got the rope, Craigin?

(Voices are still kept low.)

CRAIGIN *(pointing to bunch of loose rope on floor near him)*: It's 'ere.

BASSICK: That you, Leary?

LEARY: 'Ere, sir!

BASSICK: And McTague?

MCTAGUE: 'Ere, sir!

BASSICK: You want to be very careful with it to-night—you've got a tough one.

CRAIGIN: You ain't said who, as I've 'eard.

BASSICK *(low voice)*: Sherlock Holmes.

(Brief pause.)

CRAIGIN *(after the pause)*: You mean that, sir?

BASSICK: Indeed, I do!

CRAIGIN: We're goin' to count 'im out.

BASSICK: Well, if you *don't* and he gets away—I'm sorry for you, that's all.

CRAIGIN: I'll be cursed glad to put the gas on 'im—I tell you *that.*

LEARY: I say the same myself.

(Sound of MORIARTY *and* LARRABEE *coming.)*

BASSICK: Sh! Professor Moriarty's coming.

(MCTAGUE *places lamp on box.)*

LEARY: Not the guv'nor?
BASSICK: Yes. He wanted to see this.

(The three men retire a little up stage, waiting. BASSICK *moves to meet* MORIARTY. PRINCE *moves up out of way. Door opens. Enter* MORIARTY, *followed by* LARRABEE. *Door slowly closes behind them.* LARRABEE *waits a moment near door and then retires up near* PRINCE. *They watch the following scene. All speeches low— quiet—in undertone.)*

MORIARTY: Where's Craigin?

(CRAIGIN *steps forward.)*

Have you got your men?
CRAIGIN: All 'ere, sir.
MORIARTY: No *mistakes* to-night.
CRAIGIN: I'll be careful o' that.
MORIARTY *(quick glance about)*: That door, Bassick. *(Points up, back to audience.)*
BASSICK: A small cupboard, sir. *(Goes quickly up and opens the door wide to show it.)*

(LEARY *catches up lantern and swings it near the cupboard door.)*

MORIARTY: No outlet?
BASSICK: None whatever, sir.

(LEARY *swings lantern almost inside cupboard to let* MORIARTY *see. All this dialogue in very low tones, but distinct and impressive.* BASSICK *closes door after lantern business.)*

MORIARTY *(turns and points)*: That window?
BASSICK *(moving over a little)*: Nailed down, sir!

(LEARY *turns and swings the lantern near window so that* MORIARTY *can see.)*

MORIARTY: A man might break the glass.

BASSICK: If he did that he'd come against heavy iron bars outside.

CRAIGIN: We'll 'ave 'im tied down afore 'e could break any glass, sir.

MORIARTY *(who has turned to* CRAIGIN): Ah! You've used it before. Of course, you know if it's airtight?

BASSICK: Every crevice is caulked, sir.

MORIARTY *(turns and points as if at something directly over the footlights)*: And that door?

(LEARY *comes down and gives lantern a quick swing as if lighting place indicated.)*

BASSICK *(from same position)*: The opening is planked up solid, sir, as you can see, and double thickness.

MORIARTY: Ah! *(Satisfaction. Glances at door through which he entered.)* When the men turn the gas on him they leave by that door?

BASSICK: Yes, sir.

MORIARTY: It can be made quite secure?

BASSICK: Heavy bolts on the outside, sir, and solid bars over all.

MORIARTY: Let me see how quick you can operate them.

BASSICK: They tie the man down, sir—there's no need to hurry.

MORIARTY *(same voice)*: Let me see how quick you can operate them.

BASSICK *(quick order)*: Leary! *(Motions him to door.)*

LEARY *(handing lamp to* CRAIGIN): Yes, sir! *(He jumps to door and goes out, closing it at once, and immediately the sounds of sliding bolts and the dropping of bars are heard from outside.)*

(This is a very important effect, as it is repeated at the end of the Act. CRAIGIN *places lamp on box.)*

MORIARTY: That's all.

(Sounds of bolts withdrawn and LEARY *enters and waits.)*

(Goes to CRAIGIN.) Craigin—you'll take your men outside that door and wait till Mr. Larrabee has had a little business interview with the gentleman. Take them up the passage to the left so that Holmes does not see them as he comes in. *(To* BASSICK.) Who's driving the cab to-night?

BASSICK: I sent O'Hagan. His orders are to drive him about for an hour so he doesn't know the distance or the direction he's going, and then stop at the small door at upper Swandem Lane. He's going to get him out there and show him to this door.

MORIARTY: The cab windows were covered, of course?

BASSICK: Wooden shutters, sir, bolted and secure. There isn't a place he can see through the size of a pin.

MORIARTY *(satisfied)*: Ah! . . . *(Looks about.)* We must have a lamp here.

BASSICK: Better not, sir — there might be some gas left.

MORIARTY: You've got a light there. *(Pointing to miner's safety lamp on box.)*

BASSICK: It's a safety lamp, sir.

MORIARTY: A safety lamp! You mustn't have that here! The moment he sees that he'll know what you're doing and make trouble. *(Sniffs.)* There's hardly any gas. Go and tell Lascar we must have a good lamp.

(BASSICK *goes out.*)

(Looks about.) Bring that table over here.

(CRAIGIN *and* MCTAGUE *bring table.*)

Now, Craigin — and the rest of you — One thing remember. No shooting to-night! Not a single shot. It can be heard in the alley below. The first thing is to get his revolver away before he has a chance to use it. Two of you attract his attention in front — the other come up on him from behind and snatch it out of his pocket. Then you have him. Arrange that, Craigin.

CRAIGIN: I'll attend to it, sir.

(The three men retire. Enter BASSICK *with large lamp. Glass shade to lamp of whitish colour.* BASSICK *crosses to table and places lamp on it.)*

BASSICK *(to* MCTAGUE): Put out that lamp.

(MCTAGUE *is about to pick up lamp.)*

CRAIGIN: Stop!

(MCTAGUE *waits.)*

We'll want it when the other's taken away.

BASSICK: He mustn't see it, understand.

MORIARTY: Don't put it out—cover it with something.

CRAIGIN: Here! *(He goes up, takes lantern, and pulling out a large box from several others places lantern within and pushes the open side against the wall so that no light from lantern can be seen from front.)*

MORIARTY: That will do.

BASSICK *(approaching* MORIARTY): You mustn't stay any longer, sir. O'Hagan might be a little early.

MORIARTY: Mr. Larrabee— *(Moving a step forward.)* You understand!—they wait for you.

LARRABEE *(low—quiet)*: I understand, sir.

MORIARTY: I give you this opportunity to get what you can for your trouble. But anything that is found on him after you have finished—is subject—*(glances at* CRAIGIN *and others)*—to the usual division.

LARRABEE: That's all I want.

MORIARTY: When you have quite finished and got your money, suppose you blow that little whistle which I observe hanging from your watch chain—and these gentlemen will take *their* turn.

(BASSICK *holds door open for* MORIARTY. LARRABEE *moves up out of way as* MORIARTY *crosses.)*

(Crosses to door. At door, turning to CRAIGIN.) And, Craigin—

(CRAIGIN *crosses to* MORIARTY.)

At the proper moment present my compliments to Mr. Sherlock Holmes, and say that I wish him a pleasant journey to the other side. *(Goes out, followed by* BASSICK.)

(LARRABEE *glances about critically. As* MORIARTY *goes,* PRINCE *throws cigarette on floor in disgust, which* LEARY *picks up as he goes later, putting it in his pocket.)*

LARRABEE: You'd better put that rope out of sight.

(CRAIGIN *picks up rope, which he carries with him until he goes out later.* LEARY *and* MCTAGUE *move across noiselessly at back.* CRAIGIN *stops an instant up stage to examine the window, looking*

*at the caulking, etc., and shaking the frames to see that they are
securely spiked. Others wait near door. He finishes at window.*
LARRABEE *is examining package near lamp, which he has taken
from his pocket. As* LEARY *crosses he picks up rope which was
lying up centre and hides it in barrel.* MCTAGUE *in crossing
bumps up against* PRINCE, *and both look momentarily at each
other very much annoyed.)*

CRAIGIN *(joins* LEARY *and* MCTAGUE *at door. Speaks to*
LARRABEE *from door)*: You understand, sir, we're on this floor
just around the far turn of the passage—so 'e won't see us as 'e's
comin' up.

LARRABEE: I understand. *(Turning to* CRAIGIN.)

CRAIGIN: An' it's w'en we 'ears that whistle, eh?

LARRABEE: When you hear this whistle.

(CRAIGIN, LEARY *and* MCTAGUE *go out noiselessly. Pause. Door
remains open.* PRINCE, *who has been very quiet during foregoing
scene, begins to move a little nervously and looks about. He looks
at his watch and then glances about again.* LARRABEE *is still near
lamp, looking at package of papers which he took from his
pocket.)*

PRINCE *(coming down in a grumpy manner, head down, not
looking at* LARRABEE): Look 'ere, Jim, this sort of thing ain't so
much in my line.

LARRABEE *(at table)*: I suppose not.

PRINCE *(still eyes about without looking at* LARRABEE): When it
comes to a shy at a safe or drillin' into bank vaults, I feels perfectly
at 'ome, but I don't care so much to see a man— *(Stops—
hesitates.)* Well, it ain't my line!

LARRABEE *(turning)*: Here! *(Going to him and urging him
toward door and putting package away.)* All I want of you is to go
down on the corner below and let me know when he comes.

PRINCE *(stops and turns to* LARRABEE): 'Ow will I let you know?

LARRABEE: Have you got a whistle?

PRINCE *(pulls one out of pocket)*: Cert'nly.

LARRABEE: Well, when you see O'Hagan driving with him,
come down the alley there and blow it twice. *(Urging* PRINCE *a
little nearer door.)*

PRINCE: Yes—but ain't it quite loikely to call a cab at the same time?

LARRABEE: What more do you want—take the cab and go home.

PRINCE: Oh, then you won't need me 'ere again.

LARRABEE: No.

(PRINCE *turns to go.*)

PRINCE *(going to door—very much relieved)*: Oh, very well— then I'll tear myself away. *(Goes out.)*

(Music. Pathetic, melodramatic, agitato, pp.)

(LARRABEE *crosses to table and looks at lamp, gets two chairs and places them on either side of table. As he places second chair he stops dead as if having heard a noise outside, listens, and is satisfied all is well. Then thinking of the best way to conduct his negotiations with Holmes, takes out cigar, and holds it a moment unlighted as he thinks. Then takes out match and is about to light it when* ALICE FAULKNER *enters. He starts up and looks at her. She stands looking at him, frightened and excited.)*

(Music stops.)

LARRABEE: What do *you* want?

ALICE: It's true, then?

LARRABEE: How did you get to this place?

ALICE: I followed you—in a cab.

LARRABEE: What have you been doing since I came up here? Informing the police, perhaps.

ALICE: No—I was afraid he'd come—so I waited.

LARRABEE: Oh—to warn him very likely?

ALICE: Yes. *(Pause.)* To warn him. *(Looks about room.)*

LARRABEE: Then it's just as well you came up.

ALICE: I came to make sure— *(Glances about.)*

LARRABEE: Of what?

ALICE: That something else—is not going to be done besides— what they told me.

LARRABEE: Ah—somebody told you that something else was going to be done?

ALICE: Yes.

LARRABEE: So! We've got another spy in the house.

ALICE: You're going to swindle and deceive him — I know that. *Is there anything more? (Advancing to him a little.)*

LARRABEE: What could you do if there was?

ALICE: I could buy you off. Such men as you are always open to sale.

LARABEE: How much would you give?

ALICE: The genuine package — the real ones. All the proofs — everything.

LARRABEE *(advancing above table, quietly but with quick interest)*: Have you got it with you?

ALICE: No, but I can get it.

LARRABEE: Oh — *(Going to table. Slightly disappointed.)* So you'll do all that for this man? You think he's your friend, I suppose?

ALICE: I haven't thought of it.

LARRABEE: Look what he's doing now. Coming here to buy those things off me.

ALICE: They're false. They're counterfeit.

LARRABEE: He thinks they're genuine, doesn't he? He'd hardly come here to buy them if he didn't.

ALICE: He *may* ask my permission still.

LARRABEE: Ha! *(Sneer—turning away.)* He won't get the chance.

ALICE *(suspicious again)*: Won't get the chance. Then there *is* something else.

LARRABEE: Something else! *(Turning to her.)* Why, you see me here myself, don't you? I'm going to talk to him on a little business. How could I do him any harm?

ALICE *(advancing)*: Where are those men who came up here?

LARRABEE: What men?

ALICE: Three villainous looking men — I saw them go in at the street door —

LARRABEE: Oh — those men. They went up the other stairway. *(Pointing over shoulder.)* You can see them in the next building — if you look out of this window. *(Indicating window.)*

(ALICE *at once goes rapidly toward the window and making a hesitating pause near table as she sees* LARRABEE *crossing above her, but moving on again quickly.* LARRABEE *at same time crosses well up stage, keeping his eye on* ALICE *as she moves towards the window and tries to look out, but finding she cannot she turns at once to* LARRABEE. *He is standing near door.)*

(Music. Melodramatic. Danger. Keep down pp. Agitato.)

(Hold this an instant where they stand looking at one another, ALICE *beginning to see she has been trapped.)*

ALICE *(starting toward door)*: I'll look in the passage-way, if you please.

LARRABEE *(taking one step down before door, quietly)*: Yes — but I don't please.

ALICE *(stops before him)*: You wouldn't *dare* to keep me here.

LARRABEE: I might *dare* — but I won't. *You'd be in the way.*

ALICE: Where are those men?

LARRABEE: Stay where you are and you'll see them very soon.

(LARRABEE *goes to door and blows whistle as quietly as possible. Short pause. No footsteps heard, as the men move noiselessly. Enter* CRAIGIN, MCTAGUE *and* LEARY, *appearing suddenly and noiselessly. They stand looking in some astonishment at* ALICE.)

(Music stops.)

ALICE: I knew it. *(Moving back a step, seeing from this that they are going to attack Holmes.)* Ah! *(Under breath. After slight pause she turns and hurries to window, trying to look out or give an alarm. Then runs to cupboard door.* LARRABEE *waits, watching her movements. Desperately.)* You're going to do him some harm.

LARRABEE: Oh no, it's only a little joke — at his expense.

ALICE *(moving toward him a little)*: You wanted the letters, the package I had in the safe! I'll get it for you. Let me go and I'll bring it here — or whatever you tell me —

(LARRABEE *sneers meaningly.)*

I'll give you my word not to say anything to anyone — not to him — not to the policemen — not *anyone!*

LARRABEE *(without moving)*: You needn't take the trouble to *get* it — but you can *tell me where it is* — and you'll have to be quick about it too —

ALICE: Yes—if you'll promise not to go on with this.

LARRABEE: Of course! That's understood.

ALICE *(excitedly)*: You promise!

LARRABEE: Certainly I promise. Now where is it?

ALICE: Just outside my bedroom window—just outside on the left, fastened between the shutter and the wall—you can easily find it.

LARRABEE: Yes—I can easily find it.

ALICE: Now tell them—tell them to go.

LARRABEE *(going down to men)*: Tie her up so she can't make a noise. Keep her out there until we have Holmes in here, and then let O'Hagan keep her in his cab. She mustn't get back to the house —not till I've been there.

(ALICE *listens dazed, astonished.*)

CRAIGIN *(speaks low)*: Go an' get a hold, Leary. Hand me a piece of that rope.

(MCTAGUE *brings rope from under his coat. Business of getting rapidly ready to gag and tie* ALICE. *Much time must not be spent on this; quick, business-like.* MCTAGUE *takes handkerchief from pocket to use as gag.*)

LARRABEE *(taking a step or two down before* ALICE *so as to attract her attention front)*: Now then, my pretty bird—

(ALICE *begins to move back in alarm and looking at* LARRABEE.)

ALICE: You said—you said if I *told* you—

LARRABEE: Well—we haven't done him any harm yet, have we?

(LEARY *is moving quietly round behind her.*)

ALICE: Then send them away.

LARRABEE: Certainly. Go away now, boys, there's no more work for you to-night.

ALICE *(looking at them terrified)*: They don't obey you. They are—

(LEARY *seizes her. She screams and resists, but* CRAIGIN *and* MCTAGUE *come at once, so that she is quickly subdued and gagged with handkerchief, etc., and her hands tied. As the struggle takes place, men work up to near cupboard with* ALICE.

LARRABEE *also eagerly watching them tie* ALICE *up. This is not prolonged more than is absolutely necessary. Just as they finish, a shrill whistle is heard in distance outside at back, as if from street far below. All stop—listening—picture.)*

CRAIGIN: Now out of the door with her— *(Starting to door.)*

(The prolonged shrill whistle is heard again.)

LARRABEE: By God, he's *here.*
CRAIGIN: What!
LARRABEE: That's Sid Prince, I put him on the watch.
CRAIGIN: We won't have time to get her out.
LARRABEE: Shut her in there. *(Pointing to cupboard.)*
LEARY: Yes—that'll do.
CRAIGIN: In with her.

(LEARY *and* CRAIGIN, *almost on the word, take her towards cupboard.* MCTAGUE *goes and keeps watch at door.)*

(As he holds ALICE.) Open that door! Open that door!

(LEARY *goes and opens cupboard door. As* LEARY *leaves* ALICE *she breaks away from* CRAIGIN *and gets almost to right when* CRAIGIN *catches her again. As he takes hold of her she faints, and he throws her into cupboard in a helpless condition.* LEARY *closes cupboard door and they stand before it.)*

LEARY *(still at cupboard door. Others have turned so as to avoid suspicion if Holmes comes in on them)*: There ain't no lock on this 'ere door.
LARRABEE: No lock!
LEARY: No.
LARRABEE: Drive something in.
CRAIGIN: Here, this knife. *(Hands* LEARY *a large clasp-knife opened ready.)*
LARRABEE: A knife won't hold it.
CRAIGIN: Yes, it will. Drive it in strong.

(LEARY *drives blade in door frame with all his force.)*

LEARY: 'E'll have to find us 'ere.
CRAIGIN: Yes—and he won't either—we'll go on and do 'im up. *(Going to door.)*

LARRABEE: No, you won't.

(Men stop. Pause.)

I'll see him first, if you please.

(CRAIGIN *and* LARRABEE *facing each other savagely an instant well down stage.)*

McTAGUE: Them was orders, Craigin.

LEARY: So it was.

McTAGUE: There might be time to get back in the passage. *(He listens at door and cautiously looks off—turns back into room.)* They ain't got up one flight yet.

LEARY: Quick then. *(Moving toward door.)*

(McTAGUE, LEARY *and* CRAIGIN *go out. Door does not close.* LARRABEE *glances at door anxiously. Makes a quick dash up to it, and forces knife in with all his strength. Quickly pulls off coat and hat, throwing them on boxes, and sits quietly chewing an end of cigar. Enter* SHERLOCK HOLMES *at door, walking easily as though on some ordinary business.)*

(Stop music.)

HOLMES *(seeing the apartment with a glance as he enters and pausing, disappointed. His little laugh, with no smile)*: How the devil is it that you crooks always manage to hit on the same places for your scoundrelly business? *(Chuckles of amusement.)* Well! I certainly thought, after all this driving about in a closed cab you'd show me something new.

LARRABEE *(looking up nonchalantly)*: Seen it before, have you?

HOLMES *(standing still)*: Well, I should think so! *(Moves easily about recalling dear old times.)* I nabbed a friend of yours in this place while he was trying to drop himself out of that window. Ned Colvin, the cracksman.

LARRABEE: Colvin. I never heard of him before.

HOLMES: No? Ha! ha! Well, you certainly never heard of him after. A brace of counterfeiters used these regal chambers in the spring of '90. One of them hid in the cupboard. We pulled him out by the heels.

LARRABEE *(trying to get in on the nonchalance)*: Ah! Did you? And the other?

HOLMES: The other? He was more fortunate.

LARRABEE: Ah—he got away, I suppose.

HOLMES: Yes, he got away. We took his remains out through that door to the street. *(Indicating door.)*

LARRABEE: Quite interesting. *(Drawled a little—looks at end of his cigar.)*

(HOLMES *is looking about.)*

Times have changed since then.

(HOLMES *darts a lightning glance at* LARRABEE. *Instantly easy again and glancing about as before.)*

HOLMES *(dropping down near* LARRABEE): So they have, Mr. Larrabee—so they have. *(A little confidentially.)* Then it was only cracksmen, counterfeiters, and petty swindlers of various kinds— Now— *(Pause, looking at* LARRABEE.)

(LARRABEE *turns and looks at* HOLMES.)

LARRABEE: Well? What now?

HOLMES: Well— *(Mysteriously.)* Between you and me, Mr. Larrabee—we've heard some not altogether agreeable rumours; rumours of some pretty shady work not far from here—a murder or two of a very peculiar kind—and I've always had a suspicion— *(Stops. Sniffs very delicately. Motionless pause. Nods ominously to* LARRABEE, *who is looking about, and gets over towards window. When within reach he runs his hand lightly along the frame.)* My surmise was correct—it is.

LARRABEE *(turning to* HOLMES): It is what?

HOLMES: Caulked.

LARRABEE: What does that signify to us?

HOLMES: Nothing to us, Mr. Larrabee, nothing to us, but it might signify a good deal to some poor devil who's been caught in this trap.

LARRABEE: Well, if it's nothing to us, suppose we leave it alone and get to business. My time is limited.

HOLMES: Quite so, of course. I should have realized that these reflections could not possibly appeal to you. But it so happens that I take a deep interest in anything that pertains to what are known as the criminal classes and this same interest makes me rather curious to know — *(looking straight at* LARRABEE, *who looks up at him)* — how you happened to select such a singularly gruesome place for an ordinary business transaction.

LARRABEE *(looking at* HOLMES *across the table)*: I selected this place, Mr. Holmes, because I thought you might not be disposed to take such liberties here as you practised in my own house last night.

HOLMES: Quite so, quite so. *(Looks innocently at* LARRABEE.) But why not?

(They look at one another an instant.)

LARRABEE *(significantly)*: You might not feel quite so much at home.

HOLMES: Oh — ha! *(A little laugh.)* You've made a singular miscalculation. I feel perfectly at home, Mr. Larrabee! Perfectly! *(He seats himself at table in languid and leisurely manner, takes cigar from pocket and lights it.)*

LARRABEE *(looks at him an instant)*: Well, I'm very glad to hear it.

(LARRABEE *now takes out the counterfeit package of papers, etc., and tosses it on the table before them.* HOLMES *looks on floor slightly by light of match, unobserved by* LARRABEE.)

Here is the little packet which is the object of this meeting. *(He glances at* HOLMES *to see effect of its production.)*

(HOLMES *looks at it calmly as he smokes.)*

I haven't opened it yet, but Miss Faulkner tells me everything is there.

HOLMES: Then there is no need of opening it, Mr. Larrabee.

LARRABEE: Oh, well — I want to see you satisfied.

HOLMES: That is precisely the condition in which you now behold me. Miss Faulkner is a truthful young lady. Her word is sufficient.

LARRABEE: Very well. Now what shall we say, Mr. Holmes? *(Pause.)* Of course, we want a pretty large price for this. Miss Faulkner is giving up everything. She would not be satisfied unless the result justified it.

HOLMES *(pointedly)*: Suppose, Mr. Larrabee, that as Miss Faulkner knows nothing whatever about this affair, we omit her name from the discussion.

(Slight pause of two seconds.)

LARRABEE: Who told you she doesn't know?

HOLMES: You did. Every look, tone, gesture—everything you have said and done since I have been in this room has informed me that she has never consented to this transaction. It is a little speculation of your own. *(Tapping his fingers on end of table.)*

LARRABEE: Ha! *(Sneer.)* I suppose you think you can read me like a book.

HOLMES: No—like a primer.

LARRABEE: Well, let that pass. How much'll you give?

HOLMES: A thousand pounds.

LARRABEE: I couldn't take it.

HOLMES: What do you ask?

LARRABEE: Five thousand.

HOLMES *(shakes head)*: I couldn't give it.

LARRABEE: Very well— *(Rises.)* We've had all this trouble for nothing. *(As if about to put up the packet.)*

HOLMES *(leaning back in chair and remonstrating)*: Oh—don't say that, Mr. Larrabee! To me the occasion has been doubly interesting. I have not only had the pleasure of meeting you again, but I have also availed myself of the opportunity of making some observations regarding this place which may not come amiss.

(LARRABEE *looks at* HOLMES *contemptuously. He places chair under table.)*

LARRABEE: Why, I've been offered four thousand for this little—

HOLMES: Why didn't you take it?

LARRABEE: Because I intend to get more.

HOLMES: That's too bad.

LARRABEE: If they offered four thousand they'll give five.

HOLMES: They won't give anything.

LARRABEE: Why not?

HOLMES: They've turned the case over to me.

LARRABEE: Will you give three thousand?

HOLMES *(rising)*: Mr. Larrabee, strange as it may appear, my time is limited as well as yours. I have brought with me the sum of one thousand pounds, which is all that I wish to pay. If it is your desire to sell at this figure kindly appraise me of the fact at once. If not, permit me to wish you a very good evening.

(Pause. LARRABEE *looks at him.)*

LARRABEE *(after the pause glances nervously round once, fearing he heard something)*: Go on! *(Tosses packet on table.)* You can have them. It's too small a matter to haggle over.

(HOLMES *reseats himself at once, back of table, and takes wallet from his pocket, from which he produces a bunch of bank notes.* LARRABEE *stands watching him with glittering eye.* HOLMES *counts out ten one hundred pound notes and lays the remainder of the notes on the table with elbow on them, while he counts the first over again.)*

(Sneeringly.) Oh—I thought you said you had brought just a thousand.

HOLMES *(not looking up; counting the notes)*: I did. This is it.

LARRABEE: You brought a trifle more, I see.

HOLMES *(counting notes)*: Quite so. I didn't say I hadn't brought any more.

LARRABEE: Ha! *(Sneers.)* You can do your little tricks when it comes to it, can't you?

HOLMES: It depends on who I'm dealing with. *(Hands* LARRABEE *one thousand pounds in notes.)*

(LARRABEE *takes money and keeps a close watch at same time on the remaining pile of notes lying at* HOLMES'S *left.* HOLMES, *after handing the notes to* LARRABEE, *lays cigar he was smoking on the table, picks up packet which he puts in his pocket with his right hand, and is almost at the same time reaching with his left hand for the notes he placed upon the table when* LARRABEE *makes a sudden lunge and snatches the pile of bank notes, jumping back on the instant.* HOLMES *springs to his feet at the same time.)*

Now I've got you where I want you, Jim Larrabee! You've been so cunning and so cautious and so wise, we couldn't find a thing to hold you for—but this little slip will get you in for *robbery*—

LARRABEE: Oh! You'll have me in, will you? *(Short sneering laugh.)* What are your views about being able to get away from here yourself?

HOLMES: I do not anticipate any particular difficulty.

LARRABEE *(significantly)*: Perhaps you'll change your mind about that.

HOLMES: Whether I change my mind or not, I certainly shall leave this place, and your arrest will shortly follow.

LARRABEE: My arrest? Ha, ha! Robbery, eh— Why, even if you got away from here you haven't got a witness. Not a witness to your *name*.

HOLMES *(slowly backing, keeping his eyes sharply on* LARRABEE *as he does so)*: I'm not so sure of that, Mr. Larrabee!—*Do you usually fasten* that door with a *knife? (Pointing toward door with left arm and hand, but eyes on* LARRABEE.)

(LARRABEE *turns front as if bewildered. Tableau an instant. Very faint moan from within cupboard.* HOLMES *listens motionless an instant, then makes quick dash to door and seizing knife wrenches it out and flings it on the floor.* LARRABEE *seeing* HOLMES *start toward door of cupboard springs up to head him off.)*

LARRABEE: Come away from that door.

(But HOLMES *has the door torn open and* ALICE FAULKNER *out before* LARRABEE *gets near.)*

HOLMES: Stand back! *(Turning to* LARRABEE, *supporting* ALICE *at same time.)* You contemptible scoundrel! What does this mean!

LARRABEE: I'll show you what it means cursed quick. *(Taking a step or two, blows the little silver whistle attached to his watch chain.)*

HOLMES *(untying* ALICE *quickly)*: I'm afraid you're badly hurt, Miss Faulkner.

(Enter CRAIGIN. *He stands there a moment near door, watching* HOLMES. *He makes a signal with hand to others outside door and then moves noiselessly.* MCTAGUE *enters noiselessly, and remains a little behind* CRAIGIN *below door.* ALICE *shakes her head quickly, thinking of what she sees, and tries to call* HOLMES'S *attention to* CRAIGIN *and* MCTAGUE.)

ALICE: No!—Mr. Holmes. *(Pointing to* CRAIGIN *and* McTAGUE.)

HOLMES *(glances round)*: Ah, Craigin—delighted to see you.

(CRAIGIN *gives slight start.)*

And you too, McTague. I infer from your presence here at this particular juncture that I am not dealing with Mr. Larrabee *alone.*

LARRABEE: Your inference is quite correct, Mr. Holmes.

HOLMES: It is not difficult to imagine who is at the bottom of such a conspiracy as this. .

(CRAIGIN *begins to steal across noiselessly.* McTAGUE *remains before door,* HOLMES *turns to* ALICE *again.)*

I hope you're beginning to feel a little more yourself, Miss Faulkner—because we shall leave here very soon.

ALICE *(who has been shrinking from the sight of* CRAIGIN *and* McTAGUE): Oh yes—do let us go, Mr. Holmes.

CRAIGIN *(low, deep voice, intense)*: You'll 'ave to wait a bit, Mr. 'Olmes. We 'ave a little matter of business we'd like to talk over.

(HOLMES *turning to* CRAIGIN.)

(Enter LEARY *and glides up side in the shadow and begins to move towards* HOLMES. *In approaching from corner he glides behind door of cupboard as it stands open, and from there down on* HOLMES *at cue. As* HOLMES *turns to* CRAIGIN, ALICE *leans against wall of cupboard.)*

HOLMES: All right, Craigin, I'll see you to-morrow morning in your cell at Bow Street.

CRAIGIN *(threateningly)*: Werry sorry, sir, but I cawn't wait till morning. It's got to be settled to-night.

HOLMES *(looks at* CRAIGIN *an instant)*: All right, Craigin, we'll settle it to-night.

CRAIGIN: It's so werry *h*important, Mr. 'Olmes—so werry himportant indeed *that you'll 'ave to 'tend to it now.*

(At this instant ALICE *sees* LEARY *approaching rapidly from behind and screams.* HOLMES *turns, but* LEARY *is upon him at the same time. There is a very short struggle, and* HOLMES *throws*

LEARY *violently off, but* LEARY *has got* HOLMES'S *revolver. As they struggle* ALICE *steps back to side of room up stage. A short deadly pause.* HOLMES *motionless, regarding the men.* ALICE'S *back against wall. After the pause* LEARY *begins to revive.)*

(Low voice to LEARY.) 'Ave you got his revolver?

LEARY *(showing revolver)*: 'Ere it is. *(Getting slowly to his feet.)*

HOLMES *(recognizing* LEARY *in the dim light)*: Ah, Leary! This is a pleasure indeed. It needed only your blithe personality to make the party complete. *(Sits and writes rapidly on pocket pad, pushing lamp away a little and picking up cigar which he had left on the table, and which he keeps in his mouth as he writes.)* There is only one other I could wish to welcome here, and that is the talented author of this midnight carnival. We shall have him, however, by to-morrow night.

CRAIGIN: Though 'e ain't 'ere, Mr. 'Olmes, 'e gave me a message for yer. 'E presented his koindest compliments and wished yer a pleasant trip across.

HOLMES *(writing—cigar in mouth)*: That's very kind of him, I'm sure. *(Writes.)*

LARRABEE *(sneeringly)*: You're writing your will, I suppose?

HOLMES *(writing—with quick glances at the rest)*: No. *(Shakes head.)* Only a brief description of one or two of you gentlemen — for the police. We know the rest.

LEARY: And when will you give it 'em, Mr. 'Olmes?

HOLMES *(writes)*: In nine or nine and a half minutes, Mr. Leary.

LARRABEE: Oh, you expect to leave here in nine minutes, eh?

HOLMES: No. *(Writing.)* In one. It will take me eight minutes to find a policeman. This is a dangerous neighbourhood.

LARRABEE: Well, when you're ready to start, let us know.

HOLMES *(rising and putting pad in pocket)*: I'm ready now. *(Buttoning up coat.)*

(CRAIGIN, MCTAGUE *and* LEARY *suddenly brace themselves for action, and stand ready to make a run for* HOLMES. LARRABEE *also is ready to join in the struggle if necessary.* HOLMES *moves backward from table a little to* ALICE*—she drops down a step towards* HOLMES.)

CRAIGIN: Wait a bit. You'd better listen to me, Mr. 'Olmes. We're going to tie yer down nice and tight to the top o' that table.

HOLMES: Well, by Jove! I don't think you *will*. That's my idea, you know.

CRAIGIN: An' you'll save yourself a deal of trouble if ye submit quiet and easy like—because if ye don't ye moight get knocked about a bit—

ALICE *(under her breath)*: Oh—Mr. Holmes! *(Coming closer to* HOLMES.*)*

LARRABEE *(to* ALICE*)*: Come away from him! Come over here if you don't want to get hurt.

(Love music.)

HOLMES *(to* ALICE, *without looking round, but reaching her with left hand)*: My child, if you don't want to get hurt, don't leave me for a second.

(ALICE *moves closer to* HOLMES.)

LARRABEE: Aren't you coming?

ALICE *(breathlessly)*: No!

CRAIGIN: You'd better look out, Miss—he might get killed.

ALICE: Then you can kill me too.

(HOLMES *makes a quick turn to her, with sudden exclamation under breath. For an instant only he looks in her face—then a quick turn back to* CRAIGIN *and men.)*

HOLMES *(low voice—not taking eyes from men before him)*: I'm afraid you don't mean that, Miss Faulkner.

ALICE: Yes, I *do*.

HOLMES *(eyes on men—though they shift about rapidly, but never toward* ALICE*)*: No. *(Shakes head a trifle.)* You would not say it—at another time or place.

ALICE: I would say it anywhere—always.

(Music stops.)

CRAIGIN: So you'll 'ave it out with us, eh?

HOLMES: Do you imagine for one moment, Craigin, that I won't have it out with you?

CRAIGIN: Well then—I'll 'ave to give you one—same as I did yer right-'and man this afternoon. *(Approaching* HOLMES.)

HOLMES *(to* ALICE *without turning—intense, rapid)*: Ah!

(CRAIGIN *stops dead.*)

You heard him say that. *Same as he did my right-hand man this afternoon.*

ALICE *(under breath)*: Yes! yes!

HOLMES: Don't forget that face. *(Pointing to* CRAIGIN.) In three days I shall ask you to identify it in the prisoner's dock.

CRAIGIN *(enraged)*: Ha! *(Turning away as if to hide his face.)*

HOLMES *(very sharp—rapid)*: Yes—and the rest of you with him. You surprise me, gentlemen—thinking you're sure of anybody in this room, and never once taking the trouble to look at that window. If you wanted to make it perfectly safe, you should have had those *missing bars put in.*

(HOLMES *whispers something to* ALICE, *indicating her to make for door.*)

(Music till end of Act.)

(CRAIGIN, LEARY, MCTAGUE *and* LARRABEE *make very slight move and say* "Eh?" *but instantly at tension again, and all motionless, ready to spring on* HOLMES. HOLMES *and* ALICE, *motionless, facing them. This is held an instant.)*

LARRABEE: Bars or no bars, you're not going to get out of here as easy as you expect.

(HOLMES *moves easily down near table.*)

HOLMES: There are so many ways, Mr. Larrabee, I hardly know which to choose.

CRAIGIN *(louder—advancing)*: Well, you'd better choose quick —I can tell you that.

HOLMES *(sudden—strong—sharp)*: I'll choose at once, Mr. Craigin—and my choice—*(quickly seizing chair)*—falls on this. *(On the word he brings the chair down upon the lamp with a frightful crash, extinguishing light instantly.)*

(Every light out. Only the glow of HOLMES'S *cigar remains visible where he stands at the table. He at once begins to move toward window, keeping cigar so that it will show to men and to front.)*

CRAIGIN *(loud sharp voice to others)*: Trace 'im by the cigar. *(Moving at once toward window.)* Follow the cigar.

LARRABEE: Look out. He's going for the window.

(LEARY *goes quickly to window.* MCTAGUE *goes and is ready by safety lamp.* HOLMES *quickly fixes cigar in a crack or joint at side of window so that it is still seen—smash of the window glass is heard. Instantly glides across, well up stage, and down side to the door where he finds* ALICE. *On crash of window* CRAIGIN *and* LEARY *give quick shout of exclamation—they spring up stage toward the light of cigar—sound of quick scuffle and blows in darkness.)*

LARRABEE: Get that light.

CRAIGIN *(clear and distinct)*: The safety lamp. Where is it?

(Make this shout for lantern very strong and audible to front. MCTAGUE *kicks over box which concealed the safety lamp—lights up.* HOLMES *and* ALICE *at door.* ALICE *just going out.)*

HOLMES *(turning at door and pointing to window)*: You'll find that cigar in a crevice by the window.

(All start towards HOLMES *with exclamations, oaths, etc. He makes quick exit with* ALICE *and slams door after him. Sounds of heavy bolts outside sliding quickly into place, and heavy bars dropping into position.* CRAIGIN, MCTAGUE *and* LEARY *rush against door and make violent efforts to open it. After the first excited effort they turn quickly back. As* MCTAGUE *crosses he throws safely lamp on table.* LARRABEE, *who has stopped near when he saw door closed, turns front with a look of hatred on his face and mad with rage.)*

CURTAIN.

ACT IV

SCENE. — DR. WATSON'S *house in Kensington. The consulting-room. Oak panelling. Solid furniture. Wide double-doors opening to the hall and street door. Door communicating with doctor's inner medicine room. Another door, centre, opens to private hallway of house. The windows are supposed to open at side of house upon an area which faces the street. These windows have shades or blinds on rollers which can quickly be drawn down. At the opening of the Act they are down, so that no one could see into the room from the street.*

There is a large operating chair with high back, cushions, etc.

Music for curtain, which stops an instant before rise.

DR. WATSON *is seated behind his desk and* MRS. SMEEDLEY, *a seedy-looking middle-aged woman, is seated in the chair next to the desk with a medicine bottle in her hand.*

WATSON: Be careful to make no mistake about the medicine. If she's no better to-morrow I'll call. You will let me know, of course?

MRS. SMEEDLEY: Oh yes, indeed I will. Good evening, sir.

WATSON: Good night, Mrs. Smeedley.

(MRS. SMEEDLEY *goes out. Sound of door closing heard after she is off. Pause. The doctor turns to his desk, and ringing bell then busies himself with papers.*)

(Enter PARSONS — *a servant.)*

Parsons!

(PARSONS *comes a little towards* WATSON.)

(Lower voice.) That woman who just left — do you know her?

PARSONS *(trying to recollect)*: I can't say as I recollect 'avin' seen 'er before. Was there anything — ?

WATSON: Oh no! Acted a little strange, that's all. I thought I saw her looking about the hall before she went out.

PARSONS: Yes sir, she did give a look. I saw that myself, sir.

WATSON *(after an instant's thought)*: Oh well — I dare say it was nothing. Is there anyone waiting, Parsons?

PARSONS: There's one person in the waiting-room, sir—a gentleman.

WATSON *(looks at watch)*: I'll see him, but I've only a short time left. If any more come you must send them over to Doctor Anstruther. I spoke to him this afternoon about taking my cases. I have an important appointment at nine.

PARSONS: Very well, sir. Then you'll see this gentleman, sir?

WATSON: Yes.

(PARSONS *goes out. Short pause.* WATSON *busy at desk.* PARSONS *opens door and shows in* SID PRINCE. *He comes in a little way and pauses.* PARSONS *all through this Act closes the door after his exit, or after showing anyone in.* WATSON *looks up.)*

PRINCE *(speaking in the most dreadful husky whisper)*: Good evenin', sir!

WATSON: Good evening. *(Indicating chair.)* Pray be seated.

PRINCE *(same voice all through)*: Thanks, I don't mind if I do. *(Coughs, then sits in chair near desk.)*

WATSON *(looking at him with professional interest)*: What seems to be the trouble?

PRINCE: Throat, sir. *(Indicating his throat to assist in making himself understood.)* Most dreadful sore throat.

WATSON: Sore throat, eh? *(Glancing about for an instrument.)*

PRINCE: Well, I should think it is. It's the most 'arrowing thing I ever 'ad! It pains me that much to swallow that I—

WATSON: Hurts you to swallow, does it? *(Finding and picking up an instrument on the desk.)*

PRINCE: Indeed it does. Why, I can 'ardly get a bit of food down.

(WATSON *rises and goes to cabinet, pushes gas burner out into position and lights it.)*

WATSON: Just step this way a moment, please. (PRINCE *rises and goes up to* WATSON, *who adjusts reflector over eye, etc. He has an instrument in his hand which he wipes with a napkin.)* Now, mouth open—wide as possible. (PRINCE *opens mouth and* WATSON *places tongue holder on his tongue.)* That's it. *(Picks up dentist's mirror and warms it over gas burner.)*

PRINCE (WATSON *is about to examine throat when* PRINCE *sees instrument and is a trifle alarmed)*: Eh!

(Business of WATSON *putting in tongue holder and looking down* PRINCE'S *throat—looking carefully this way and that.)*

WATSON: Say "Ah!"

PRINCE *(husky voice)*: Ah! *(Steps away and places handkerchief to mouth as if the attempt to say* "Ah!" *hurt him.)*

(WATSON *discontinues, and takes instrument out of* PRINCE'S *mouth.)*

WATSON *(a slight incredulity in his manner)*: Where do you feel this pain?

PRINCE *(indicating with his finger)*: Just about there, doctor. Inside about there.

WATSON: That's singular. I don't find anything wrong. *(Pushes gas burner back to usual position—and placing instrument on cabinet.)*

PRINCE: You may not foind anything wrong, but I feel it wrong. If you would only give me something to take away this awful agony.

WATSON: That's nothing. It'll pass away in a few hours. *(Reflectively.)* Singular thing it would have affected your voice in this way. Well, I'll give you a gargle—it may help you a little.

PRINCE: Yes—if you only would, doctor.

(WATSON *goes into surgery,* PRINCE *watching him like a cat. Music. Dramatic agitato, very pp.* WATSON *does not close the door of the room, but pushes it part way so that it is open about a foot.* PRINCE *moves toward door, watching* WATSON *through it. Stops near door. Seems to watch for his chance, for he suddenly turns and goes quickly down and runs up blinds of both windows and moves back quickly, watching* WATSON *through the door again. Seeing that he still has time to spare, he goes to centre door and opens it, looking and listening off. Distant sound of a piano when door is open which stops when it is closed.* PRINCE *quickly turns back and goes off a little way at centre door, leaving it open so that he is seen peering up above and listening. Turns to come back, but just at the door he sees* WATSON *coming on and stops.* WATSON *suddenly enters and sees* PRINCE *in centre door and stops, with a bottle in his hand, and looks at* PRINCE.)

(Music stops.)

WATSON: What are you doing there?

PRINCE: Why, nothing at all, doctor. I felt such a draught on the back o' my neck, don't yer know, that I opened the door to see where it came from!

(WATSON *goes down and rings bell on his desk, placing bottle on papers. Pause. Enter* PARSONS.)

WATSON: Parsons, show this man the shortest way to the street door and close the door after him.

PRINCE: But, doctor, ye don't understand.

WATSON: I understand quite enough. Good evening.

PRINCE: Yer know, the draught plays hell with my throat, sir— and seems to affect my—

WATSON: Good evening. *(He sits and pays no further attention to* PRINCE.)

PARSONS: This way, sir, if you please.

PRINCE: I consider that you've treated me damned outrageous, that's wot I do, and ye won't hear the last of this very soon.

PARSONS *(approaching him)*: Come, none o' that now. *(Takes* PRINCE *by the arm.)*

PRINCE *(as he walks toward door with* PARSONS, *turns head back and speaks over his shoulder, shouting out in his natural voice)*: Yer call yerself a doctor an' treats sick people as comes to see yer this 'ere way. *(Goes out with* PARSONS *and continues talking until slam of door outside.)* Yer call yerself a doctor! A bloomin' foine doctor you are! *(Etc.)*

(PARSONS *has forced* PRINCE *out by the arm during foregoing speech. Door closes after* PRINCE. *Sound of outside door closing follows shortly.* WATSON, *after short pause, looks round room, not observing that window shades are up. He rings bell. Enter* PARSONS.)

WATSON *(rises and gathers up a few things as if to go)*: I shall be at Mr. Holmes's in Baker Street. If there's anything special, you'll know where to send for me. The appointment was for nine. *(Looks at watch.)* It's fifteen minutes past eight now—I'm going to walk over.

PARSONS: Very well, sir.

(Bell of outside door rings. PARSONS *looks at* WATSON, *who shakes his head.)*

WATSON: No. I won't see any more to-night. They must go to Doctor Anstruther.

PARSONS: Yes, sir. *(He starts towards door to answer bell.)*

(WATSON *looks and sees blinds up.)*

WATSON: Parsons! (PARSONS *turns.)* Why aren't those blinds down?

PARSONS: They was down a few minutes ago, sir!

WATSON: That's strange! Well, you'd better pull them down now.

PARSONS: Yes, sir.

(Bell rings twice as PARSONS *pulls second blind down. He goes out to answer bell. Pause. Then enter* PARSONS *in a peculiar manner.)*

If you please, sir, it isn't a patient at all, sir.

WATSON: Well, what is it?

PARSONS: A lady sir—(WATSON *looks up)*—and she wants to see you most particular, sir!

WATSON: What does she want to see me about?

PARSONS: She didn't say, sir. Only she said it was of the hutmost himportance to 'er, if you could see 'er, sir.

WATSON: Is she there in the hall?

PARSONS: Yes, sir.

WATSON: Very well—I was going to walk for the exercise—but I can take a cab.

PARSONS: Then you'll see the lady, sir.

WATSON: Yes. (PARSONS *turns to go.* (WATSON *continues his preparations.)* And call a cab for me at the same time—have it wait.

PARSONS: Yes, sir.

(PARSONS *goes out. Pause.* PARSONS *appears, ushering in a lady—and goes when she has entered. Enter* MADGE LARRABEE. *Her manner is entirely different from that of the former scenes. She is an impetuous gushing society lady, with trouble on her mind.)*

MADGE *(as she comes in)*: Ah! Doctor—it's awfully good of you to see me. I know what a busy man you must be but I'm in *such* trouble — oh, it's really too dreadful — You'll excuse my troubling you in this way, won't you?

WATSON: Don't speak of it, madam.

MADGE: Oh, thank you so much! For it did look frightful my coming in like this — but I'm not alone — oh no! — I left my maid in the cab — I'm Mrs. H. de Witte Seaton — *(Trying to find card-case.)* Dear me — I didn't bring my card-case — or if I did I lost it.

WATSON: Don't trouble about a card, Mrs. Seaton. *(With gesture to indicate chair.)*

MADGE: Oh, thank you. *(Sitting as she continues to talk.)* You don't know what I've been through this evening — trying to find some one who could tell me what to do. (WATSON *sits in chair at desk.)* It's something that's happened, doctor — it has just simply happened — I know that it wasn't his fault! I know it!

WATSON: Whose fault?

MADGE: My brother's — my poor, dear, youngest brother — he couldn't have done such a thing, he simply couldn't and —

WATSON: Such a thing as what, Mrs. Seaton?

MADGE: As to take the plans of our defences at Gibraltar from the Admiralty Offices. They think he stole them, doctor — and they've arrested him for it — you see, he works there. He was the only one who knew about them in the whole office — because they trusted him so. He was to make copies and — Oh, doctor, it's really too dreadful! *(Overcome, she takes out her handkerchief and wipes her eyes. This must all be perfectly natural, and not in the least particular overdone.)*

WATSON: I'm very sorry, Mrs. Seaton —

MADGE *(mixed up with sobs)*: Oh, thank you so much! They said you were Mr. Holmes's friend — several people told me that, several — they advised me to ask you where I could find him — and everything depends on it, doctor — everything.

WATSON: Holmes, of course. He's just the one you want.

MADGE: That's *it!* He's just the one — and there's hardly any time left! They'll take my poor brother away to prison to-morrow! *(Shows signs of breaking down again.)*

WATSON: There, there, Mrs. Seaton — pray control yourself.

MADGE *(choking down sobs)*: Now what would you advise me to do?

WATSON: I'd go to Mr. Holmes at once.

MADGE: But I've been. I've been, and he wasn't *there!*

WATSON: You went to his house?

MADGE: Yes—in Baker Street. That's why I came to you! They said he might be here!

WATSON: No—he isn't here! *(Turns away slightly.)*

(MADGE *looks deeply discouraged.)*

MADGE: But don't you expect him some time this evening?

WATSON: No. *(Shaking head.)* There's no possibility of his coming—so far as I know.

MADGE: But couldn't you *get* him to come? *(Pause.)* It would be such a great favour to me—I'm almost worn out with going about —and with this dreadful anxiety! If you could get word to him to—*(sees that* WATSON *is looking at her strangely and sharply)*— to come.

(Brief pause.)

WATSON *(rising—rather hard voice)*: I could *not* get him to come, madam. And I beg you to excuse me. I am going out myself—*(looks at watch)*—on urgent business. *(Rings bell.)*

MADGE *(rising)*: Oh, certainly! Don't let me detain you! And you think I had better call at his house again?

WATSON *(coldly)*: That will be the wisest thing to do.

MADGE: Oh, thank you so much. *(Extends her hand.)* You don't *know* how you've encouraged me!

(WATSON *withdraws his hand, as he still looks at her. Enter* PARSONS. *He stands at door.)*

Well—good night, doctor.

(WATSON *simply bows coldly.* MADGE *turns to go. The crash of a capsizing vehicle, followed by excited shouts of men, is heard. This effect must be as if outside the house with doors closed, and not close at hand.* MADGE *stops suddenly on hearing the crash and shouts.* WATSON *looks at* PARSONS.)

WATSON: What's that, Parsons?

PARSONS: I really can't say, sir, but it sounded to me like a haccident.

MADGE *(turning to* WATSON): Oh *dear!* I do hope it isn't anything serious! It affects me terribly to know that anyone is hurt.

WATSON: Probably nothing more than a broken-down cab. See what it is, Parsons.

(Bell and knock. MADGE *turns and looks toward door again, anxiously.* PARSONS *turns to go. Sudden vigorous ringing of door bell, followed by the sound of a knocker violently used.)*

PARSONS: There's the bell, sir! There's somebody 'urt, sir, an' they're a-wantin' *you!*

WATSON: Well, don't allow anybody to come in! *(Looks at watch.)* I have no more time. *(Hurriedly gathers papers up.)*

PARSONS: Very well, sir. *(Goes leaving door open.)*

*(*MADGE *turns from looking off at door, and looks at* WATSON *anxiously. Looks toward door again.)*

MADGE: But they're coming *in,* doctor. *(Retreats backward.)*

WATSON *(moving toward door)*: Parsons! Parsons!

(Sound of voices. Following speeches outside are not in rotation, but jumbled together, so that it is all over over very quickly.)

VOICE *(outside)*: We 'ad to bring 'im in, man.

VOICE *(outside)*: There's nowhere else to go!

PARSONS *(outside)*: The doctor can't see anybody.

VOICE *(outside)*: Well let the old gent lay 'ere awhile can't yer. It's common decency. Wot 'ave yer got a red lamp 'angin' outside yer bloomin' door for?

VOICE *(outside)*: Yes! yes! let him stay.

(Enter PARSONS *at door. Door closes and noise stops.)*

PARSONS: They would bring 'im in, sir. It's an old gentleman as was 'urt a bit w'en the cab upset!

MADGE: Oh!

(Sound of groans, etc. outside, and the old gentleman whining out complaints and threats.)

WATSON: Let them put him here. *(Indicating operating chair.)* And send at once for Doctor Anstruther.

PARSONS: Yes, sir!

WATSON: Help him in, Parsons.

(PARSONS *goes out.*)

MADGE: Oh, doctor, isn't it frightful.

WATSON *(turning to centre door)*: Mrs. Seaton, if you will be so good as to step this way, you can reach the hall, by taking the first door to your left.

MADGE *(hesitating)*: But I — I may be of some use, doctor.

WATSON *(with a trifle of impatience)*: None whatever. *(Holds door open.)*

MADGE: But, doctor — I *must see* the poor fellow — I haven't the *power* to go!

WATSON *(facing* MADGE*)*: Madam, I believe you have some ulterior motive in coming here! You will kindly —

(Enter at door a white-haired old gentleman in black clerical clothes, white tie, etc., assisted by PARSONS *and the* DRIVER. *He limps as though his leg were hurt. His coat is soiled. His hat is soiled as if it had rolled in the street.* MADGE *has retired above desk, and watches old gent closely from there without moving.* WATSON *turns toward the party as they come in.)*

HOLMES *(as he comes in)*: Oh, oh! *(He limps so that he hardly touches his right foot to floor.)*

PARSONS *(as he helps* HOLMES *in)*: This way, sir! Be careful of the sill, sir! That's it. *(Etc.)*

DRIVER *(as he comes in, and also beginning outside before entrance)*: Now we'll go in 'ere. You'll see the doctor an' it'll be all right.

HOLMES: No, it won't be all right.

DRIVER: It was a haccident. You cawn't 'elp a haccident.

HOLMES: Yes, you can.

DRIVER: He was on the wrong side of the street. I turned hup — *(Etc.)*

PARSONS: Now over to this chair. *(Indicating operating chair.)*

HOLMES *(pushing back and trying to stop at the desk chair)*: No, I'll sit here.

PARSONS: No, this is the chair, sir.

HOLMES: Don't I know where I want to sit?

DRIVER *(impatiently)*: You'll sit 'ere.

(They lead him up to operating chair.)

DRIVER *(as they lead him up)*: Now, the doctor'll have a look at ye. 'Ere's the doctor.

HOLMES: That isn't a doctor.

DRIVER: It is a doctor. *(Seeing WATSON.)* 'Ere, doctor, will you just come and have a look at this old gent? (HOLMES *trying to stop him.)* He's hurt 'isself a little, an' — an' —

HOLMES *(trying to stop DRIVER)*: Wait, wait, wait!

DRIVER: Well, well?

HOLMES *(still standing back to audience and turned · to DRIVER)*: Are you the driver?

DRIVER: Yes, I'm the driver.

HOLMES: Well, I'll have you arrested for this.

DRIVER: Arrested?

HOLMES: Arrested, arrested, arrested!

DRIVER: You cawn't arrest me.

HOLMES: I can't, but somebody else can.

DRIVER: 'Ere, 'ere. *(Trying to urge HOLMES to chair.)*

HOLMES: You are a very disagreeable man! You are totally uninformed on every subject! I wonder you are able to live in the same house with yourself.

(The DRIVER is trying to talk back and make HOLMES sit down. HOLMES turns suddenly on PARSONS. WATSON is trying to attract PARSONS' attention.)

Are you a driver?

PARSONS: No, sir!

PARSONS: Well, what are you?

PARSONS: I'm the butler, sir.

HOLMES: *Butler! Butler!*

DRIVER: He's the doctor's servant.

HOLMES: Who'd have such a looking butler as you! What fool would —

DRIVER *(turning HOLMES toward him roughly)*: He is the doctor's servant!

HOLMES: Who asked you who he was?

DRIVER: Never mind who asked me — I'm telling you.

HOLMES: Well, go and tell somebody else.

DRIVER *(trying to push* HOLMES *into chair)*: Sit down here! Sit down and be quiet.

WATSON *(to* PARSONS): Have a cab ready for me. I must see if he's badly hurt.

PARSONS: Yes, sir. *(Goes.)*

HOLMES *(resisting)*: Quiet! quiet! Where's my hat? My hat! My hat!

DRIVER: Never mind your 'at.

HOLMES: I will mind my hat! and I hold you responsible —

DRIVER: There's your hat in your 'and.

HOLMES *(looks at hat)*: That isn't my hat! Here! (DRIVER *trying to push him into chair.)* You're responsible. *(In chair.)* I'll have you arrested. *(Clinging to* DRIVER'S *coat tail as he tries to get away to door.)* Here, come back. *(Choking with rage.)*

DRIVER *(first wrenching away coat from* HOLMES'S *grasp; at door)*: I cawn't stay around 'ere, you know! Some one'll be pinching my cab. *(Exit.)*

HOLMES *(screaming after him)*: Then bring your cab in here. I want— *(Lapses into groans and remonstrances.)* Why didn't somebody stop him? These cabmen! What did he bring me in here for? I know where I am, it's a conspiracy. I won't stay in this place. If I ever get out of here alive— *(Etc.)*

WATSON *(steps quickly to door, speaking off)*: Parsons—take that man's number. *(Quickly to old gent.)* Now, sir, if you'll sit quiet for one moment, I'll have a look at you! *(Crosses to end of cabinet as if to look for instrument.)*

*(*MADGE *advances near to the old gentleman, looking at him closely. She suddenly seems to be satisfied of something, backs away, and reaching out as if to get to the window and give signal, then coming face to face with* WATSON *as he turns, and smiling pleasantly at him. Business with glove. She begins to glide down stage, making a sweep around toward door as if to get out. She shows by her expression that she has recognized* HOLMES, *but is instantly herself again, thinking possibly that* HOLMES *is watching her, and she wishes to evade suspicion regarding her determination to get off at door. Quick as a flash the old gentleman springs to the door and stands facing her. She stops suddenly on finding him facing her, then wheels quickly about and goes rapidly across toward window.)*

HOLMES *(sharp)*: Don't let her get to that window.

(WATSON, *who had moved up a little above windows, instantly springs before the windows.* MADGE *stops on being headed off in that direction.)*

WATSON: Is that *you,* Holmes?

(MADGE *stands motionless.)*

HOLMES: Quite so. *(Takes off his wig, etc.)*

WATSON: What do you want me to do?

HOLMES *(easily)*: That's all, you've done it. Don't do anything more just now.

(MADGE *gives a sharp look at them, then goes very slowly for a few steps and suddenly turns and makes a dash for centre door.)*

WATSON: Look out, Holmes! *She can get out that way. (A step or two up.)*

(MADGE *runs off.* HOLMES *is unmoved.)*

HOLMES: I don't think so. *(Saunters over to above* WATSON'S *desk.)* Well, well, what remarkable weather we're having, doctor, eh? *(Suddenly seeing cigarettes on desk.)* Ah! I'm glad to see that you keep a few prescriptions carefully done up. *(Picks up a cigarette and sits on desk.)* Good for the nerves! (HOLMES *finds matches and lights cigarette.)* Have you ever observed, Watson, that those people are always making—   .

(Enter the DRIVER.)

FORMAN *(speaking at once—so as to break in on* HOLMES): I've got her, sir!

(Very brief pause.)

WATSON: Good heavens! Is that *Forman?*

(HOLMES *nods* "Yes.")

HOLMES: Yes, that's Forman all right. Has Inspector Bradstreet come with his men?

FORMAN: Yes, sir. One of 'em's in the hall there 'olding her. The others are in the kitchen garden. They came in over the back wall from Mortimer Street.

HOLMES: One moment. *(Sits in thought.)* Watson, my dear fellow— (WATSON *moves toward* HOLMES *at desk.)* As you doubtless gather from the little episode that has just taken place, we are making the arrests. The scoundrels are hot on my track. To get me out of the way is the one chance left to them—and I'm taking advantage of their mad pursuit to draw them where we can quietly lay our hands on them—one by one. We've made a pretty good haul aready—four last night in the gas chamber—seven this afternoon in various places, and one more just now, but I regret to say that up to this time the Professor himself has so far not risen to the bait.

WATSON: Where do you think he is now?

HOLMES: In the open streets—under some clever disguise— watching for a chance to get at me.

WATSON: And was this woman sent in here to—

HOLMES: Quite so. A spy—to let them know by some signal, probably at that window—*(pointing)*—if she found me in the house. And it has just occurred to me that it might not be such a bad idea to try the Professor with *that* bait. Forman! *(Motions him to come down.)*

FORMAN: Yes, sir!

HOLMES *(voice lower)*: One moment. *(Business.)* Bring that Larrabee woman back here for a moment, and when I light a fresh cigarette—let go your hold on her—carelessly—as if your attention was attracted to something else. Get hold of her again when I tell you.

FORMAN: Very well, sir!

(Goes quickly to re-enter bringing in MADGE LARRABEE. *They stop.* MADGE *calm, but looks at* HOLMES *with the utmost hatred. Brief pause.)*

HOLMES: My dear Mrs. Larrabee—(MADGE, *who has looked away, turns to him angrily)*—I took the liberty of having you brought in for a moment—*(puffs cigarette, which he has nearly finished)*—in order to convey to you in a few fitting words—my sincere sympathy in your rather—unpleasant—predicament.

MADGE *(hissing it out angrily between her teeth)*: It's a lie! It's a lie! There's no predicament.

HOLMES: Ah—I'm charmed to gather—from your rather forcible—observation—that you do not regard it as such. Quite right, too. Our prisons are so well conducted now. Many consider them quite as comfortable as most of the hotels. Quieter and more orderly.

MADGE: How the prisons are conducted is no concern of mine! There is nothing they can hold me for—nothing.

HOLMES: Oh—to be sure. *(Putting fresh cigarette in mouth.)* There may be something in that. Still—it occurred to me that you might prefer to be near your unfortunate husband—eh? *(Rises from table and goes to gas burner. Slight good-natured chuckle.)* We hear a great deal about the heroic devotion of wives, and all that—*(lights cigarette at gas)*—rubbish. You know, Mrs. Larrabee, when we come right down to it—

(FORMAN carelessly relinquishes his hold on MADGE'S arm, and seems to have his attention called to door. Stands as if listening to something outside. MADGE gives a quick glance about and at HOLMES who is lighting a cigarette at the gas, and apparently not noticing anything. She makes a sudden dash for the window, quickly snaps up blind and makes a rapid motion up and down before window with right hand—then turns quickly, facing HOLMES with triumphant defiance. HOLMES is still lighting cigarette.)

Many thanks. *(To* FORMAN.*)* That's all, Forman. Pick her up again.

(FORMAN at once goes to MADGE and turns her and waits in front of window—holding her right wrist.)

Doctor, would you kindly pull the blind down once more. I don't care to be shot from the street.

(WATSON instantly pulls down blind.)

(NOTE.—Special care must be exercised regarding these window blinds. They must be made specially strong and solid, so that no failure to operate is possible.)

MADGE *(in triumph)*: Ah! It's too late.

HOLMES: Too late, eh? *(Strolling a little.)*

MADGE: The signal is given. You will near from him soon.
HOLMES: It wouldn't surprise me at all.

(Door bell rings.)

(Voices of BILLY *and* PARSONS *outside. Door at once opened, and* BILLY *on a little way, but held back by* PARSONS *for an instant. He breaks away from* PARSONS. *All very quick,* BILLY *dressed as a street gamin, and carrying a bunch of evening papers.)*

(As BILLY *comes.)* I think I shall hear from him *now. (Shout.)* Let—(BILLY *stands panting)*—him go, Parsons. Quick, Billy. (BILLY *comes close to* HOLMES.)

BILLY: He's just come, sir.

HOLMES: From where?

BILLY: The house across the street; he was in there a-watchin' these windows. He must 'ave seen something, for he's just come out— *(Breathlessly.)* There was a cab waitin' in the street for the doctor—and he's changed places with the driver.

HOLMES: Where did the driver go?

BILLY: He slunk away in the dark, sir, but he ain't gone far, an' there's two or three more 'angin' about.

HOLMES *(slight motion of the head towards* FORMAN): Ah— another driver to-night.

BILLY: They're all in it, sir, an' they're a-layin' to get you in that cab w'en you come out, sir! But don't you do it, sir!

HOLMES: On the contrary, sir, I'll have that new driver *in* here, sir! Get out again quick, Billy, and keep your eyes on him!

BILLY: Yes, sir—thank you, sir! *(Goes.)*

HOLMES: Yes, sir! Watson, can you let me have a heavy port-manteau for a few moments—?

(MADGE now watching for another chance to get at the window.)

WATSON: Parsons—my large Gladstone—bring it here!

PARSONS: Yes, sir. *(Goes out.)*

WATSON: I'm afraid it's a pretty shabby looking—

(MADGE suddenly tries to break loose from FORMAN *and attempts to make a dash for window.* FORMAN *turns and pulls her a step or two away. Slight pause.)*

HOLMES: Many thanks, Mrs. Larrabee, but your *first* signal is all that we require. By it you informed your friend Moriarty that I was here in the house. You are now aware of the fact that he is impersonating a driver, and that it is my intention to have him in *here*. You wish to signal that there is danger. There *is* danger, Mrs. Larrabee, but we don't care to have you let him know it. Take her out, Forman, and make her comfortable and happy.

(FORMAN *leads* MADGE *up to centre door as if to take her out. She pulls him to a stop and gives* HOLMES *a look of the most violent hatred.)*

And by the way, you might tell the inspector to wait a few moments. I may send him another lot. You can't tell!

FORMAN: Come along now! *(Takes her off.)*

(As MADGE *is pulled up, she snaps her fingers in* HOLMES'S *face and goes off laughing hysterically.)*

HOLMES: Fine woman!

(Enter PARSONS, *carrying a large portmanteau or Gladstone valise.)*

Put it down there. *(Pointing down before him at floor.)* Thank you so much.

(PARSONS *puts portmanteau down as indicated.)*

Parsons, you ordered a cab for the doctor a short time ago. It has been waiting, I believe.

PARSONS: Yes, sir, I think it 'as.

HOLMES: Be so good as to tell the driver, the one you'll now find there, to come in here and get a valise. See that he comes in himself. When he comes tell him that's the one.

(PARSONS *goes.)*

WATSON: But surely he won't come in.

HOLMES: Surely he will! It's his only chance to get me into that cab! He'll take almost any risk for that. *(Goes to above desk.)* In times like this you should tell your man never to take the first cab that comes on a call—*(smokes)*—nor yet the second—the third may be safe!

WATSON: But in this case—

HOLMES: My dear fellow, I admit that in this case I have turned it to my advantage, but I speak for your future guidance.

(Music. Melodramatic, danger, agitato, very subdued.)

(Door opens. PARSONS *enters, pointing the portmanteau out to some one who is following.)*

PARSONS: 'Ere it is—right in, this way.

HOLMES *(goes to* WATSON *above table. In rather a loud voice to* WATSON):* Well, good-bye, old fellow! *(Shakes hands with him warmly and bringing him down left a little.)* I'll write you from Paris—and I hope you'll keep fully informed of the progress of events.

(MORIARTY *enters in the disguise of a cabman, and goes at once to valise which* PARSONS *points out, trying to hurry it through and keeping face away from* HOLMES *but fidgeting about, not touching valise.* PARSONS *goes out.)*

(Speaks right on, apparently paying no attention to MORIARTY.) As for these papers, I'll attend to them personally. Here, my man—*(to* MORIARTY)—just help me to tighten up these straps a bit—* (He slides over to valise and kneels, pulling at strap, and* MORIARTY *bending over and doing same.)* There are a few little things in this bag—*(business)*—that I wouldn't like to lose—*(business)*—and it's just as well to— Eh—*(looking round for an instant)*—who's that at the window?

(MORIARTY *quickly looks up without lifting hands from valise, and at the same instant the snap of handcuffs is heard, and he springs up with the irons on his wrists, making two or three violent efforts to break loose. He then stands motionless.* HOLMES *drops into chair, a cigarette in his mouth.* MORIARTY *in rising knocks his hat off and stands facing audience.)*

(Music stops.)

(In a very quiet tone.) Doctor, will you kindly strike the bell two or three times in rapid succession.

(WATSON *steps to desk and gives several rapid strokes of the bell.)*

Thanks!

(Enter FORMAN. FORMAN *goes down to* MORIARTY *and fastens handcuffs which he has on his own wrists to chain attached to that of* MORIARTY'S. *This is held an instant—the two men looking at each other.)*

Forman!

FORMAN: Yes, sir.

HOLMES: Got a man there with you?

FORMAN: Yes, sir. the inspector came in himself.

HOLMES: Ah—the inspector himself. We shall read graphic accounts in to-morrow's papers of a very difficult arrest he succeeded in making at Dr. Watson's house in Kensington. Take him out, Forman, and introduce him to the inspector — they'll be pleased to meet.

(FORMAN *starts to force* MORIARTY *off.* MORIARTY *hangs back and endeavours to get at* HOLMES—*a very slight struggle.)*

Here! Wait! Let's see what he wants!

MORIARTY *(low voice to* HOLMES): Do you imagine, Sherlock Holmes, *that this is the end?*

HOLMES: I ventured to dream that it might be.

MORIARTY: Are you quite sure the police will be able to hold me?

HOLMES: I am quite sure of nothing.

MORIARTY: Ah! *(Slight pause.)* I have heard that you are planning to take a little trip—you and your friend here—a little trip on the Continent.

HOLMES: And if I do?

MORIARTY *(a step to* HOLMES): I shall meet you there. *(Slight pause.)*

HOLMES: That's all, Forman.

(FORMAN *moves up to door, quietly with* MORIARTY.)

MORIARTY *(stopping at door)*: I shall meet you there. You will change your course — you will try to elude me — but whichever way you turn—there will be eyes that see and wires that tell. I shall meet you there—and you know it. You know it!—and you know it. *(Goes with* FORMAN.)

(Pause.)

HOLMES: Did you hear that, Watson?

WATSON: Yes—but surely you don't place any importance on such—

HOLMES *(stopping him with wave of hand)*: Oh! no importance! But I have a fancy that he spoke the truth.

WATSON: We'll give up the trip.

HOLMES *(a negative wave of the hand at* WATSON): It would be quite the same. What matters it here or there—if *it must* come. *(Sits meditative.)*

WATSON *(calling)*: Parsons!

(PARSONS *comes in.* WATSON *points to the valise.* PARSONS *removes it and goes.)*

HOLMES: Watson, my dear fellow—*(smokes)*—it's too bad. Now that this is all over, I suppose you imagine that your room will no longer be required. Let me assure—let me assure you— *(voice trembles)*—that the worst is yet to come.

WATSON *(stands in front of desk)*: The worst to— *(Suddenly thinks of something. Pulls out watch hurriedly.)* Why, good heavens, Holmes. We've barely five minutes.

HOLMES *(looks up innocently at him)*: For what?

WATSON: To get to Baker Street—your rooms!

(HOLMES *still looks at him.)*

Your appointment with Sir Edward and the Count! They were to receive that packet of letters from you.

HOLMES *(nods assent)*: They're coming here.

(Pause. WATSON *looking at* HOLMES.)

WATSON: Here!

HOLMES: That is—if you will be so good as to permit it.

WATSON: Certainly—but why not there?

HOLMES: The police wouldn't allow us inside the ropes.

WATSON: Police! Ropes!

HOLMES: Police — ropes -- ladders — hose — crowds — fire engines—

WATSON: Why, you don't mean that—

HOLMES *(nods)*: Quite so—the devils have burned me out.

WATSON: Good heavens—burned you—

(Pause. HOLMES *nods.)*

Oh, that's too bad. What did you lose?

HOLMES: Everything!—everything! I'm so glad of it! *I've had enough.* This one thing—*(right hand strong gesture of emphasis —he stops in midst of sentence—a frown upon his face as he thinks—then in a lower voice)*—ends it! This one thing—that I shall do—here in a few moments—is the finish. (HOLMES *rises.)*

WATSON: You mean—Miss Faulkner?

(HOLMES *nods slightly in affirmative without turning to* WATSON.)

(Love music. Very pp.)

HOLMES *(turning suddenly to* WATSON): Watson—she trusted me! She—clung to me! There were four to one against me! They said *"Come here,"* I said *"Stay close to me,"* and she did! She clung to me—I could feel her heart beating against mine—and I was playing a game!—*(lower—parenthetical)*—a dangerous game —but I was playing it!—It will be the same to-night! She'll be there—I'll be here! She'll listen—she'll believe—and she'll trust me—and I'll—be playing—a game. *No more*—I've had enough! It's my last case!

(WATSON *has been watching him narrowly.)*

Oh well! what does it matter? Life is a small affair at the most—a little while—a few sunrises and sunsets—the warm breath of a few summers—the cold chill of a few winters— *(Looking down on floor a little way before him in meditation.)* And then—·

(Pause.)

WATSON: And then—?

(HOLMES *glances up at him. Upward toss of hand before speaking.)*

HOLMES: And then.

(The music stops.)

WATSON *(going to* HOLMES): My dear Holmes—I'm afraid that plan of—gaining her confidence and regard went a little further than you intended—

(HOLMES *nods assent slightly.*)

HOLMES *(mutters after nodding)*: A trifle!

WATSON: For — her — or for you?

HOLMES: For her — *(looks up at* WATSON *slowly)* — and — for me.

WATSON *(astonished. After an instant's pause)*: But — if you both love each other —

HOLMES *(putting hand on* WATSON *to stop him sharply)*: Sh —! Don't say it! *(Pause.)* You mustn't tempt me — with such a thought. That girl! — young — exquisite — just beginning her sweet life — I — seared, drugged, poisoned, almost at an end! No! no! I must cure her! I must stop it, now — while there's time! *(Pause.)* She's coming here.

WATSON: She won't come alone?

HOLMES: No, Térèse will be with her.

(HOLMES *turns and goes to door to surgery, getting a book on the way, and placing it in the way of door closing. Turns to* WATSON.)

When she comes let her wait in that room. You can manage that, I'm quite sure.

WATSON: Certainly — Do you intend to leave that book there?

HOLMES *(nods* "Yes")*: To keep that door from closing. She is to overhear.

WATSON: I see.

HOLMES: Sir Edward and the Count are very likely to become excited. I shall endeavour to make them so. You must not be alarmed, old fellow.

(Bell of outside door rings off. HOLMES *and* WATSON *look at one another.)*

(Going to centre door.) She may be there now. I'll go to your dressing-room, if you'll allow me, and brush away some of this dust.

WATSON: By all means! *(Goes to door.)* My wife is in the drawing-room. Do look in on her a moment — it will please her so much.

HOLMES *(at door)*: My dear fellow, it will more than please me! *(Opens door. Piano heard off when the door is opened.)* Mrs.

Watson! Home! Love! Life! Ah, Watson! *(Eyes glance about thinking. He sighs a little absently, suddenly turns and goes out.)*

(WATSON *turns and goes to his desk—not to sit. Enter* PARSONS.)

PARSONS: A lady sir, wants to know if she can speak to you. If there's anyone 'ere she won't come in.

WATSON: Any name?

PARSONS: No, sir. I asked her and she said it was unnecessary — as you wouldn't know 'er. She 'as 'er maid with 'er, sir.

WATSON: Then it must be — Show her in.

(PARSONS *turns to go.)*

And Parsons —

(PARSONS *stops and turns.)*

(Lower voice.) Two gentlemen, Count von Stalburg and Sir Edward Leighton will call. Bring them here to this room at once, and then tell Mr. Holmes. You'll find him in my dressing-room.

PARSONS: Yes, sir.

WATSON: Send everybody else away — I'll see that lady.

PARSONS: Yes, sir.

(He goes, leaving door open. Brief pause. PARSONS *appears outside door, showing some one to the room. Enter* ALICE FAULKNER. ALICE *glances apprehensively about, fearing she will see Holmes. Seeing that* WATSON *is alone, she is much relieved and goes towards him.* PARSONS *closes door from outside.)*

ALICE *(with some timidity)*: Is this—is this Doctor Watson's room?

WATSON *(encouragingly—and advancing a step or two)*: Yes, and I am Doctor Watson.

ALICE: Is—would you mind telling me. if Mr. Holmes—Mr.— Sherlock Holmes—is here?

WATSON: He will be before long, Miss—er—

ALICE: My name is Alice Faulkner.

WATSON: Miss Faulkner. He came a short time ago, but has gone upstairs for a few moments.

ALICE: Oh!—*(with an apprehensive look)*—and is he coming down—soon?

WATSON: Well, the fact is, Miss Faulkner, he has an appointment with two gentlemen here, and I was to let him know as soon as they arrived.

ALICE: Do you suppose I could wait — without troubling you too much — and see him — *afterwards?*

WATSON: Why, certainly.

ALICE: Thank you — and I — I don't want him to know — that — I — that I came.

WATSON: Of course, if you wish, there's no need of my telling him.

ALICE: It's — very important *indeed* that you *don't,* Dr. Watson. I can explain it all to you afterwards.

WATSON: No explanation is necessary, Miss Faulkner.

ALICE: Thank you. *(Glances about.)* I suppose there is a waiting-room for patients?

WATSON: Yes, or you could sit in there. *(Indicating surgery door.)* You'll be less likely to be disturbed.

ALICE: Yes, thank you. (ALICE *glances toward door.)* I think I would rather be — where it's entirely quiet.

(Bell of front door outside rings.)

WATSON *(going to surgery door)*: Then step this way. I think the gentlemen have arrived.

ALICE *(goes to door and turns)*: And when the business between the gentlemen is over, would you please have some one tell me?

WATSON: I'll tell you myself, Miss Faulkner.

ALICE: Thank you. *(She goes.)*

(PARSONS *enters.)*

PARSONS: Count von Stalburg. Sir Edward Leighton.

(Enter SIR EDWARD *and* COUNT VON STALBURG. PARSONS *goes, closing door after him.)*

WATSON: Count — Sir   Edward —   *(Bowing   and   coming forward.)*

SIR EDWARD: Dr. Watson. *(Bows.)* Good evening. *(Placing his hat on pedestal.)*

(VON STALBURG *bows slightly and stands.)*

Our appointment with Mr. Holmes was changed to your house, I believe.

WATSON: Quite right, Sir Edward. Pray be seated, gentlemen.

(SIR EDWARD and WATSON sit.)

VON STALBURG: Mr. Holmes is a trifle late. *(Sits.)*

WATSON: He has already arrived, Count. I have sent for him.

VON STALBURG: Ugh!

(Slight pause.)

SIR EDWARD: It was quite a surprise to receive his message an hour ago changing the place of meeting. We should otherwise have gone to his house in Baker Street.

WATSON: You would have found it in ashes, Sir Edward.

SIR EDWARD: What! Really!

VON STALBURG: Ugh!

(Both looking at WATSON.)

SIR EDWARD: The—the house burnt!

WATSON: Burning now, probably.

SIR EDWARD: I'm very sorry to hear this. It must be a severe blow to him.

WATSON: No, he minds it very little.

SIR EDWARD *(surprised)*: Really! I should hardly have thought it.

VON STALBURG: Did I understand you to say, doctor, that you had sent for Mr. Holmes?

WATSON: Yes, Count, and he'll be here shortly. Indeed, I think I hear him on the stairs now.

(Pause. Enter HOLMES at centre door. He is very pale. His clothing is re-arranged and cleansed, though he still, of course, wears the clerical suit, white tie, etc. He stands near door a moment. SIR EDWARD and COUNT rise and turn to him. WATSON rises and goes to desk, where he soon seats himself in chair behind desk. SIR EDWARD and the COUNT stand looking at HOLMES. Brief pause.)

HOLMES *(coming forward and speaking in a low clear voice, entirely calm, but showing some suppressed feeling or anxiety at the back of it)*: Gentlemen, be seated again, I beg.

(Brief pause. SIR EDWARD and the COUNT reseat themselves. HOLMES remains standing. He stands looking down before him for quite a while, others looking at him. He finally begins to speak in a low voice without first looking up.)

Our business to-night can be quickly disposed of. I need not tell you, gentlemen — for I have already told you — that the part which I play in it is more than painful to me. But business is business — and the sooner it is over the better. You were notified to come here this evening in order that I might — *(pause)* — deliver into your hands the packet which you engaged me — on behalf of your exalted client —

(COUNT *and* SIR EDWARD *bow slightly at* "exalted client.")

— to recover. Let me say, in justice to myself, that but for that agreement on my part, and the consequent steps which you took upon the basis of it, I would never have continued with the work. As it was, however, I felt bound to do so, and therefore pursued the matter — to the very end — and I now have the honour to deliver it into your hands.

(HOLMES *goes toward* SIR EDWARD *with the packet.* SIR EDWARD *rises and meets him.* HOLMES *places the packet in his hands.* COUNT VON STALBURG *rises and stands at his chair.)*

SIR EDWARD *(formally)*: Permit me to congratulate you, Mr. Holmes, upon the marvellous skill you have displayed, and the promptness with which you have fulfilled your agreement.

(HOLMES *bows slightly and turns away.* SIR EDWARD *at once breaks the seals of the packet and looks at the contents. He begins to show some surprise as he glances at one or two letters or papers and at once looks closer. He quickly motions to* COUNT, *who goes at once to him. He whispers something to him, and they both look at two or three things together.)*

VON STALBURG: Oh! No! No!

SIR EDWARD *(stopping examination and looking across to* HOLMES): What does this mean? *(Pause.)*

(HOLMES *turns to* SIR EDWARD *in apparent surprise.)*

These letters! And these — other things. *Where did you get them?*

HOLMES: I purchased them — last night.

SIR EDWARD: Purchased them?

HOLMES: Quite so — quite so.

VON STALBURG: From whom — if I may ask?

HOLMES: From whom? From the parties interested — by consent of Miss Faulkner.

SIR EDWARD: You have been deceived.

HOLMES: What!

(WATSON *rises and stands at his desk.*)

SIR EDWARD *(excitedly)*: This packet contains *nothing* — not a single letter or paper that we wanted. All clever imitations! The photographs are of another person! You have been *duped*. With all your supposed cleverness, they have *tricked* you! Ha! ha! ha!

VON STALBURG: Most decidedly duped, Mr. Holmes!

(HOLMES *turns quickly to* SIR EDWARD.)

HOLMES: Why, this is terrible! *(Turns back to* WATSON. *Stands looking in his face.)*

SIR EDWARD *(astonished)*: Terrible! Surely, sir, you do not mean by that, that there is a possibility you may not be able to recover them!

(Enter ALICE *and stands listening.)*

HOLMES: It's quite true!

SIR EDWARD: After your positive assurance! After the steps we have taken in the matter by your advice! Why — why, this is — *(Turns to* COUNT, *too indignant to speak.)*

VON STALBURG *(indignantly)*: Surely, sir, you don't mean there is no hope of it?

HOLMES: None whatever, Count. It is too late now! I can't begin all over again!

SIR EDWARD: Why, this is scandalous! It is criminal, sir! You had no right to mislead us in this way, and you shall *certainly suffer the consequences.* I shall see that you are brought into court to answer for it, Mr. Holmes. It will be such a blow to your reputation that you —

HOLMES: There is nothing to do, Sir Edward — I am ruined — ruined —

ALICE *(coming forward)*: He is not ruined, Sir Edward. *(In a quiet voice, perfectly calm and self-possessed; she draws the genuine packet from her dress.)* It is entirely owing to him and what he said to me that I now wish to give you the— *(Starting toward* SIR EDWARD *as if to hand him the packet.)*

(HOLMES *steps forward and intercepts her with left hand extended. She stops surprised.)*

HOLMES: One moment— *(Pause.)* Allow me. *(He takes packet from her hand.)*

(WATSON *stands looking at the scene. Pause.* HOLMES *stands with the package in his hand, looking down for a moment. He raises his head, as if he overcame weakness—glances at his watch, and turns to* SIR EDWARD *and the* COUNT. *He speaks quietly as if the climax of the tragedy were passed—the deed done.* ALICE'S *questioning gaze he plainly avoids.)*

Gentlemen— *(putting watch back in pocket)* — I notified you in my letter of this morning that the package should be produced at a quarter-past nine. It is barely fourteen past—and this is it. The one you have there, as you have already discovered, is a counterfeit.

(Love music.)

(HOLMES *turns a little, sees* ALICE, *stands looking at her.* ALICE *is looking at* HOLMES *with astonishment and horror. She moves back a little involuntarily.)*

SIR EDWARD *and* VON STALBURG *(staring up with admiration and delight as they perceive the trick)*: Ah! excellent! Admirable, Mr. Holmes! It is all clear now! Really marvellous! *(To one another, etc.)* Yes—upon my word!

(On SIR EDWARD *and* COUNT *breaking into expressions of admiration,* WATSON *quickly moves up to them, and steps them with a quick "Sh!" All stand motionless.* HOLMES *and* ALICE *looking at one another.* HOLMES *goes quickly to* ALICE *and puts the package into her hands.)*

HOLMES *(as he does this)*: Take this, Miss Faulkner. Take it away from me, quick! It is *yours*. Never give it up. Use it only for what you wish!

(Stop music.)

SIR EDWARD *(springing forward with a mild exclamation)*: What! We are not to have it? *(Throwing other package up stage.)*

(VON STALBURG *gives an exclamation or look with foregoing.)*

HOLMES *(turning from* ALICE—*but keeping left hand back upon her hands into which he put the package—as if to make her keep it. Strong—breathless—not loud—with emphatic shake of head)*: No, you are not to have it.

SIR EDWARD: After all this?

HOLMES: After all this.

VON STALBURG: But, my dear sir—

SIR EDWARD: This is outrageous! Your agreement?

HOLMES: I break it! Do what you please—warrants—summons —arrests—will find me here! *(Turns up and says under his breath to* WATSON.) Get them out! Get them away! *(Stands by* WATSON'S *desk, his back to the audience.)*

(Brief pause. WATSON *moves toward* SIR EDWARD *and the* COUNT *at the back of* HOLMES.)

WATSON: I'm sure, gentlemen, that you will appreciate the fact—

ALICE *(stepping forward—interrupting)*: Wait a moment, Doctor Watson! *(Going to* SIR EDWARD.) Here is the package, Sir Edward! *(Hands it to* SIR EDWARD *at once.)*

(WATSON *motions to* PARSONS, *off, to come on.)*

HOLMES *(turning to* ALICE): No!

ALICE *(to* HOLMES): Yes— *(Turning to* HOLMES. *Pause.)* I much prefer that he should have them. Since you last came that night and asked me to give them to you, I have thought of what you said. You were right—it was *revenge. (She looks down a moment—then suddenly turns away.)*

(HOLMES *stands motionless, near corner of desk, his eyes down.* PARSONS *enters and stands waiting with* SIR EDWARD'S *hat in his hand, which he took from off pedestal.)*

SIR EDWARD: We are greatly indebted to you, Miss Faulkner— *(Looks at* VON STALBURG.)*

VON STALBURG: To be sure!

SIR EDWARD: And to you, too, Mr. Holmes—if this was a part of the game. *(Motionless pause all round. Examining papers carefully.* COUNT *looking at them also.)* It was certainly an extraordinary method of obtaining possession of valuable papers —but we won't quarrel with the method as long as it accomplished the desired result! Eh, Count? *(Placing package in breast pocket and buttoning coat.)*

VON STALBURG: Certainly not, Sir Edward.

SIR EDWARD *(turning to* HOLMES): You have only to notify me of the *charge for your services*—(ALICE *gives a little look of bitterness at the word* "charge")—Mr. Holmes, and you will receive a cheque. I have the honour to wish you—*good night.*

(Music till end of Act.)

(Bowing punctiliously.) Dr. Watson. *(Bowing at* WATSON.) This way, Count.

(WATSON *bows and follows them to door.* HOLMES *does not move.* COUNT VON STALBURG *bows to* HOLMES *and to* WATSON *and goes, followed by* SIR EDWARD. PARSONS *exits after giving* SIR EDWARD *his hat.* WATSON *quietly turns and sees* HOLMES *beckoning to him.* WATSON *goes to* HOLMES, *who whispers to him, after which he quietly goes.* HOLMES, *after a moment's pause, looks at* ALICE.)

HOLMES *(speaks hurriedly)*: Now that you think it over, Miss Faulkner, you are doubtless beginning to realize the series of tricks by which I sought to deprive you of your property. I couldn't take it out of the house that night like a straightforward thief—because it could have been recovered at law, and for that reason I resorted to a cruel and cowardly device which should induce you to relinquish it.

ALICE *(not looking at him)*: But you—you did not give it to them—

(Pause.)

HOLMES *(in a forced cynical hard voice)*: No—I preferred that you should do as you did.

(ALICE *looks suddenly up at him in surprise and pain, with a breathless* "What?" *scarcely audible.* HOLMES *meets her look without a tremor.)*

(Slowly, distinctly.) You see, Miss Faulkner, it was a trick—a deception—to the very—end.

(ALICE *looks in his face a moment longer and then down.)*

Your maid is waiting.

ALICE *(stopping him by speech—no action)*: And was it—a trick—last night—when they tried to kill you?

HOLMES *(hearing* ALICE, *stops dead)*: I went there to purchase the counterfeit package—to use as you have seen.

ALICE: And—did you know I would come?

(Pause.)

HOLMES: No.

(ALICE *gives a subdued breath of relief.)*

But it fell in with my plans notwithstanding. Now that you see me in my true light, Miss Faulkner, we have nothing left to say but good night—and good-bye—which you ought to be very glad to do. Believe me, I meant no harm to you—it was purely business— with me. For that you see I would sacrifice everything. Even my supposed—friendship for you—was a pretense—a sham—every- thing that you—

(She has slowly turned away to the front during his speech. She turns and looks him in the face.)

ALICE *(quietly but distinctly)*: I don't believe it.

(They look at one another.)

HOLMES *(after a while)*: Why not?

ALICE: From the way you speak—from the way you—look— from all sorts of things!— *(With a very slight smile.)* You're not the only one—who can tell things—from small details.

HOLMES *(coming a step closer to her)*: Your faculty—of observation—is—is somewhat remarkable, Miss Faulkner—and your deduction is quite correct! I suppose—indeed I *know*—that I love you. I love you. But I know as well what I am—and what you are—

(ALICE *begins to draw nearer to him gradually, but with her face turned front.)*

I know that no such person as I should ever dream of being a part of your sweet life! It would be a crime for me to think of such a thing! There is every reason why I should say good-bye and farewell! There is every reason —

(ALICE *gently places her right hand on* HOLMES'S *breast, which stops him from continuing speech. He suddenly stops. After an instant he begins slowly to look down into her face. His left arm gradually steals about her. He presses her head close to him and the lights fade away with* ALICE *resting in* HOLMES'S *arms, her head on his breast.)*

(Music swells gradually.)

CURTAIN.

The Painful Predicament
of Sherlock Holmes

A Fantasy in about One-Tenth of an Act

by William Gillette

GWENDOLYN COBB
SHERLOCK HOLMES
BILLY
and two valuable assistants
are the people most concerned

It all transpires in Sherlock Holmes's Baker Street apartments
somewhere about the date of day before yesterday.

The time of day is not stated.

DARK CURTAIN.

SHERLOCK HOLMES *is discovered seated on the floor before the fire, smoking. There is a table with various things on it, an arm chair right of it. A high upholstered stool is at its left. Firelight from fire. Moonlight from window.*

Strange lights from door when it is open. After the curtain is up and the firelight on, there is a pause.

Sudden loud ringing at front door bell outside in distance, continuing impatiently. After time for opening of door, loud talking and protestations heard, GWENDOLYN *pouring forth a steady stream in a high key insisting that she must see Mr. Holmes, that it is very important, a matter of life and death, etc.,* BILLY *trying to tell her she cannot come up and shouting louder and louder in his efforts to make her hear. This continues a moment and then suddenly grows louder as the two come running up the stairs and approach the door;* BILLY *leading and the voice after him.*

Enter BILLY, *very excited. He pulls the door shut after him, and holds it while he turns to speak to* HOLMES.

BILLY: I beg your pardon, sir —

(The door is pulled from outside and BILLY *turns to hold it, but turns again quickly to* HOLMES.)

(Same business.)

I beg your pardon, sir — If you please, sir! — It's a young lady 'as just came in, an' says she must see you — she's 'ere now, sir, a-tryin' to pull the door open — but I don't like 'er eye, sir! . . . I don't like it at all, sir!

*(*HOLMES *rises and turns up lamp. Lights on.)*

'Er eye is certainly bad, sir! An' she — she don't seem to be able to leave off talkin' long enough fer me to tell 'er as 'ow she can't see you, sir!

*(*HOLMES *watches* BILLY *and the door with interest.)*

I tried to tell 'er as you give orders not to see no one. I shouted it out tremendous — but she was talkin' so loud it never got to 'er — so I run up to warn you — an' she come runnin' after me — an' — an' —

(Door suddenly pulled upon from outside while BILLY *is talking to* HOLMES.*)*

An'. . . an' 'ere she is, sir!

(Enter GWENDOLYN COBB *with unrestricted enthusiasm.)*

GWENDOLYN *(entering joyously)*: Oh! There you are! This is Mr. Holmes, I know! Oh — I've heard so much about you! You really can't imagine! *(Going toward* HOLMES.*)* And I've simply longed to see you myself and see if. . . oh, do shake hands with me. *(They shake hands.)* Isn't it wonderful to realize I'm shaking hands with Sherlock Holmes! It's simply ripping! To think that I've lived to see this day! *(Looks at him.)* Of course, I suppose you're the real one — detectives have so many disguises and things that it might be you were only pretending — but still, why should you?

(He motions her to seat, she does not pause an instant for any business.)

Oh, thank you. Yes — I will sit down.

(She moves to chair beside table and sits on arm of it.)

(HOLMES *motions* BILLY *to go.)*

(Exit BILLY.*)*

Because I came to ask your advise about something! Oh yes, it wasn't just curiosity that brought me here — I'm in a dreadful predicament — that's what you like, isn't it? — predicaments! Well, this is one — it is a lolla! It's simply awful! You've no idea! I don't suppose you ever had such a frightful affair to unravel. It isn't a murder or anything like that — it's a thousand times worse! Oh — millions of times worse. There are worse things than murder — aren't there, Mr. Holmes?

(HOLMES *nods again to indicate that he thinks so too.)*

Oh, how nice of you to agree with me about it — few would do it so soon. But you can fathom my inmost soul — I feel that you are doing it now—and it gives me strength to go on—indeed it does, Mr. Holmes! Just your presence and your sympathy encourages me! *(Looking at him admiringly.)* And it's really you. And there's the fire.

(GWENDOLYN *jumps up and runs to it, going around the table.)*

(HOLMES *stands regarding her.)*

I suppose it's a real fire, isn't it? You know can never tell in these days when everything seems to be adulterated—you don't know what you're getting, do you?

(HOLMES *shakes head emphatically.)*

No, you don't! There you go again agreeing with me. How nice of you! It's inspiring! *(Looking at him in rapture.)* And it's so perfectly ripping to see you there before my eyes! But you're not smoking. Oh, I do wish you'd smoke. I always think of you that way! It doesn't seem right! Do smoke!

(HOLMES *lights pipe.)*

Where's the tobacco? *(Looking on mantel, takes jar.)* Here! *(Smells.)* It is true you smoke that terrible shag tobacco? What is it like? *(Drops jar.)* Oh, I'm so sorry! *(Steps back and breaks violin.)* Oh! Isn't that too bad!

(Stamps about on violin trying to extricate herself. Continues talking and apologizing all the while. Suddenly sits on lounge to get loose from violin and breaks bow which lies across the arm of lounge.)

Oh, dear me! I'm so sorry! Mercy, what was that?

(Takes out broken violin bow.)

I'm afraid you won't want me to come again—if I go on like this! Oh! *(Springs to her feet.)* What have you got there cooking over that lamp—I would so like a cup of tea!

(Goes up to retort, etc.)

But I suppose— *(Smells of thing.)* No—it isn't tea! What a funny thing you're boiling in it! It looks like a soap bubble with a handle! I'm going to see what— *(Takes up retort and instantly drops it on floor.)* Oh! it was hot! Why didn't you tell me it was hot? *(Gesturing excitedly.)* How could I know — I've never been here before — one can't know everything about things, alone and unprotected . . .

(Backing up in her excitement upsets lamp, etc. which goes over with a crash.)

(Lights off, firelights again. Moonlight from window.)

There goes something else! It does seem to me you have more loose truck lying about — oh — I see! It's to trap people! What a splendid idea! They break the glass and you have them. *(Moving toward him admiringly.)* And you can tell from the kind of glass they break where they were born and why they murdered the man! Oh, it's perfectly thrilling! Now I suppose you know just from the few little things I've done since I've been here exactly what sort of a person I am — do you?

(HOLMES *nods quietly. He lights a candle.)*

(Lights on.)

Oh, how wonderful! Everything seems wonderful! All the things about here . . . only it's so . . . oh! Why that looks just like a friend of mine!

(Turning up papers on wall.)

And there's another! What a handsome man! But what has he got all those lines running across his face for? I should think it would hurt — and here's — oh, this is beautiful! *(Tears it off.)* You must let me keep this — it looks so much like a young man I know.

(The other sketches fall down.)

Oh, dear, there go the rest of them. But you've got plenty more, haven't you? *(Looks about.)* See that lady's foot? Why do you have such an ugly foot hung up here! It isn't nice at all!

(Pulls it down. Other sketches hung up fall with it.)

I'll send you a pretty water-colour of cows drinking at a stream — it'll look so much better! Mercy — did that man's fingers grow together like that? How it must have hurt. . . . What did you do for him? I suppose Dr. Watson attended to him—oh, if I could only see him! And I want him to help you about this dreadful affair of mine! It needs you both! And if Dr. Watson wasn't with you it wouldn't seem as if you were detecting at all. It's a terrible thing—I'm in such trouble.

(HOLMES *motions her to sit.*)

Oh thank you. I suppose I'd better tell you about it now—and—

(She is sitting on stool by table. HOLMES *remains standing.)*

—then you can talk it over with Dr. Watson and ask him what his idea is, and then it'll turn out that he was wrong and you knew all the time. . .oh—that's so wonderful—it gives me that delicious crawly, creepy feeling as if mice were running up and down my spine—oh! *(Facing toward front.)* Oh!. . .

(HOLMES *has edged round on the upper side of table and as she shudders, etc. he quietly takes a handkerchief out of her dress or pocket and moves quietly to other side of table and sits. He examines the handkerchief while she is not looking, using magnifying glass, etc.)*

Now this is what I came to ask you about—I'm sure you've never had such a painful case to attend to—because it affects two human souls. . .not bodies. . .pah. . .what are bodies. . .merely mud. . . . But souls. . .they are immortal—they live forever. . . . His name is Levi Lichenstein. He's what they call a Yankee. Of course you know, without my telling you, that we adore each other! Oh, Mr. Holmes, we adore each other. It couldn't be expressed in words! Poets couldn't do it! . . . What are poets? Pooh! *(Snaps fingers.)* We adore each other. Do I need to say more?

(HOLMES *shakes head.*)

No! Of course I don't. . .ah, how you understand! It's perfectly wonderful! Now listen—I want to tell you my troubles.

(HOLMES *quietly scribbles on a pad of paper.*)

That's right—take down what I say. Every word is important. He's in jail! Put that down! It's outrageous. And my own father did it. I'm not ashamed of it—but if—*(affected)*—if— Oh, my God!

(Grabs for handkerchief to weep but is unable to find it.) There!
(Springs to her feet.) It's been stolen. I *knew* I should lose
something if I came here. . .where the air seems simply charged
with thugs and pickpockets.

(HOLMES *rises and politely passes her handkerchief to her and sits
again as before.)*

Oh, thank you! *(Sits.)* My father put him there! *(She sobs.)*

(HOLMES *rings bell on table.)*

(GWENDOLYN *gives a convulsive sob on ringing of bell. But she
goes right on talking, not paying any attention to the business and
going on excitedly through her sobs and eye-wipings.)*

(Enter BILLY. HOLMES *motions him. He comes down back of*
HOLMES. HOLMES *hands him the paper he has been scribbling
upon and motions him off.)*

(Exit BILLY.)

Oh, Mr. Holmes—think of one's own father being the one to bring
disgrace upon one! Think of one's own father doing these cruel
and shameful things. But it's always one's own father—he is the
one out of the world who jumps headlong at the chance to be
heartless and cruel and—and—

*(Three heavy and resounding thuds heard in distance, as if
someone were pounding a heavy beam on the floor.)*

(GWENDOLYN *springs to her feet with a scream.)*

(Melodramatic music.)

Oh! . . . There it is. . .those awful three knocks! Something is
going to happen. Is there any danger—do tell me. . .

(HOLMES *scribbles on piece of paper.)*

Oh, don't keep me in this dreadful suspense—I have dreamt of
those three awful knocks. . . but why should they come to me? Oh,
heaven. . . you're not going to let them. . .

(HOLMES *pushes the paper across to her. She snatches it up and
reads it in a loud voice.)*

"Plumbers—in—the—house."

(Stop music.)

Oh, I see! Plumbers! *(She sits again.)* And you knew it. . .you could tell it was the plumbers without once leaving your chair! Oh, how wonderful. . .do you know, Levi is a little that way. He really is, Mr. Holmes. That's the reason I adore him so! Perhaps he can see too much! Do you think there's any danger of that?. . . Oh, Mr. Holmes—tell me—do you think we'll be happy together? Oh—I'm sure you know—and you will tell me, won't you?

(HOLMES *scribbles on piece of paper.)*

It's perfectly clear to you without even seeing him. I know it is— and so much depends upon it. . .when two souls seem drawn to each other. Tell me. . .I can bear anything. . .and I'd so like to know if we shall be happy together or not.

(HOLMES *pushes piece of paper toward her. She picks it up quickly and reads it in a slow, loud, distinct voice.)*

"Has—he—ever—spoken—to—you?" Oh, yes! Indeed he has. . . He once told me. . .

(Melodramatic music.)

Oh, heavens. . . And he's in jail. He'll never speak again. I haven't told you yet. . .take down all these things. . .my father put him there. Yes—my own father! Levi has lent a friend of mine some money—a mere pittance—scarcely as much as that—say half a pittance. My friend gave him a mortgage on some furniture his grandmother had left him and he couldn't pay, the furniture came to Levi. Then they found another will and it left all this furniture to a distant aunt out in America and the lawyers issued a writ of replevin and then Levi sued out a habeas corpus and signed a bond so that he was responsible—and my father went on this bond—and the furniture was taken back! Levi had to get another bond, and while he was swearing it the distant aunt arrived from America and had him arrested for obtaining a habeas corpus under false pretenses and he brought suit against her for defamation of character—and he was right—she said the most *frightful things.* Why—*(rising)*—she stood there—in the office of his own barristers and spoke of him as a reprobate and a right angle triable!

*(Raises voice in excitement and mo*ᵢ *is about wildly.)*

That miserable woman—with painted face and horrible American accent actually accused him of having *falsified some of the furniture.* And my father, hearing that we loved each other, swore out a warrant and he is in jail! *(Screams, etc.)*

(Enter two uniformed men, followed by BILLY. *They stop an instant, looking at* GWENDOLYN. *In the height of her excitement she sees them and stops dead with a wild moan. They go down to her at once and get her quickly off at door. She goes without resistance.)*

BILLY: It was the *right* asylum, sir! *(Exits.)*

(HOLMES *rises. Takes an injection of cocaine. Lights pipe with candle which he then blows out.)*

(Lights off except red light of fire, etc.)

(HOLMES *goes to lounge before fire, and sinks down upon it, leaning back on the cushions.)*

(Lights gradually off.)

(Stop music.)

CURTAIN.

Conan Doyle as Dramatist

Conan Doyle himself next brought Sherlock Holmes to the stage. The theatre had gotten well into his blood by now. He sold a one-act play called A STORY OF WATERLOO to Henry Irving of the Lyceum; adapted his Napoleonic hero, Brigadier Gerard, to the stage; and dramatized his novel THE TRAGEDY OF THE KOROSKO, about a boatload of European tourists kidnapped by Sudanese rebels, as THE FIRES OF FATE. All were moderately successful. Holmes was back in harness as well, Doyle having surrendered to public opinion and resurrected his character with the publication of THE HOUND OF THE BASKERVILLES in 1901.

He was Sir Arthur now, a national figure—knighted less for his writing than for his vigorous public defense of British conduct in the Boer War—wealthy, respected. With his money came a penchant for financial speculation, in which he lost thousands, and it was only a question of time before he hit upon the idea of backing his own plays.

He had written a drama based on his prizefighting novel RODNEY STONE, which he retitled THE HOUSE OF TEMPERLEY, and took a six-months' lease on the Adelphi Theatre, where the play opened in the spring of 1910. Prizefighting was illegal in England at the time, so discredited as a sport that Doyle had with difficulty persuaded the solidly middle-class STRAND to serialize the novel, and London's more genteel theatre-going public would have nothing to do with a play version that actually depicted boxing matches on stage.

Much more than his pride was at stake this time. The theatre rental and salaries were costing him £600 a week, and there were still four months to go on the lease when THE HOUSE OF TEMPERLEY closed. "I determined to play a bold and energetic game," he recalled in his autobiography. "When I saw the course that things were taking I shut myself up and devoted my whole mind to making a sensational Sherlock Holmes drama."

201

The play was an elaboration of "The Adventure of the Speckled Band," the Holmes story Doyle had always considered his best and which forever remained his favourite. He wrote it, he claimed, in a single week—he had always been a fast worker—and within a fortnight of withdrawing THE HOUSE OF TEMPERLEY *from the Adelphi, he had an all-new company in ,rehearsals of* THE SPECKLED BAND.

H. A. Saintsbury, who had acted Holmes more than a thousand times on tour with the Gillette play, was cast as the great detective, but the real star of the show was the popular Shakespearian actor Lyn Harding, playing Dr. Grimesby Rylott, the murderer. Harding also served as producer of the piece.

"There were heated arguments at rehearsals between author and producer," Hesketh Pearson wrote in CONAN DOYLE: HIS LIFE AND ART. *"Doyle had pictured Rylott as an old-fashioned melodramatic villain in a frock coat; but ·Harding wanted to create a character and asked Doyle to write in lines that would bring out more boldly certain dramatic moments. Doyle, slow to see another point of view, refused. . . while Harding, convinced that the character needed some extraneous decoration, set to work on his own account, building up the villain by degrees as a neurotic, now blinking an eye, now making a leg tremble, now pulling at a lock of hair on his forehead. Doyle never lost his temper, but he was displeased and told Harding in his calm way that he thought the part was being burlesqued. For a few days their relations, which had previously been pleasant, became strained."*

As the first night drew near, the impasse was broken by none other than J. M. Barrie, a good friend of Harding as well as Doyle. Barrie was a giant of the theatre now, having written his best plays, THE LITTLE MINISTER, THE ADMIRABLE CRICHTON, LITTLE MARY, *and of course* PETER PAN, *to enormous popular and critical acclaim, a state of affairs Doyle forever regretted, saying the world had lost a great novelist when Barrie turned his talents to the stage. The little man came to one of the rehearsals, and at the end of the second act, after the gripping confrontation scene between Holmes and Rylott, he turned to Doyle and said: "Let Harding have his own way."*

Sir Arthur relented, and when THE SPECKLED BAND *opened on 4 June 1910, Harding electrified the audience with his extra-*

ordinary characterization and took more than a dozen curtain calls. By way of apology, Doyle wrote the actor a gracious letter of congratulation, and in his autobiography he praised Harding's "most masterful" handling of the part.

"We had a fine rock boa to play the title-rôle," Doyle remarked in MEMORIES AND ADVENTURES, "a snake which was the pride of my heart, so one can imagine my disgust when I saw that one critic ended his disparaging review by the words 'The crisis of the play was produced by the appearance of a palpably artificial serpent.' I was inclined to offer him a goodly sum if he were to undertake to go to bed with it."

If the play's notices were mixed, the public's response to it was not. "Before the end of the run I had cleared off all that I had lost upon the other play, and I had created a permanent property of some value," Doyle wrote. When the Adelphi lease expired, he moved THE SPECKLED BAND up the Strand to the Globe, where it ran for another three months, though without Lyn Harding. And even before it finally closed on 29 October 1910, yet another company had begun a successful engagement in Boston.

Far less is known about THE CROWN DIAMOND, and nothing at all about how and why, or even when, it was written. It débuted 2 May 1921 in a single performance at a theatre in Bristol and later that month played a one-week stand at the Coliseum in London. During the last week of August it returned to the Coliseum for another seven-day run, two shows a day, for a total of twenty-eight performances in London and the one in Bristol. Dennis Neilson-Terry portrayed Holmes in each. It has never again been performed.

Having adapted any number of his stories and novels to the stage, Doyle now reversed himself and made THE CROWN DIAMOND into a short story, the much better known "The Adventure of the Mazarin Stone," which appeared in the STRAND for October 1921 and was collected in THE CASE-BOOK OF SHERLOCK HOLMES. With minor differences of names and incident, the play and the story are identical in plot, persona, and presentation—right down to "The Mazarin Stone" having been written in the third person and from a "fourth-wall" perspective, an observation shrewdly made by critic Anthony Boucher in 1949, long after the very existence of THE CROWN DIAMOND had been forgotten.

The incredible events of "The Mazarin Stone" are indeed more suited to matinée melodrama than to the kind of magazine fiction Doyle habitually wrote. With its unbelievable plot, its inconsistencies as to the details of the Baker Street flat, and its poor exposition, it is often mentioned as the prime candidate for the very worst Sherlock Holmes story ever. Yet awful as "The Mazarin Stone" is, THE CROWN DIAMOND *is worse.*

The play would almost seem to be an effort on Doyle's part to out-do Gillette in improbability. In fact, it was the opinion of Adrian Conan Doyle, the author's son, that THE CROWN DIAMOND *had actually been written in the early 1900s, about the time of* THE RETURN OF SHERLOCK HOLMES *and in the afterglow of the Gillette drama's success. This belief was based on an analysis of the text and the author's handwriting, and it is a reasonable enough conclusion. The wax bust and the allusion to air-guns are clearly lifted straight from the discarded climax to* SHERLOCK HOLMES. *The character name Colonel Sebastian Moran (altered to Count Negretto Sylvius in the short-story version) evokes "The Adventure of the Empty House," the first episode of the* RETURN *of 1903. It is not difficult to surmise that* THE CROWN DIAMOND *was written after Gillette's play but before "The Empty House," perhaps as a sort of experiment, and was then abandoned when its major plot elements were transferred to "The Empty House."*

If that is so, then the question is why Doyle, who was always so protective of his lesser efforts, permitted THE CROWN DIAMOND *to be produced at all, albeit twenty years later, and then adapted it into a decidedly inferior magazine story. But if it is not so, then the even greater mystery is why he would write such a thing as* THE CROWN DIAMOND *at all, once he had attained the playwrighting skill demonstrated in* THE SPECKLED BAND *and his other successful dramas. It is a conundrum worthy of Holmes himself.*

Another indicator of an early date for THE CROWN DIAMOND *is the token treatment Watson receives. As author Isaac Asimov recently pointed out, in this case, just as the moment of danger approaches, Holmes uncharacteristically* sends Watson away *and is left to face his enemies alone, even as Gillette's hero does. Watson doesn't even re-appear at the end, as in "The Mazarin Stone." The story could just as well be told without him.*

This abandonment of the celebrated Holmes-Watson relationship, so central to the success of the original tales, was a mistake

Doyle did not make in THE SPECKLED BAND. *Here the good doctor is present from the beginning. He, not Holmes's adversaries, provides the foil for his friend's exposition of the case, and so the detective is not reduced to the smart-talking boor he can so easily become in a less-than-masterful portrayal in the Gillette play. Watson moves the plot—he introduces the heroine to Holmes, chloroforms the Indian henchman with his own hands—and at the climax of the play he is satisfyingly where he belongs, right at Sherlock Holmes's side.*

On balance, in fact, THE SPECKLED BAND *is a better play than* SHERLOCK HOLMES. *Written as it was by Conan Doyle himself, perhaps it could not be otherwise. Sir Arthur eschewed Gillette's torturous plotting and spectacular effects and did what he had always done best of his contemporaries—he told a simple, straightforward story and textured it with character rather than incident.*

Old Rodgers, the self-pitying butler, and the pompous, meddling, yet courageous juryman Armitage are examples of the kind of depth which Doyle habitually brought to even minor characters, and the latter provides some typically Doylesque humour as well. There are no comparable rôles in SHERLOCK HOLMES. *The parade of clients through Holmes's consulting-room, and the tantalizing allusions to overlapping cases, are pure "Sherlockiana." If Doyle makes concessions to the expectations raised by Gillette—he gives us Holmes in disguise not once but twice, and inserts Billy (who was invented by Gillette, not Doyle) in the third act to no purpose at all—he does so without detracting from the play's dramatic force. And if the climactic scene is too abrupt and too melodramatic to be wholly satisfying, as has been charged, it is a small disappointment in contrast to seeing Holmes depicted on the stage precisely as his creator intended him to be.*

THE SPECKLED BAND *was first published in an acting edition by Samuel French in 1912 and remained in print for decades owing to the play's popularity as a repertory and summer-stock piece, but it has not been available for many years now. No reading edition was ever published, and the version which follows was specially prepared for this book.*

The Speckled Band

An Adventure of Sherlock Holmes

Cast of Characters

MR. SHERLOCK HOLMES
  The great Detective.

DR. WATSON
  His Friend.

BILLY
  Page to SHERLOCK HOLMES.

DR. GRIMESBY RYLOTT
  A retired Anglo-Indian Surgeon,
  Owner of Stoke Moran Manor.

ENID STONOR
  His Step-daughter.

ALI
  An Indian, valet to DR. RYLOTT.

RODGERS
  Butler to DR. RYLOTT.

MRS. STAUNTON
  Housekeeper to DR. RYLOTT.

MR. SCOTT WILSON
  Engaged to ENID's sister.

MR. LONGBRACE
  Coroner.

MR. BREWER
  Foreman of the Jury.

MR. ARMITAGE
  A Juror.

MR. HOLT LOAMING
MR. MILVERTON
MR. JAMES B. MONTAGUE
  Clients of MR. SHERLOCK HOLMES.

CORONER'S OFFICER
INSPECTOR DOWNING

ACT I

The Hall of Stoke Place, Stoke Moran.

Two years elapse between Acts I and II.

ACT II

Scene 1
DR. RYLOTT'S *Study, Stoke Place.*

Scene 2
MR. SHERLOCK HOLMES'S *Rooms, Upper Baker Street, London.*

ACT III

Scene 1
The Hall of Stoke Place.

Scene 2
ENID'S *Bedroom, Stoke Place.*

ACT I

SCENE. —*Stoke Place at Stoke Moran. A large, oak-lined, gloomy hall, with everything in disrepair. At the back, centre, is a big double door which leads into the morning-room. To its right, but also facing the audience, is another door which leads to the outside entrance hall. A little down, right, is the door to* DR. RYLOTT'S *study. Farther down, right, a large opening gives access to the passageway of the bedroom wing. A fifth entrance, up left, leads to the servants' hall. There is a long table in the middle of the room, with chairs round.*

ENID STONOR *sits on a couch at one side, her face buried in the cushion, sobbing.* RODGERS *also discovered, the butler, a broken old man. He looks timidly about him and then approaches* ENID.

RODGERS: Don't cry, my dear young lady. You're so good and kind to others that it just goes to my heart to see such trouble to you. Things will all change for the better now.

ENID: Thank you, Rodgers, you are very kind.

RODGERS: Life can't be all trouble, Miss Enid. There must surely be some sunshine somewhere, though I've waited a weary time for it.

ENID: Poor old Rodgers!

RODGERS: Yes, it used to be poor *young* Rodgers, and now it's poor *old* Rodgers; and there's the story of my life.

(Enter ALI, *an Indian servant, from the servants' hall.)*

ALI: Mrs. Staunton says you are to have beer and sandwiches for the jury, and tiffin for the coroner.

RODGERS: Very good.

ALI: Go at once.

RODGERS: You mind your own business. You think you are the master.

ALI: I carry the housekeeper's order.

RODGERS: Well, I've got my orders.

ALI: And I see they are done.

RODGERS: You're only the valet, a servant—same as me; same as Mrs. Staunton for that matter.

ALI: Shall I tell master? Shall I say you will not take the order?

RODGERS: There, there, I'll do it.

(Enter DR. GRIMESBY RYLOTT *from his study.)*

RYLOTT: Well, what's the matter? What are you doing here, Rodgers?

RODGERS: Nothing, sir, nothing.

ALI: I tell him to set out tiffin.

RYLOTT: Go this instant! What do you mean?

(RODGERS *exits into servants' hall.)*

Ali, stand at the door and show people in. *(To* ENID.) Oh! for God's sake stop your snivelling! Have I not enough to worry me without that? *(Shakes her.)* Stop it, I say! I'll have no more. They'll all be in here in a moment.

ENID: Oh! don't be so harsh with me.

RYLOTT: Hark! I think I hear them. *(Crossing toward bedroom passage.)* What can they be loitering for? They won't learn much by looking at the body. I suppose that consequential ass of a coroner is giving them a lecture. If Professor Van Donop and Doctor Watson are satisfied, surely that is good enough for him. Ali!

ALI: Yes, Sahib.

RYLOTT: How many witnesses have come?

ALI: Seven, Sahib.

RYLOTT: All in the morning-room?

ALI: Yes, Sahib.

RYLOTT: Then put any others in there also.

(ALI *salaams.)*

Woman, *will* you dry your eyes and try for once to think of other people besides yourself? Learn to stamp down your private emotions. Look at me. I was as fond of your sister Violet as if she had really been my daughter, and yet I face the situation now like a man. Get up and do your duty.

ENID *(drying her eyes)*: What can I do?

RYLOTT *(sitting on the settee beside her)*: There's a brave girl. I did not mean to be harsh. Thirty years of India sends a man home

with a cayenne pepper temper. Did I ever tell you the funny story
of the Indian judge and the cabman?

ENID: Oh, how can you?

RYLOTT: Well, well, I'll tell it some other time. Don't look so
shocked. I meant well, I was trying to cheer you up. Now look
here, Enid! be a sensible girl and pull yourself together — and I say!
be careful what you tell them. We may have had our little
disagreements — every family has — but don't wash our linen in
public. It is a time to forgive and forget. I always loved Violet in
my heart.

ENID: Oh! if I could only think so!

RYLOTT: Since your mother died you have both been to me as
my own daughters; in every way the same; mind you say so. D'you
hear?

ENID: Yes, I hear.

RYLOTT: Don't forget it. *(Rising, turns her face.)* Don't forget
it. Curse them! are they never coming, the carrion crows! I'll see
what they are after.

(Exits into bedroom passage.)

(SCOTT WILSON *enters at the hall door and is shown by* ALI *into
the morning-room. While he is showing him in,* DR. WATSON
enters, and, seeing ENID *with her face in the cushions, he comes
across to her.)*

WATSON: Let me say how sorry I am, Miss Stonor. *(Shaking
hands.)*

ENID *(rises to meet him)*: I am so glad to see you, Dr. Watson.
(Sinks on stool and sobs.) I fear I am a weak, cowardly creature,
unfit to meet the shocks of life. It is all like some horrible
nightmare.

WATSON: I think you have been splendidly brave. What woman
could fail to feel such a shock?

ENID: Your kindness has been the one gleam of light in these
dark days. There is such bad feeling between my stepfather and
the country doctor that I am sure he would not have come to us.
But I remembered the kind letter you wrote when we came home,
and I telegraphed on the chance. I could hardly dare hope that
you would come from London so promptly.

WATSON: Why, I knew your mother well in India, and I remember you and your poor sister when you were schoolgirls. I was only too glad to be of any use—if indeed I was of any use. Where is your stepfather?

ENID: He has gone in to speak with the coroner.

WATSON: I trust that he does not visit you with any of that violence of which I hear so much in the village. Excuse me if I take a liberty; it is only that I am interested. You are very lonely and defenceless.

ENID: Thank you. I am sure you mean well, but indeed I would rather not discuss this matter.

ALI *(advancing)*: This way, sir.

WATSON: In a minute.

ALI: Master's orders, sir. *(Coming down.)*

WATSON: In a minute, I say.

ALI: Very sorry, sir. Must go now.

WATSON *(pushing him away)*: Stand back, you rascal. I will go in my own time. Don't you dare to interfere with me.

(ALI *shrugs shoulders and withdraws.*)

Just one last word. It is a true friend who speaks, and you will not resent it. If you should be in any trouble, if anything should come which made you uneasy—which worried you—

ENID: What should come? You frighten me.

WATSON: You have no one in this lonely place to whom you can go. If by chance you should want a friend you will turn to me, will you not?

ENID: How good you are! But you mean more than you say. What is it that you fear?

WATSON: It is a gloomy atmosphere for a young girl. Your stepfather is a strange man. You would come to me, would you not?

ENID: I promise you I will. *(Rising.)*

WATSON: I can do little enough. But I have a singular friend—a man with strange powers and a very masterful personality. We used to live together, and I came to know him well. Holmes is his name—Mr. Sherlock Holmes. It is to him I should turn if things looked black for you. If any man in England could help you it is he.

ENID: But I shall need no help. And yet it is good to think that I am not all alone. Hush! they are coming. Don't delay! Oh! I beg you to go.

WATSON: I take your promise with me.

(He goes into the morning-room.)

(DR. RYLOTT *enters from the bedroom wing, conversing with the* CORONER. *The* JURY, *in a confused crowd, come behind. There are a* CORONER'S OFFICER *and a police* INSPECTOR.)

CORONER: Very proper sentiments, sir; very proper sentiments. I can entirely understand your feelings.

RYLOTT: At my age it is a great thing to have a soothing female influence around one. I shall miss it at every turn. She had the sweet temperament of her dear mother. Enid, my dear, have you been introduced to Mr. Longbrace, the Coroner?

CORONER: How do you do, Miss Stonor? You have my sympathy, I am sure. Well, well, we must get to business. Mr. Brewer, I understand that you have been elected as foreman. Is that so, gentlemen?

ALL: Yes, yes.

CORONER: Then perhaps you would sit here. *(Looks at watch.)* Dear me! it is later than I thought. Now, Dr. Rylott — *(sits at table)* — both you and your stepdaughter are witnesses in this inquiry, so your presence here is irregular.

RYLOTT: I thought, sir, that under my own roof —

CORONER: Not at all, sir, not at all. The procedure is entirely unaffected by such a consideration.

RYLOTT: I am quite in your hands.

CORONER: Then you will kindly withdraw.

RYLOTT: Come, Enid.

CORONER: Possibly the young lady would wish to be free, so we could take her evidence first.

RYLOTT: That would be most considerate. You can understand, sir, that I would wish her spared in this ordeal. I leave you, dear girl. *(Aside.)* Remember!

(RYLOTT *is about to go into his study but is directed by the* INSPECTOR *into the morning-room.)*

CORONER: Put a chair, there, officer.

(OFFICER *places chair.*)

That will do. Now, Miss Stonor! Thank you. The officer will swear you —

(ENID *is sworn by the* OFFICER.)

OFFICER: — The truth and nothing but the truth. Thank you.

(ENID *kisses the Book.*)

CORONER: Now, gentlemen, before I take the evidence, I will remind you of the general circumstances connected with the sudden decease of this unhappy young lady. She was Miss Violet Stonor, the elder of the stepdaughters of Dr. Grimesby Rylott, a retired Anglo-Indian doctor, who has lived for several years at this ancient house of Stoke Place, in Stoke Moran. She was born and educated in India, and her health was never robust. There was, however, no actual physical lesion, nor has any been discovered by the doctors. You have seen the room on the ground floor at the end of this passage, and you realize that the young lady was well guarded, having her sister's bedroom on one side of her and her stepfather's on the other. We will now take the evidence of the sister of the deceased as to what actually occurred. Miss Stonor, do you identify the body of the deceased as that of your sister, Violet Stonor?

ENID: Yes.

CORONER: Might I ask you to tell us what happened upon the night of April 14? I understand that your sister was in her ordinary health when you said good-night to her?

ENID: Yes, she seemed as usual. She was never strong.

CORONER: Had she some mental trouble?

ENID *(hesitating)*: She was not very happy in her mind.

CORONER: I beg that you will have no reserves. I am sure you appreciate the solemnity of this occasion. Why was your sister unhappy in her mind?

ENID: There were obstacles to her engagement.

CORONER: Yes, yes, I understand that this will be dealt with by another witness. Your sister was unhappy in her mind because she was engaged to be married and there were obstacles. Proceed.

ENID: I was awakened shortly after midnight by a scream. I ran into the passage. As I reached her door I heard a sound like low music, then the key turn in the lock, and she rushed out in her nightdress. Her face was convulsed with terror. She screamed out a few words and fell into my arms, and then slipped down upon the floor. When I tried to raise her I found that she was dead. Then — then I fainted myself, and I knew no more.

CORONER: When you came to yourself — ?

ENID: When I came to myself I had been carried by my stepfather and Rodgers, the butler, back to my bed.

CORONER: You mentioned music. What sort of music?

ENID: It was a low, sweet sound.

CORONER: Where did this music come from?

ENID: I could not tell. I may say that once or twice I thought that I heard music at night.

CORONER: You say that your sister screamed out some words. What were the words?

ENID: It was incoherent raving. She was wild with terror.

CORONER: But could you distinguish nothing?

ENID: I heard the word "band" — I also heard the word "speckled." I cannot say more. I was myself almost as terrified as she.

CORONER: Dear me. Band — speckled — it sounds like delirium. She mentioned no name?

ENID: None.

CORONER: What light was in the passage?

ENID: A lamp against the wall.

CORONER: You could distinctly see your sister?

ENID: Oh, yes.

CORONER: And there was at that time no trace of violence upon her?

ENID: No, no!

CORONER: You are quite clear that she unlocked her door before she appeared?

ENID: Yes, I can swear it.

CORONER: And her window? Did she ever sleep with her window open?

ENID: No, it was always fastened at night.

CORONER: Did you examine it after her death?

ENID: I saw it next morning; it was fastened then.

CORONER: One other point, Miss Stonor. You have no reason to believe that your sister contemplated suicide?

ENID: Certainly not.

CORONER: At the same time when a young lady—admittedly of a nervous, highly-strung disposition—is crossed in her love affairs, such a possibility cannot be excluded. You can throw no light upon such a supposition?

ENID: No.

FOREMAN: Don't you think, Mr. Coroner, if the young lady had designs upon herself she would have stayed in her room and not rushed out into the passage?

CORONER: Well, that is for your consideration and judgment. You have heard this young lady's evidence. Have any of you any questions to put?

ARMITAGE *(rising)*: Well, I'm a plain man, a Methodist and the son of a Methodist—

CORONER: What is your name, sir?

ARMITAGE: I'm Mr. Armitage, sir. I own the big shop in the village.

CORONER: Well, sir?

ARMITAGE: I'm a Methodist and the son of a Methodist—

CORONER: Your religious opinions are not under discussion, Mr. Armitage.

ARMITAGE: But I speaks my mind as man to man. I pays my taxes the same as the rest of them.

CORONER: Have you any questions to ask?

ARMITAGE: I would like to ask this young lady whether her stepfather uses her ill, for there are some queer stories got about in the village.

CORONER: The question would be out of order. It does not bear upon the death of the deceased.

FOREMAN: Well, sir, I will put Mr. Armitage's question in another shape. Can you tell us, Miss, whether your stepfather ever ill-used the deceased young lady?

ENID: He—he was not always gentle.

ARMITAGE: Does he lay hands on you?—that's what I want to know.

CORONER: Really, Mr. Armitage.

ARMITAGE: Excuse me, Mr. Coroner. I've lived in this village, boy and man, for fifty years; and I can look any man in the face.

(ARMITAGE *sits.*)

CORONER: You have heard the question, Miss Stonor. I don't know that we could insist upon your answering it.

ENID: Gentlemen, my stepfather has spent his life in the tropics. It has affected his health. There are times—there are times—when he loses control over his temper. At such times he is liable to be violent. My sister and I thought—hoped—that he was not really responsible for it. He is sorry for it afterwards.

CORONER: Well, Miss Stonor, I am sure I voice the sentiments of the Jury when I express our profound sympathy for the sorrow which has come upon you.

(JURY *all murmur,* "Certainly," "Quite so," *etc.)*

Call Mr. Scott Wilson. We need not detain you any longer.

(ENID *rises and goes into the morning-room.)*

OFFICER *(at door)*: Mr. Scott Wilson.

(Enter SCOTT WILSON—*a commonplace young gentleman.)*

CORONER: Swear him, officer—

(SCOTT WILSON *mumbles and kisses the Book.)*

I understand, Mr. Scott Wilson, that you were engaged to be married to the deceased.

WILSON: Yes, sir.

CORONER: Since how long?

WILSON: Six weeks.

CORONER: Was there any quarrel between you?

WILSON: None.

CORONER: Were you in a position to marry?

WILSON: Yes.

CORONER: Was there any talk of an immediate marriage?

WILSON: Well, sir, we hoped before the summer was over.

CORONER: We hear of obstacles. What were the obstacles?

WILSON: Dr. Rylott. He would not hear of the marriage.

CORONER: Why not?

WILSON: He gave no reason, sir.

CORONER: There was some scandal, was there not?

WILSON: Yes, sir, he assaulted me.

CORONER: What happened?

WILSON: He met me in the village. He was like a raving madman. He struck me several times with his cane, and he set his boar-hound upon me.

CORONER: What did you do?

WILSON: I took refuge in one of the little village shops.

ARMITAGE *(jumping up)*: I beg your pardon, young gentleman, you took refuge in my shop.

WILSON: Yes, sir, I took refuge in Mr. Armitage's shop.

(ARMITAGE *sits.)*

CORONER: And a police charge resulted?

WILSON: I withdrew it, sir, out of consideration for my fiancée.

CORONER: But you continued your engagement?

WILSON: I would not be bullied out of that.

CORONER: Quite so. But this opposition, and her fears as to your safety, caused Miss Stonor great anxiety?

WILSON: Yes.

CORONER: Apart from that, you can say nothing which throws any light on this sad event?

WILSON: No. I had not seen her for a week before her death.

CORONER: She never expressed any particular apprehension to you?

WILSON: She was always nervous and unhappy.

CORONER: But nothing definite?

WILSON: No.

CORONER: Any questions, gentlemen. *(Pause.)* Very good. Call Dr. Watson! You may go.

(SCOTT WILSON *goes out through the entrance hall.)*

OFFICER *(at morning-room door)*: Dr. Watson!

(Enter DR. WATSON.)

CORONER: You will kindly take the oath. Gentlemen, at the opening of this Court, and before you viewed the body, you had read to you the evidence of Professor Van Donop, the pathologist, who is unable to be present to-day. Dr. Watson's evidence is supplementary to that. You are not in practice, I understand, Dr. Watson?

WATSON: No, sir.

CORONER: A retired Army Surgeon, I understand?

WATSON: Yes.

CORONER: Dear me! you retired young.

WATSON: I was wounded in the Afghan Campaign.

CORONER: I see, I see. You knew Dr. Rylott before this tragedy?

WATSON: No, sir. I knew Mrs. Stonor when she was a widow, and I knew her two daughters. That was in India. I heard of her re-marriage and her death. When I heard that the children, with their stepfather, had come to England, I wrote and reminded them that they had at least one friend.

CORONER: Well, what then?

WATSON: I heard no more until I received a wire from Miss Enid Stonor. I at once came down to Stoke Moran.

CORONER: You were the first medical man to see the body?

WATSON: Dr. Rylott is himself a medical man.

CORONER: Exactly. You were the first independent medical man?

WATSON: Oh, yes, sir.

CORONER: Without going too far into painful details, I take it that you are in agreement with Professor Van Donop's report and analysis?

WATSON: Yes, sir.

CORONER: You found no physical lesion?

WATSON: No.

CORONER: Nothing to account for death?

WATSON: No.

CORONER: No signs of violence?

WATSON: No.

CORONER: Nor of poison?

WATSON: No.

CORONER: Yet there must be a cause?

WATSON: There are many causes of death which leave no sign.

CORONER: For instance — ?

WATSON: Well, for instance, the subtler poisons. There are many poisons for which we have no test.

CORONER: No doubt. But you will remember, Dr. Watson, that this young lady died some five or six hours after her last meal. So far as the evidence goes it was only then that she could have taken poison, unless she took it of her own free will; in which case we should have expected to find some paper or bottle in her room. But it would indeed be a strange poison which could strike her

down so suddenly many hours after it was taken. You perceive the
difficulty?

WATSON: Yes, sir.

CORONER: You could name no such poison?

WATSON: No.

CORONER: Then what remains?

WATSON: There are other causes. One may die of nervous
shock, or one may die of a broken heart.

CORONER: Had you any reason to think that the deceased had
undergone nervous shock?

WATSON: Only the narrative of her sister.

CORONER: You have formed no conjecture as to the nature of
the shock?

WATSON: No, sir.

CORONER: You spoke of a broken heart. Have you any reason
for using such an expression?

WATSON: Only my general impression that she was not happy.

CORONER: I fear we cannot deal with "general impressions."

(Murmurs of acquiescence from the JURY.)

You have no definite reason?

WATSON: None that I can put into words.

CORONER: Has any juror any question to ask?

ARMITAGE *(rising)*: I'm a plain, downright man; and I want to
get to the bottom of this thing.

CORONER: We all share your desire, Mr. Armitage.

ARMITAGE: Look here, Doctor, you examined this lady. Did
you find any signs of violence?

WATSON: I have already said I did not.

ARMITAGE: I mean bruises, or the like.

WATSON: No, sir.

CORONER: Any questions?

ARMITAGE: I would like to ask the Doctor whether he wrote to
these young ladies because he had any reason to think they were
ill-used.

WATSON: No, sir. I wrote because I knew their mother.

ARMITAGE: What did their mother die of?

WATSON: I have no idea.

CORONER: Really, Mr. Armitage, you go too far!

(ARMITAGE sits.)

Anything else?

FOREMAN: May I ask, Dr. Watson, whether you examined the window of the room to see if any one from outside could have molested the lady?

WATSON: The window was bolted.

FOREMAN: Yes, but had it been bolted all night?

WATSON: Yes, it had.

CORONER: How do you know?

WATSON: By the dust on the window-latch.

CORONER: Dear me, Doctor, you are very observant!

WATSON: I have a friend, sir, who trained me in such matters.

CORONER: Well, your evidence seems final on that point. We are all obliged to you, Dr. Watson, and will detain you no longer.

(Exit DR. WATSON into the morning-room.)

OFFICER *(at door)*: Mr. Rodgers!

(Enter RODGERS.)

CORONER: Swear him! *(Business of swearing.)* Well, Mr. Rodgers, how long have you been in the service of Dr. Rylott?

RODGERS: For many years, sir.

CORONER: Ever since the family settled here?

RODGERS: Yes, sir. I'm an old man, sir, too old to change. I don't suppose I'd get another place if I lost this one. He tells me it would be the gutter or the workhouse.

CORONER: Who tells you?

RODGERS: Him, sir—the master. But I am not saying anything against him, sir. No, no, don't think that—not a word against the master. You won't misunderstand me?

CORONER: You seem nervous?

RODGERS: Well, I'm an old man, sir, and things like this—

CORONER: Quite so, we can understand. Now, Rodgers, upon the night of April 14, you helped to carry the deceased to her room.

RODGERS: Did I, sir? Who said that?

CORONER: We had it in Miss Stonor's evidence. Was it not so?

RODGERS: Yes, yes, if Miss Enid said it. What Miss Enid says is true. And what the master says is true. It's all true.

CORONER: I suppose you came when you heard the scream?

RODGERS: Yes, yes, the scream in the night; I came to it.

CORONER: And what did you see?

RODGERS: I saw—I saw— *(Puts his hands up as if about to faint.)*

CORONER: Come, come, man, speak out.

RODGERS: I'm—I'm frightened.

CORONER: You have nothing to fear. You are under the protection of the law. Who are you afraid of? Your master?

RODGERS *(rising)*: No, no, gentlemen, don't think that! No, no!

CORONER: Well, then—what did you see?

RODGERS: She was on the ground, sir, and Miss Enid beside her —both in white night clothes. My master was standing near them.

CORONER: Well?

RODGERS: We carried the young lady to her room and laid her on her couch. She never spoke nor moved. I know no more— indeed I know no more. *(Sinking into his chair.)*

CORONER: Any questions, gentlemen?

ARMITAGE: You live in the house all the time?

RODGERS: Yes, sir.

ARMITAGE: Does your master ever knock you about?

RODGERS: No, sir, no.

ARMITAGE: Well, Mr. Scott Wilson told us what happened to him, and I know he laid the under gardener up for a week and paid ten pound to keep out of court. You know that yourself.

RODGERS: No, no, sir, I know nothing of the kind.

ARMITAGE: Well, every one else in the village knows. What I want to ask is—was he ever violent to these young ladies?

FOREMAN: Yes, that's it. Was he violent?

RODGERS: No, not to say violent. No, he's a kind man, the master.

(Pause.)

CORONER: Call Mrs. Staunton, the housekeeper. That will do.

(Exit RODGERS *into the servant's hall.)*

(Enter MRS. STAUNTON *from the morning-room.)*

CORONER: You are housekeeper here?

MRS. STAUNTON: Yes, sir. *(Standing.)*

CORONER: How long have you been here?

MRS. STAUNTON: Ever since the family settled here.

CORONER: Can you tell us anything of this matter?

MRS. STAUNTON: I knew nothing of it, sir, till after the poor young lady had been laid upon the bed. After that it was I who took charge of things, for Dr. Rylott was so dreadfully upset that he could do nothing.

CORONER: Oh! he was very upset, was he?

MRS. STAUNTON: I never saw a man in such a state of grief.

CORONER: Living in the house you had numerous opportunities of seeing the relations between Dr. Rylott and his two step-daughters.

MRS. STAUNTON: Yes, sir.

CORONER: How would you describe them?

MRS. STAUNTON: He was kindness itself to them. No two young ladies could be better treated than they have been.

CORONER: It has been suggested that he was sometimes violent to them.

MRS. STAUNTON: Never, sir. He was like a tender father.

ARMITAGE: How about that riding switch? We've heard tales about that.

MRS. STAUNTON: Oh, it's you, Mr. Armitage? There are good reasons why you should make mischief against the Doctor. He told you what he thought of you and your canting ways.

CORONER: Now, then, I cannot have these recriminations. If I had known, Mr. Armitage, that there was personal feeling between the Doctor and you—

ARMITAGE: Nothing of the sort, sir. I'm doing my public duty.

CORONER: Well, the evidence of the witness seems very clear in combating your assertion of ill-treatment. Any other Juror? Very good, Mrs. Staunton.

(Exit MRS. STAUNTON *into the servants' hall.)*

Call Dr. Grimesby Rylott.

OFFICER *(calls at morning-room door)*: Dr. Rylott.

(Enter DR. RYLOTT.)

CORONER: Dr. Rylott, do you identify the body of the deceased as that of your stepdaughter, Violet Stonor?

RYLOTT: Yes, sir.

CORONER: Can you say anything which will throw any light upon this unhappy business?

RYLOTT: You may well say unhappy, sir. It has completely unnerved me.

CORONER: No doubt.

RYLOTT: She was the ray of sunshine in the house. She knew my ways; I am lost without her.

CORONER: No doubt. But we must confine ourselves to the facts. Have you any explanation which will cover the facts of your stepdaughter's death?

RYLOTT: I know just as much of the matter as you do. It is a complete and absolute mystery to me.

CORONER: Speaking as a doctor, you had no misgivings as to her health?

RYLOTT: She was never robust, but I had no reason for uneasiness.

CORONER: It has come out in evidence that her happiness had been affected by your interference with her engagement?

RYLOTT *(rising)*: That is entirely a misunderstanding, sir. As a matter of fact, I interfered in order to protect her from a man who I had every reason to believe was a mere fortune hunter. She saw it herself in that light and was relieved to see the last of him.

CORONER: Excuse me, sir, but this introduces a new element into the case. Then the young lady had seperate means?

RYLOTT: An annuity under her mother's will. *(Sits.)*

CORONER: And to whom does it now go?

RYLOTT: I believe that I might have a claim upon it, but I am waiving it in favour of her sister.

CORONER: Very handsome, I am sure.

(Murmurs from the JURY.)

ARMITAGE *(rising)*: I expect, sir, so long as she lives under your roof you have the spending of it.

CORONER: Well, well, we can hardly go into that.

ARMITAGE: Had the young lady her own cheque book?

CORONER: Really, Mr. Armitage, you get away from the subject.

ARMITAGE: It is the subject.

RYLOTT *(rising)*: I am not here, sir, to submit to impertinence. *(Sits.)*

CORONER: I must ask you, Mr. Armitage— *(Holds up hand.)*

(ARMITAGE sits.)

Now, Dr. Rylott, the medical evidence, as you are aware, gives us no cause of death. You can suggest none?

RYLOTT: No, sir.

CORONER: Your stepdaughter has affirmed that her sister unlocked her door before appearing in the passage. Can you confirm this?

RYLOTT: Yes, I heard her unlock the door.

CORONER: You arrived in the passage simultaneously with the lady?

RYLOTT: Yes.

CORONER: You had been aroused by the scream?

RYLOTT: Yes.

CORONER: And naturally you came at once?

RYLOTT: Quite so. I was just in time to see her rush from her room and fall into her sister's arms. I can only imagine that she had some nightmare or hideous dream which had been too much for her heart. That is my own theory of her death.

CORONER: We have it on record that she said some incoherent words before she died.

RYLOTT: I heard nothing of the sort.

CORONER: She said nothing so far as you know?

RYLOTT: Nothing.

CORONER: Did you hear any music?

RYLOTT: Music, sir? No, I heard none.

CORONER: Well, what happened next?

RYLOTT: I satisfied myself that the poor girl was dead. Rodgers, my butler, had arrived, and together we laid her on her couch. I can really tell you nothing more.

CORONER: You did not at once send for a doctor?

RYLOTT: Well, sir, I was a doctor myself. To satisfy Enid I consented in the morning to telegraph for Dr. Watson, who had been the girls' friend in India. I really could do no more.

CORONER: Looking back, you have nothing with which to reproach yourself in your treatment of this lady?

RYLOTT: She was the apple of my eye, I would have given my life for her.

CORONER: Well, gentlemen, any questions?

ARMITAGE: Yes, a good many. *(Rising.)*

(The other JURYMEN *show some impatience.)*

Well, I pay my way, the same as the rest of you, and I claim my rights. Mr. Coroner, I claim my rights.

CORONER: Well, well, Mr. Armitage, be as short as you can. *(Looks at his watch.)* It is nearly two.

ARMITAGE: See here, Dr. Rylott, what about that great hound of yours? What about that whip you carry. What about the tales we hear down in the village of your bully-raggin' them young ladies?

RYLOTT *(rising)*: Really, Mr. Coroner, I must claim your protection. This fellow's impertinence is intolerable.

CORONER: You go rather far, Mr. Armitage. You must confine yourself to definite questions upon matters of fact.

(RYLOTT *sits.)*

ARMITAGE: Well, then, do you sleep with a light in your room?

RYLOTT: No, I do not.

ARMITAGE: How was you dressed in the passage?

RYLOTT: In my dressing-gown.

ARMITAGE: How did you get it?

RYLOTT: I struck a light, of course, and took it from a hook.

ARMITAGE: Well, if you did all that, how did you come into the passage as quick as the young lady who ran out just as she was?

RYLOTT: I can only tell you it was so.

ARMITAGE: Well, I can only tell *you* I don't believe it.

CORONER: You must withdraw that, Mr. Armitage.

ARMITAGE: I says what I mean, Mr. Coroner, and I say it again, I don't believe it. I've got common sense if I haven't got education.

RYLOTT *(rising)*: I can afford to disregard his remarks, Mr. Coroner.

CORONER: Anything else, Mr. Armitage?

ARMITAGE: I've said my say, and I stick to it.

CORONER: Then that will do, Dr. Rylott.

(Pause. DR. RYLOTT *is going up towards the morning-room door.)*

By the way, can your Indian servant help us at all in the matter?

RYLOTT *(coming down again)*: Ali sleeps in a garret and knew nothing till next morning. He is my personal valet.

CORONER: Then we need not call him. Very good, Dr. Rylott. You can remain if you wish. *(To* JURY.) Well, gentlemen, you have heard the evidence relating to this very painful case. There are several conceivable alternatives. There is death by murder. Of this I need not say there is not a shadow or tittle of evidence. There is death by suicide. Here, again, the presumption is absolutely against it. Then there is death by accident. We have nothing to lead us to believe that there has been an accident. Finally, we come to death by natural causes. It must be admitted that these natural causes are obscure, but the processes of nature are often mysterious, and we cannot claim to have such an exact knowledge of them that we can always define them. You have read the evidence of Professor Van Donop and you have heard that of Dr. Watson. If you are not satisfied it is always within your competence to declare that death arose from unknown causes. It is for you to form your own conclusions.

(The JURY *buzz together for a moment. The* CORONER *looks at his watch, rises, and goes over to* DR. RYLOTT.)

We are later than I intended.

RYLOTT: These absurd interruptions—!

CORONER: Yes, at these country inquests we generally have some queer fellows on the jury.

RYLOTT: Lunch must be ready. Won't you join us.

CORONER: Well, well, I shall be delighted.

FOREMAN: We are all ready, sir.

(CORONER *returns to table.)*

CORONER: Well, gentlemen? *(Sits.)*

FOREMAN: We are for unknown causes.

CORONER: Quite so. Unanimous?

ARMITAGE: No, sir. I am for further investigation. I don't say it's unknown, and I won't say it's unknown.

CORONER: I entirely agree with the majority finding. Well, gentlemen, that will finish our labours. Officer —

(The OFFICER *comes to him.* ARMITAGE *sits.)*

You will all sign the inquisition before you leave this room. The officer will take your signatures as you pass out.

(The JURY *rise—sign book as they go out into the entrance hall.)*

(Crossing to ARMITAGE.) Mr. Armitage. One moment, Mr. Armitage, I'm sorry that you are not yet satisfied.

ARMITAGE: No, sir, I am not.

CORONER: You are a little exacting. *(Turns away.)*

RYLOTT *(touching* ARMITAGE *on the shoulder)*: I have only one thing to say to you, sir. Get out of my house. D'you hear?

ARMITAGE: Yes, Dr. Rylott, I hear. And I seem to hear something else. Something crying from the ground, Dr. Rylott, crying from the ground.

(Exits slowly into the entrance hall.)

RYLOTT: Impertinent rascal! *(Turns away.)*

(Enter WATSON, ENID *and the other witnesses from the morning-room. They all file out towards the entrance hall.)*

*(*ENID *has come down stage.* DR. WATSON *comes back from the door.)*

WATSON: Good-bye, Miss Enid. *(Shakes hands. Then in a lower voice.)* Don't forget that you have a friend.

(He goes out.)

(Business of CORONER *and* RYLOTT *lighting cigarettes—*ENID *catches* RYLOTT'S *eye across* CORONER, *and shrinks down on to a chair.)*

CURTAIN.

ACT II

SCENE I. — DR. RYLOTT'S *study at Stoke Place. The door at one side, a pair of French windows on the other. It is two years later.*

Enter MRS. STAUNTON, *showing in* ARMITAGE.

MRS. STAUNTON: I can't tell how long the Doctor may be. It's not long since he went out.

ARMITAGE: Well, I'll wait for him, however long it is.

MRS. STAUNTON: It's nothing I could do for you, I suppose.

ARMITAGE: No, it is not.

MRS. STAUNTON: Well, you need not be so short. Perhaps, after you've seen the Doctor, you may be sorry.

ARMITAGE: There's the law of England watching over me, Mrs. Staunton. I advise you not to forget it — nor your master either. I fear no man so long as I am doing my duty.

(Enter ENID.)

Ah, Miss Stonor, I am very glad to see you.

ENID *(bewildered)*: Good-day, Mr. Armitage. What brings you up here?

ARMITAGE: I had a little business with the Doctor. But I should be very glad to have a chat with you also.

MRS. STAUNTON: I don't think the Doctor would like it, Miss Enid.

ARMITAGE: A pretty state of things. Isn't this young lady able to speak with whoever she likes? Do you call this a prison, or a private asylum, or what? These are fine doings in a free country.

MRS. STAUNTON: I am sure the Doctor would not like it.

ARMITAGE: Look here, Mrs. Staunton, two is company and three is none. If I'm not afraid of your master, I'm not afraid of you. You're a bit beyond your station, you are. Get to the other side of that door and leave us alone, or else —

MRS. STAUNTON: Or what, Mr. Armitage?

ARMITAGE: As sure as my father was a Methodist I'll go down to the J.P. and swear out an information that this young lady is under constraint.

MRS. STAUNTON: Oh—well, you need not be so hot about it. It's nothing to me what you say to Miss Enid. But the Doctor won't like it.

(She goes out.)

ARMITAGE *(looking at the door)*: You haven't such a thing as a hatpin? *(Crossing over to door.)*

ENID: No.

ARMITAGE: If I were to jab it through that keyhole—

ENID: Mr. Armitage, please don't.

ARMITAGE: You'd hear Sister Jane's top note. But we'll speak low, for I don't mean she shall hear. First of all, Miss Enid, how are they using you? Are you all right?

ENID: Mr. Armitage, I know you mean it all for kindness, but I cannot discuss my personal affairs with you. I hardly know you.

ARMITAGE: Only the village grocer. I know all about that. But I've taken an interest in you, Miss Stonor, and I'm not the kind of man that can't leave go his hold. I came here not to see you, but your stepfather.

ENID: Oh, Mr. Armitage, I beg you to go away at once. You have no idea how violent he is if any one thwarts him. Please, please go at once.

ARMITAGE: Well, Miss Stonor, your only chance of getting me to go is to answer my questions. When my conscience is clear I'll go, and not before. My conscience tells me that it is my duty to stay here till I have some satisfaction.

ENID *(crossing to settee and sitting)*: What is it, Mr. Armitage? Let's sit down.

ARMITAGE *(bringing chair over to settee)*: Well, I'll tell you. I make it my business to know what is going on in this house. It may be that I like you, or it may be that I dislike your stepfather. Or it may be that it's just my nature, but so it is. I've got my own way of finding out, and I find out.

ENID: What have you found out?

ARMITAGE: Now look here, Miss. Cast your mind back to that inquest two years ago.

ENID: Oh! *(Turning away.)*

ARMITAGE: I'm sorry if it hurts you, but I must speak plain. When did your sister meet her death? It was shortly after her engagement, was it not?

ENID: Yes, it was.

ARMITAGE: Well, you're engaged now, are you not?

ENID: Yes, I am.

ARMITAGE: Point number one. Well, now, have there not been repairs lately, and are you not forced to sleep in the very room your sister died in?

ENID: Only for a few nights.

ARMITAGE: Point number two. In your evidence you said you heard music in the house at night. Have you never heard music of late?

ENID: Good God! only last night I thought I heard it; and then persuaded myself that it was a dream. But how do you know these things, Mr. Armitage, and what do they mean?

ARMITAGE: Well, I won't tell you how I know them, and I can't tell you what they mean. But it's devilish, Miss Stonor, devilish! *(Rising.)* Now I've come up to see your stepfather and to tell him, as man to man, that I've got my eye on him, and that if anything happens to you it will be a bad day's work for him.

ENID *(rising)*: Oh, Mr. Armitage, he would beat you within an inch of your life. Mr. Armitage, you cannot think what he is like when the fury is on him. He is terrible.

ARMITAGE: The law will look after me.

ENID: It might avenge you, Mr. Armitage, but it could not protect you. Besides, there is no possible danger. You know of my engagement to Lieutenant Curtis?

ARMITAGE: I hear he leaves to-morrow.

ENID: That is true. But the next day I am going on a visit to his mother, at Fenton. Indeed, there is no danger.

ARMITAGE: Well, I won't deny that I am consoled by what you say, but there's just one condition on which I would leave this house.

ENID: What is that?

ARMITAGE: Well, I remember your friend, Dr. Watson, at the inquest — and we've heard of his connexion with Mr. Sherlock Holmes. If you'll promise me that you'll slip away to London to-morrow, see those two gentlemen, and get their advice, I'll wash my hands of it. I should feel that some one stronger than me was looking after you.

ENID: Oh, Mr. Armitage, I couldn't.

ARMITAGE *(folding his arms)*: Then I stay here.

ENID: It is Lieutenant Curtis's last day in England.

ARMITAGE: When does he leave?

ENID: In the evening.

ARMITAGE: Well, if you go in the morning, you'd be back in time.

ENID: But how can I get away?

ARMITAGE: Who's to stop you? Have you money?

ENID: Yes, I have enough.

ARMITAGE: Then go.

ENID: It is really impossible.

ARMITAGE *(sitting)*: Very good. Then I'll have it out with the Doctor.

ENID *(crossing to him)*: There, there! I'll promise. I'll go. I won't have you hurt. I'll write and arrange it all, somehow.

ARMITAGE: Word of honour?

ENID: Yes, yes. I'll write to Dr. Watson. Oh, do go. This way. *(Goes to the French window.)* If you keep among the laurels you can get to the high road and no one will meet you.

ARMITAGE *(going up to the windows. Pause. Returning)*: That dog about?

ENID: It is with the Doctor. Oh, do go! and thank you — thank you with all my heart.

ARMITAGE: My wife and I can always take you in. Don't you forget it.

(ARMITAGE *goes out.* ENID *stands looking after him. As she does so,* MRS. STAUNTON *enters the room.)*

MRS. STAUNTON: I saw Mr. Armitage going off through the shrubbery. *(Looks out of window.)*

ENID: Yes, he has gone.

MRS. STAUNTON: But why did he not wait to see the Doctor?

ENID: He's changed his mind.

MRS. STAUNTON: He is the most impertinent busybody in the whole village. Fancy the insolence of him coming up here without a with-your-leave or by-your-leave. What was it he wanted, Miss Enid?

ENID: It is not your place, Mrs. Staunton, to ask such questions.

MRS. STAUNTON: Oh, indeed! For that matter, Miss Enid, I should not have thought it was your place to have secrets with the village grocer. The Doctor will want to know all about it.

ENID: What my stepfather may do is another matter. I beg, Mrs. Staunton, that you will attend to your own affairs and leave me alone.

MRS. STAUNTON *(putting her arms akimbo)*: High and mighty, indeed! I'm to do all the work of the house, but the grocer can come in and turn me out of the room. If you think I am nobody you may find yourself mistaken some of these days.

ENID: How dare you —

(She makes for the door, as RYLOTT *enters.)*

RYLOTT: Why, Enid, what's the matter? Any one been upsetting you? What's all this, Mrs. Staunton?

ENID: Mrs. Staunton has been rude to me.

RYLOTT: Dear, dear! Here's a storm in a teacup. Well, now, come and tell me all about it. No one shall bother my little Enid. What would her sailor boy say?

MRS. STAUNTON: Mr. Armitage has been here. He would speak with Miss Enid alone. I didn't think it right. That is why Miss Enid is offended.

RYLOTT: Where is the fellow?

MRS. STAUNTON: He is gone. He went off through the shrubbery.

RYLOTT: Upon my word, he seems to make himself at home. What did he want, Enid?

ENID: He wanted to know how I was.

RYLOTT: This is too funny! You have made a conquest, Enid. You have a rustic admirer.

ENID: I believe he is a true friend who means well to me.

RYLOTT: Astounding! Perhaps it is as well for him that he did not prolong his visit. But now, my dear girl, go to your room until I send for you. I am very sorry that you have been upset, and I will see that such a thing does not happen again. Tut, tut! my little girl shall not be worried. Leave it to me. *(Goes up to door with* ENID.)*

*(*ENID *goes out.)*

Well, what is it, then? Why have you upset her?

MRS. STAUNTON: Why has she upset me? Why should I be always the last to be considered?

RYLOTT: Why should you be considered at all?

MRS. STAUNTON: You dare to say that to me—you that promised me marriage only a year ago. If I was what I should be, then there would be no talk as to who is the mistress of this house. I'll put up with no more of her tantrums, talking to me as if I was the kitchen-maid. *(Turning from him.)*

RYLOTT: You forget yourself.

MRS. STAUNTON: I forget nothing. I don't forget your promise, and it will be a bad day for you if you don't keep it.

RYLOTT: I'll put you out on the roadside if you dare speak so to me.

MRS. STAUNTON: You will, will you? Try it, and see. I saved you once. Maybe I could do the other thing, if I tried.

RYLOTT: Saved me!

MRS. STAUNTON: Yes, saved you. If it hadn't been for my evidence at that inquest, that fellow Armitage would have taken the Jury with him. Yes, he would. I've had it from them since.

RYLOTT: Well, you only spoke the truth.

MRS. STAUNTON: The truth! Do you think I don't know?

RYLOTT: What do you know?

(She is silent, and looks hard at him.)

What do you know?

(She is still silent.)

Don't look at me like that, woman. What *do* you know?

MRS. STAUNTON: I know enough.

(Pause.)

RYLOTT: Tell me, then—how did she die?

MRS. STAUNTON: Only you know that. I may not know how she died, but I know very well—

RYLOTT *(interrupting)*: You were always fanciful, Kate, but I know very well that you have only my own interests at heart. Put it out of your head if I have said anything unkind. Don't quarrel with this little fool, or you may interfere with my plans. Just wait a little longer, and things will come straight with us. You know that I have a hasty temper, but it is soon over.

MRS. STAUNTON: You can always talk me round, and you know it. Now, listen to me, for I am the only friend you've got. Don't try it again. You've got clear once. But a second would be too dangerous.

RYLOTT: They would make no more of the second than of the first. No one in the world can tell. It's impossible, I tell you. If she marries, half my income is gone.

MRS. STAUNTON: Yes, I know. Couldn't she sign it to you?

RYLOTT: She can be strong enough when she likes. She would never sign it to me. I hinted at it once, and she talked of a lawyer. *(Pause.)* But if anything should happen to her—well, there's an end to all our trouble.

MRS. STAUNTON: They must suspect.

RYLOTT: Let them suspect. But they can prove nothing.

MRS. STAUNTON: Not yet.

RYLOTT: On Wednesday she goes a-visiting, and who knows when she may return? No, it's to-morrow or never.

MRS. STAUNTON: Then let it be never.

RYLOTT: And lose half my income without a struggle? No, Kate, it's all or nothing with me now.

MRS. STAUNTON: Well, look out for Armitage.

RYLOTT: What about him?

MRS. STAUNTON: He must have known something before he dared to come here.

RYLOTT: What can he know of our affairs?

MRS. STAUNTON: There's Rodgers. You think he's half-witted. So he is. But he may know more and say more than we think. He talks and Armitage talks. Maybe Armitage gets hold of him.

RYLOTT: We'll soon settle that. *(Crossing to bell-pull.)* I'll twist the old rogue's neck if he has dared to play me false. There's one thing—he can't hold anything in if I want it to come out. Did you ever see a snake and a white mouse? You just watch.

(Enter RODGERS.)

Come here, Rodgers.

RODGERS: Yes, sir.

RYLOTT: Stand here, where the light falls on your face, Rodgers. I shall know then if you are telling me the truth.

RODGERS: The truth, sir. Surely I would tell that.

RYLOTT *(takes chair from behind settee)*: Sit there! Don't move! Now look at me. That's right. You can't lie to me now. You've been down to see Mr. Armitage.

RODGERS: Sir—I hope—there was no harm in that.

RYLOTT: How often?

RODGERS: Two or three times.

RYLOTT: How often?

RODGERS: Two or three —

RYLOTT: How often?

RODGERS: When I go to the village I always see him.

MRS. STAUNTON: That's nearly every day.

RYLOTT: What have you told him about me?

RODGERS: Oh, sir, nothing.

RYLOTT: What have you told him?

RODGERS: Just the news of the house, sir.

RYLOTT: What news?

RODGERS: Well, about Miss Enid's engagement, and Siva biting the gardener, and the cook giving notice, and the like.

RYLOTT: Nothing more than this.

RODGERS: No, sir.

RYLOTT: Nothing more about Miss Enid?

RODGERS: No, sir.

RYLOTT: You swear it?

RODGERS: No, sir, no. I said nothing more.

RYLOTT *(springing up, catching him by the neck, shaking him)*: You doddering old rascal, how came you to say anything at all? I kept you here out of charity, and you dare to gossip about my affairs. I've had enough of you — *(Throwing him off.)* I'll go to London to-morrow and get a younger man. You pack up your things and go. D'you hear?

RODGERS: Won't you look it over, sir? I'm an old man, sir, and I have no place to go to. Where am I to go?

RYLOTT: You can go to the devil for all I care, or to your friend Armitage, the grocer. There is no place for you here. Get out of the room.

RODGERS: Yes, sir. You won't reconsider it.

RYLOTT: Get out. And tell Miss Enid I want her.

RODGERS: Yes, sir.

(RODGERS *goes out.)*

MRS. STAUNTON: You have done wisely. He was not safe.

RYLOTT: The old devil suited me, too, in a way. A younger man may give more trouble.

MRS. STAUNTON: You'll soon break him in.

RYLOTT: Yes, I expect I will. *(Crossing to her.)* Now, make it right with Enid for my sake. You must play the game to the end.

MRS. STAUNTON: It's all right. I'm ready for her.

(Enter ENID.*)*

RYLOTT: My dear, Mrs. Staunton is very sorry if she has given you any annoyance. I hope you will accept her apology in the same spirit that it is offered.

MRS. STAUNTON: I meant no harm, Miss Enid, and I was only thinking of the master's interests. I hope you'll forgive me.

ENID: Certainly, I forgive you, Mrs. Staunton.

RYLOTT: There's a good little girl. Now, Mrs. Staunton, you had better leave us.

(MRS. STAUNTON *goes out.)*

Now, my dear, you must not be vexed with poor Mrs. Staunton, for she is a very hard-working woman and devoted to her duty, though, of course, her manners are often wanting in polish. Come now, dear, say that it is all right.

(ENID *sits on settee.)*

ENID: I have said that I forgive her.

RYLOTT: You must tell me anything I can do, to make you happier. Of course, you have some one else now, but I would not like you to forget your old stepfather altogether. Until the day when you have to leave me, I wish to do the very best for you.

ENID: You are very kind.

RYLOTT: Can you suggest anything that I can do?

ENID: No, no, there is nothing.

RYLOTT: I was a little too rough last week. I am sorry for that. I should wish your future husband to like me. You will tell him, when you see him, that I have done what I could to make you happy?

ENID: Yes, yes.

RYLOTT: You see him to-morrow?

ENID: Yes.

RYLOTT: And he leaves us to-morrow evening? *(Sitting beside her on settee.)*

ENID: Yes.

RYLOTT: You have all my sympathy, dear. But he will soon be back again, and then, of course, you will part no more. You will be sorry to hear that old Rodgers has been behaving badly, and that I must get rid of him.

ENID *(rising)*: Rodgers! What has he done?

RYLOTT: He grows more foolish and incompetent every day. I propose to go to London myself to-morrow to get a new butler. Would you send a line in my name to the agents to say that I shall call about two o'clock?

ENID: I will do so.

RYLOTT: There's a good little girl. *(Pause. Crossing to her and placing his hand on her shoulder.)* There's nothing on your mind, is there?

ENID: Oh, no.

RYLOTT: Well, then, run away and get your letter written. I dare bet you have another of your own to write. One a day—or two a day?—what is his allowance? Well, well, we have all done it at some time.

(Enter ALI with milk, jug, glass, and saucer on a tray.)

ALI: I beg pardon, Sahib, I go.

RYLOTT: Come in! Come in! Put my milk down on the table.

(ALI does so.)

Now, my dear, please don't forget to write the letter to the agents.

(ENID goes out.)

You fool! why did you not make sure I was alone?

ALI: I thought no one here but Sahib.

RYLOTT: Well, as it happens there's no harm done. *(Goes to door and locks it. Pulls down blind of window.)*

(While he does so ALI opens a cupboard and takes out a peculiar square wicker-work basket. RYLOTT pours milk into saucer and puts it before basket. Then he cracks his fingers and whistles while ALI plays on an Eastern flute.)

CURTAIN.

SCENE II. — MR. SHERLOCK HOLMES'S *room in Baker Street.*

Enter BILLY, *showing in* DR. WATSON.

WATSON: I particularly want to see Mr. Holmes.

BILLY: Well, sir, I expect he will be back almost immediately.

WATSON: Is he very busy just now?

BILLY: Yes, sir, we are very busy. We don't get much time to ourselves these days.

WATSON: Any particular case?

BILLY: Quite a number of cases, sir. Two German princes and the Duchess of Ferrers yesterday. The Pope's been bothering us again. Wants us to go to Rome over the cameo robbery. We are very overworked.

WATSON: Well, I'll wait for Mr. Holmes.

BILLY: Very good, sir. Here is *The Times.* There's four for him in the waiting-room now.

WATSON: Any lady among them?

BILLY: Not what I would call a lady, sir.

WATSON: All right, I'll wait. *(Lights a cigarette and looks around him.)* Just the same as ever. There are the old chemicals! Heavens! what have I not endured from those chemicals in the old days? Pistol practice on the wall. Quite so. I wonder if he still keeps tobacco in that Persian slipper? Yes, here it is. And his pipes in the coal-scuttle — black clays. Full of them — the same as ever. *(Takes one out and smells it.)* Faugh! Bottle of cocaine — Billy, Billy!

BILLY: I've done my best to break him of it, sir.

WATSON: All right, Billy, you can go.

(BILLY *goes out.*)

There's the old violin — the same old violin, with one string left. *(Sits on settee.)*

(Enter SHERLOCK HOLMES, *disguised as a workman, with tools.)*

HOLMES: You sent for me, Mr. Sherlock Holmes.

WATSON: I am not Mr. Holmes.

HOLMES: Beg pardon, sir, it was to mend the gas-bracket.

WATSON: What's wrong with it?

239

HOLMES: Leaking, sir.

WATSON: Well, go on with your work.

HOLMES: Yes, sir. *(Goes to the bracket.)* Hope I won't disturb you, sir?

WATSON *(taking up* The Times): That's all right. Don't mind me.

HOLMES: Very untidy man, Mr. Holmes, sir.

WATSON: What do you mean by that?

HOLMES: Well, sir, you can't help noticing it. It's all over the room. I've 'eard say he was as tidy as any when he started, but he learned bad 'abits from a cove what lived with him. Watson was his name.

(Slips into bedroom.)

WATSON *(rising)*: You impertinent fellow! How dare you talk in such a fashion? What do you want? *(Looks round.)* Why! what the deuce has become of him?

(The workman emerges as SHERLOCK HOLMES, *in dressing-gown, with hands in pockets.)*

Good Heavens, Holmes! I should never have recognized you.

HOLMES: My dear Watson, when you begin to recognize me it will indeed be the beginning of the end. When your eagle eye penetrates my disguise I shall retire to an eligible poultry farm.

WATSON: But why—?

HOLMES: A case, my dear Watson, a case! One of those small conundrums which a trustful public occasionally confides to my investigation. To the British workman, Watson, all doors are open. His costume is unostentatious, and his habits are sociable. A tool-bag is an excellent passport, and a tawny moustache will secure the co-operation of the maids. It may interest you to know that my humble double is courting a cook at Battersea. *(Strikes match and lights pipe.)*

WATSON: My dear Holmes! is it fair to the girl?

HOLMES: Chivalrous old Watson! It's a game of life and death, and every card must be played! But in this case I have a hated rival —the constable on the adjoining beat—so when I disappear all will readjust itself. We walk out on Saturday evenings. Oh! those walks! But the honour of a Duchess is at stake. A mad world, my masters. *(Turns to survey* WATSON.) Well, Watson, what is your news?

WATSON *(smiling)*: Well, Holmes, I came here to tell you what I am sure will please you.

HOLMES: Engaged, Watson, engaged! Your coat, your hat, your gloves, your buttonhole, your smile, your blush! The successful suitor shines from you all over. What I had heard of you, or perhaps what I had not heard of you, had already excited my worst suspicions. *(Looks fixedly at* WATSON.) But this is better and better, for I begin to perceive that it is a young lady whom I know and respect.

WATSON: But, Holmes, this is marvellous. The lady is Miss Morstan, whom you have indeed met and admired. But how could you tell —

HOLMES: By the same observation, my dear Watson, which assures me that you have seen the lady this morning. *(Picks a hair off* WATSON'S *breast, wraps it round his finger, and glances at it with his lens.)* Charming, my dear fellow, charming. There is no mistaking the Titian tint. You lucky fellow! I envy you.

WATSON: Thank you, Holmes. Some of these days I may find myself congratulating you.

HOLMES: No marriage without love, Watson.

WATSON: Then why not love? *(Placing his hand on* HOLMES'S *shoulders.)*

HOLMES: Absurd, Watson, absurd! I am not for love, nor love for me. It would disturb my reason, unbalance my faculties. Love is like a flaw in the crystal, sand in the clockwork, iron near the magnet. No, no, I have other work in the world.

WATSON: You have, indeed. Billy says you are very busy just now.

HOLMES: There are one or two small matters.

WATSON: Have you room to consider one other — the case of Miss Enid Stonor?

HOLMES: My dear fellow, if you have any personal interest in it. *(Sitting on divan.)*

WATSON: Yes, I feel keenly about it.

HOLMES *(taking out note-book)*: Let us see how I stand. There is the Baxter Square murder — I have put the police on the track. The Clerkenwell Jewel Robbery — that is now clearing. The case of

the Duchess of Ferrers—I have my material. The Pope's cameos—
His Holiness must wait. The Princess who is about to run from
home—let her run. I must see one or two who are waiting for
me—*(rings bell)*—then I am entirely at your disposal.

(Enter BILLY.*)*

BILLY: Yes, Mr. Holmes.
HOLMES: How many are waiting?
BILLY: Three, sir.
HOLMES: A light morning. Show them in now.

(BILLY *goes out.)*

WATSON: Well, I'll look in later.

HOLMES *(striking match and lighting pipe)*: No, no, my dear
fellow! I have always looked on you as a partner in the Firm—
Holmes, Watson, Billy & Co. That's our brass plate when we raise
one. If you'll sit there I shall soon be free.

(Enter BILLY, *with a card on tray.* MR. HOLT LOAMING *follows—
a rich, dissipated-looking, middle-aged man in an astrachan-
collared coat.* BILLY *goes out.)*

(Reading.) Mr. Holt Loaming. I remember the name. A racing
man, I believe?
LOAMING: Yes, sir.
HOLMES: Pray take a seat.

(LOAMING *draws up near the table.)*

What can I do for you?

LOAMING: Time's money, Mr. Holmes, both yours and mine.
I'm pretty quick off the mark, and you won't mind that. I'm not
here on the advice gratis line. Don't you think it. I've my cheque-
book here—*(takes it out)*—and there's plenty behind it. I won't
grudge you your fee, Mr. Holmes. I promise you that.

HOLMES: Well, Mr. Loaming, let us hear the business.

LOAMING: My wife, Mr. Holmes—damn her!—she's given me
the slip. Got back to her own people and they've hid her. There's
the law, of course, but she'd get out all kinds of lies about ill-
treatment. She's mine, and I'll just take her when I know where to
lay my hands on her.

HOLMES: How would you take her?

LOAMING: I just have to walk up to her and beckon. She's one of those wincing kind of nervous fillies that kick about in the paddock, but give in when once the bridle's on them and they feel the whip. You show me where she is, and I'll do the rest.

HOLMES: She is with her own people, you say?

LOAMING: Well, there's no man in the case, if that's what you're driving at. Lord! if you knew how straight she is, and how she carries on when I have a fling. She's got a cluster of aunts, and she's lyin' low somewhere among them. It's for you to put her up.

HOLMES: I fancy not, Mr. Loaming.

LOAMING: Eh? What's that?

HOLMES: I rather like to think of her among that cluster of aunts.

LOAMING: But, damn it, sir, she's my wife.

HOLMES: That's why!

LOAMING *(getting up)*: Well, it's a rum start, this. Look here, you don't know what you're missing. I'd have gone to five hundred. Here's the cheque.

HOLMES: The case does not attract me. *(Rings bell.)*

(Enter BILLY.)

Show Mr. Loaming out, Billy.

LOAMING: It's the last you'll see of me, Mr. Holmes.

HOLMES: Life is full of little consolations.

LOAMING: Damn!

(He takes his hat and goes out with BILLY.)

HOLMES: I'm afraid I shall never be a rich man, Watson.

(Re-enter BILLY.)

Well?

BILLY: Mr. James B. Montague, sir.

(Enter MONTAGUE, as BILLY goes out.)

HOLMES: Good morning, Mr. Montague. Pray take a chair.

(MONTAGUE *sits.)*

What can I do?

MONTAGUE *(a furtive-looking man with slimy ways)*: Anything fresh about the sudden death of my brother, sir? The police said it was murder, and you said it was murder; but we don't get any further, do we? *(Placing hat on floor.)*

HOLMES: I have not lost sight of it.

MONTAGUE: That man Henderson was a bad man, Mr. Holmes, an evil liver and a corruption. Yes, sir, a corruption and a danger. Who knows what passed between them? I've my suspicions — I've always had my suspicions.

HOLMES: So you said.

MONTAGUE: Have you worked any further on that line, sir? Because, if you tell me from time to time how it is shaping, I may be able to give you a word in season.

HOLMES: I have my eye on him — a very cunning rascal, as you say. We have not enough to arrest him on, but we work away in the hope.

MONTAGUE: Good, Mr. Holmes, good! Watch him; you'll get him, as safe as Judgment.

HOLMES: I'll let you know if anything comes of it. *(Rings.)*

MONTAGUE *(rising)*: That's right, sir. Watch 'im. I'm his brother, sir. It's me that should know. It's never out of my mind.

(Enter BILLY.*)*

HOLMES: Very good, Mr. Montague. Good-morning.

(MONTAGUE *and* BILLY *go out.)*

Curious little murder, Watson; done for most inadequate motive. That was the murderer.

WATSON: Good Heavens!

HOLMES: My case is almost complete. Meanwhile I amuse him and myself by the pretended pursuit of the wrong man — a very ancient device, Watson.

(Re-enter BILLY.*)*

Well, any more?

BILLY: Mr. Milverton is here, Mr. Holmes.

HOLMES: Show him in when I ring.

(BILLY *goes out.)*

I am sorry to delay the business upon which you wished to consult me; but this, I hope, will be the last. You remember Milverton?

WATSON: No.

HOLMES: Ah! it was after your time. The most crawling reptile in London — the King of the Blackmailers — a cunning, ruthless devil. I have traced seventeen suicides to that man's influence. It is he who is after the Duchess of Ferrers.

WATSON: The beautiful Duchess, whose re-marriage is announced?

HOLMES: Exactly. He has a letter which he thinks would break off the wedding. *(Rings.)* It is my task to regain it.

(Enter MILVERTON.*)*

Well, Mr. Milverton. Pray take a seat.

MILVERTON: Who is this?

HOLMES: My friend, Dr. Watson. Do you mind?

MILVERTON *(sitting)*: Oh! I have no object in secrecy. It is your client's reputation, not mine, which is at stake.

HOLMES: Your reputation! Good Heavens! *(Crossing to fireplace and filling pipe from slipper.)*

MILVERTON: Not much to lose there, is there, Mr. Holmes? I can't hurt. But she can. Hardly a fair fight, is it?

HOLMES: What are the terms now? *(Filling pipe.)*

MILVERTON: Steady at seven thousand. No money — no marriage.

HOLMES: Suppose she tells the whole story to the Marquis? Then your letter is not worth sixpence. He would condone all. Come, now, what harm is in the letter?

MILVERTON: Sprightly — very sprightly. However, it is purely a matter of business. If you think it is in the best interests of your client that the Marquis should see the letter — why, you would be very foolish to pay a large sum to regain it.

HOLMES: The lady has no great resources.

MILVERTON: But her marriage is a most suitable time for her friends and relations to make some little effort. I can assure you that this envelope would give more joy than all the tiaras and bracelets in Regent Street.

HOLMES: No, it is impossible!

MILVERTON: Dear me! Dear me! How unfortunate.

HOLMES: It can profit you in no way to push matters to an end.

MILVERTON: There you mistake. I have other cases maturing. If it were known that I had been severe on the Duchess the others would be more open to reason.

HOLMES: Well, well, you give us till noon to-morrow? *(Rings.)*

MILVERTON: But not an hour longer.

(Enter BILLY.*)*

HOLMES: We are at your mercy. Surely you won't treat us too harshly?

MILVERTON: Not a minute longer. *(Putting on hat.)*

(BILLY *and* MILVERTON *go out.)*

Terrible! Terrible! A fumigator would be useful, eh, Watson? Pah!

WATSON: What can you do?

HOLMES: My dear Watson—what have I done? It is this gentleman's cook who has honoured me. In the intervals of philandering I have made an acquaintance with the lock of his safe. Mr. Milverton spent last night at his club; when he returns home he will find there has been a little burglary at The Firs, Battersea, and his precious letter is missing. *(Rings.)*

WATSON: Holmes, you are splendid!

(Enter BILLY.*)*

HOLMES: Tut, tut! *(To* BILLY.) Well, any more?

BILLY: One lady, sir—just come—Miss Enid Stonor, of Stoke Moran.

WATSON: Ah! this is the case. *(Rising.)*

HOLMES: I'll ring, Billy.

(BILLY *goes out.)*

Now, Watson! Stonor! Stonor! Surely I associate the name with something?

WATSON: I told you of the case at the time. Sudden mysterious death of a girl at an old house in Stoke Moran, some two years ago.

HOLMES: My dear fellow! it all comes back to me. An inquest, was it not, with a string of most stupid and ineffectual witnesses?

WATSON: I was one of them.

HOLMES: Of course—so you were, so you were. I docketed the evidence. It introduced to my notice a gentleman of singular and most interesting personality. I have a few notes. *(Takes down a scrapbook from a row.)* Let's see—it's *R*—Ranter—Romanez—

Rylott! That's our man. Fifty-five years of age, killed his khitmutgar in India; once in a madhouse, married money—wife died—distinguished surgeon. Well, Watson, what has the distinguished surgeon been up to now? *(Throwing scrapbook on divan.)*

WATSON: Devilry, I fear.

HOLMES: I have the case very clear in my mind.

WATSON: Then you may remember that the death of the lady followed close upon her engagement?

HOLMES: Exactly.

WATSON: Miss Enid Stonor in turn became engaged, about a month ago, to a neighbour, Lieutenant Curtis.

HOLMES: Ah!

WATSON: Unhappily, the young man leaves for the Mediterranean to-day. She will henceforward be alone at Stoke Moran.

HOLMES: I see.

WATSON: And some circumstances have excited her alarm.

HOLMES: I gather that the amiable stepfather stands to lose in case of a marriage.

WATSON: That is so. Of course, supposing that Rylott did the other girl to death, it seems unlikely, on the face of it, that he would try it on again, as two sudden deaths in the house could hardly pass the coroner—

HOLMES: No, no, Watson! you are making the mistake of putting your normal brain into Rylott's abnormal being. The born criminal is often a monstrous egotist. His mind is unhinged from the beginning. What he wants he must have. Because he thinks a thing, it is right. Because *he* does a thing, it will escape detection. You can't say *a priori* that he will take this view or that one. Perhaps we had best have the young lady in. *(Rings bell.)* My dear fellow, you'll get into trouble if you go about righting the wrongs of distressed damsels. It won't do, Watson, it really won't.

(Enter ENID. WATSON *gets up and meets her.)*

WATSON: How do you do, Miss Enid? This is my friend, Mr. Holmes, of whom I spoke.

(HOLMES *shakes hands with* ENID.)

HOLMES: How do you do, Miss Stonor? Dear me! you must find a dog-cart a cold conveyance in this weather.

ENID: A dog-cart, Mr. Holmes?

HOLMES: One can hardly fail to observe the tell-tale splashes on the left sleeve. A white horse and clay soil are indicated. But what is this? You are trembling. Do sit down.

ENID *(looking round and sitting on settee)*: Tell me, Mr. Holmes, my stepfather has not been here?

HOLMES: No.

ENID: He saw me in the street. I dashed past him in a cab. But he saw me; our eyes met, and he waved me to stop.

HOLMES: Why is your stepfather in London?

ENID: He came up on business.

HOLMES: It would be interesting to know what the business was.

ENID: It was to get a new butler. Rodgers, our old one, is to leave us, and a new butler is to come at once. I doubt if any servant would come to such a place.

HOLMES: He may certainly find some difficulty. He would, no doubt, apply to an agent.

ENID: At two o'clock, to Patterson and Green, of Cavendish Street.

HOLMES: Exactly. I know them. But this is a digression, is it not? We get back to the fact that he saw you in the street?

ENID: Yes, it was in Pall Mall. I fancy he followed me.

HOLMES: Would he imagine you would come here?

ENID: No, he would think I was going to Dr. Watson's. He knows that Dr. Watson is my only friend in London.

HOLMES: What has been Dr. Rylott's attitude towards you since your engagement?

ENID: He has been much kinder, because he knows I have some one to protect me. But even so, there are moments — *(Raising her arm.)*

HOLMES: Good Heavens!

ENID: He does not realize his own strength. When he is angry he is like a fierce wild beast. Only last week he thrashed the blacksmith.

HOLMES: He is welcome to the blacksmith, but not to my clients. This must not occur again. Does your fiancé know of this?

ENID: I would not dare to tell him. He would do something dreadful. Besides, as I say, my stepfather has, on the whole, been kinder. But there is a look in his eyes, when I turn on him suddenly, that chills me to the bone. His kindness is from his head, not from his heart. I feel as if he were waiting — waiting —

HOLMES: Waiting for what?

ENID: Waiting for my fiancé to leave. Waiting till he has me at his mercy. That room freezes my blood. Often I cannot sleep for horror.

WATSON: What? He has changed your room? *(Rising from armchair.)*

ENID: My old room is under repair.

WATSON: You sleep, then, in the room where your sister died?

ENID: In the same room. And other things have happened. The music has come again.

HOLMES: The music? Tell me about this music.

ENID: It came before my sister's death. She spoke of it, and then I heard it myself the night she died. But it has come again. Oh, Mr. Holmes, I am terrified.

HOLMES: There, there! you've had enough to break any one's nerve. This — music — does it seem to be *inside* the house or *outside?*

ENID: Indeed, I could not say.

HOLMES: What is it like?

ENID: A sort of soft, droning sound.

HOLMES: Like a flute or pipe?

ENID: Yes. It reminds me of my childhood in India.

HOLMES: Ah — India?

ENID: And there's one other thing that puzzles me — my sister's dying words — as she lay in my arms she gasped out two words.

HOLMES: What were they?

ENID: "Band" and "Speckled."

HOLMES: Band — speckled — and Indian music. You sleep with your door and window fastened?

ENID: Yes, but so did poor Violet. It did not save *her,* and it may not save *me.*

HOLMES: Could there be anything in the nature of secret doors or panels?

ENID: No. I have searched again and again. There is nothing.

HOLMES: And nothing peculiar in the room?

ENID: No, I cannot say there is.

HOLMES: I must really drop in and have a look at this most

interesting apartment. Suggestive—very suggestive. *(Pause.)* When did you hear this music last?

ENID: Last night.

HOLMES: And your fiancé leaves to-day?

ENID: He leaves to-day. What shall I do?

HOLMES: Well, Miss Stonor, I take up your case. It presents features which commend it to me. You must put yourself into my hands.

ENID: I do—unreservedly. *(Rising, and crossing to him.)*

HOLMES *(to* WATSON): It is a question whether we are justified in letting her return at all to Stoke Moran.

ENID: I must return. At five o'clock my fiancé leaves, and I shall not see him again for months.

HOLMES: Ah! that is a complication. Where is the A.B.C.? *(Finds it in umbrella stand.)* Stonehouse—Stowell—Stoke—

ENID: I know my train, Mr. Holmes.

HOLMES: I was looking for mine.

ENID: You are coming down?

HOLMES: I shall not be content until I have seen this room of yours. Yes, that will do. I could get up to you between eleven and twelve, to-night. Would you have the goodness to leave your shutter open? The room is, I understand, upon the ground floor?

ENID: Oh! Mr. Holmes, it is not safe. You cannot think of the danger.

HOLMES: I have taken up your case, Miss Stonor, and this is part of it. Have you any friends in Stoke Moran?

ENID: Mr. Armitage and his wife.

HOLMES: That is most fortunate. Now, listen to me, Miss Stonor. When you have returned home certain circumstances may arise which will ensure your safety. In that case you will stay at Stoke Place until I come in the evening. On the other hand, things may miscarry, and you may not be safe. In that case I will so manage that a warning will reach you. You will then break away from home and take refuge with the Armitages. Is that clear?

ENID: Who will bring me the warning?

HOLMES: I cannot say. But you have my assurance that it will come.

ENID: Then, until it does, I will stay at Stoke Place.

HOLMES: And should any new development occur you could always send me a telegram, could you not?

ENID: Yes, I could do that.

HOLMES: Then it is not good-bye, but au revoir.

(Enter BILLY.)

What is it?

BILLY: Please, Mr. Holmes, a gentleman to see you, at once.

HOLMES: Who is he?

BILLY: A very impatient gentleman, sir. It was all I could do to get him to stay in the waiting-room.

ENID: Is he tall, dark, with a black beard, and a long white scar on his cheek?

BILLY: That's him, Miss.

ENID: Oh, Mr. Holmes, what shall I do? He has followed me.

WATSON: If he went to my rooms, my landlady had instructions to send any one on here.

HOLMES: Exactly.

ENID: Oh! I dare not meet him, I dare not. Can't I slip out somehow?

HOLMES: I see no reason why you should stay. Billy, show the lady out by the side passage.

BILLY: Don't be alarmed, Miss, I'll see you through.

(BILLY *and* ENID *go out.)*

WATSON: This fellow is dangerous, Holmes. You may need a weapon.

HOLMES: There's something of the kind in that drawer at your right.

(Enter BILLY.)

BILLY: Shall I stay when I show him in, Mr. Holmes?

HOLMES: Why so?

BILLY: An ugly customer, Mr. Holmes.

HOLMES: Tut, tut! show him up.

(BILLY *goes out.)*

Well, Watson, I must thank you for a most interesting morning. You are certainly the stormy petrel of crime.

(Enter DR. RYLOTT.)

RYLOTT: This is Mr. Sherlock Holmes, I believe.

HOLMES: Your belief is justified.

RYLOTT: I have reason to think that you have taken an unsolicited interest in my affairs.

HOLMES: Your name being — ?

RYLOTT: My name, sir, is Grimesby Rylott — Doctor Grimesby Rylott, of Stoke Moran. *(Throws down card.)*

HOLMES: A pretty place, I hear! And obviously good for the lungs.

RYLOTT: Sir, you are trifling with me. I have come here to ask whether you have had a visit from my stepdaughter, Miss Enid Stonor —

HOLMES: The first law in my profession, Doctor, is never to answer questions.

RYLOTT: Sir, you *shall* answer me.

HOLMES: We could do with warmer weather.

RYLOTT: I insist upon an answer.

HOLMES: But I hear the crocuses are coming on.

RYLOTT: *Curse your crocuses!* I've heard of you, you meddling busybody. And you, Dr. Watson — I expected to find you here. What do you mean by interfering with my lawful affairs?

WATSON: So long as they are lawful, Dr. Rylott, no one is likely to interfere with them.

RYLOTT: Now look here, Mr. Holmes, perhaps I may seem to you a little hot-headed —

HOLMES: Dear me, Dr. Rylott, what put that idea into your head?

RYLOTT: I apologize if I have seemed rude — *(Sitting.)*

HOLMES: Robust — a little robust — nothing more.

RYLOTT: I wish to put the matter to you as man to man. You know what girls are, how sudden and unreasonable their prejudices may be. Imagine, sir, how hurt I should feel to be distrusted by one whom I have loved.

HOLMES: You have my deep sympathy, Dr. Rylott.

RYLOTT *(pleased)*: Ah!

HOLMES: You are a most unfortunate man. There was that sad tragedy two years ago —

RYLOTT: Yes, indeed!

HOLMES: I think I could help you in that matter.

RYLOTT: How so?

HOLMES: As a friend, and without a fee.

RYLOTT: You are very good.

HOLMES: I am very busy, but your case seems so hard that I will put everything aside to assist you.

RYLOTT: In what way, sir?

HOLMES: I will come down at once, examine the room in which the tragedy occurred, and see if such small faculties as I possess can throw any light upon the matter.

RYLOTT: Sir, this is an intolerable liberty. *(Rising.)*

HOLMES: What! you don't want help?

RYLOTT: It is intolerable, I say. What I ask you to do—what I order you to do is to leave my affairs alone. Alone, sir—do you hear me?

HOLMES: You are perfectly audible.

RYLOTT: I'll have no interference—none! Don't dare to meddle with me. D'you hear, the pair of you? You—Holmes, I'm warning you.

HOLMES *(looking at his watch)*: I fear I must end this interview. Times flies when one is chatting. Life has its duties as well as its pleasures, Doctor.

RYLOTT: Insolent rascal! I'll—I'll— *(Turns to the grate and picks up the poker.)*

(WATSON *jumps up.*)

HOLMES: No, Watson, no! It does need poking, but perhaps you would put on a few coals first.

RYLOTT: You laugh at me? You don't know the man you are dealing with. You think that my strength fails because my hair is turned. I was the strongest man in India once. See that! *(Bends the poker and throws it down at* HOLMES'S *feet.)* I am not a safe man to play with, Mr. Holmes.

HOLMES: Nor am I a safe man to play with, Dr. Rylott. Let me see—what were we talking about before the Sandow performance?

RYLOTT: You shall not overcrow me with your insolence! I tell you now, and you, too, Dr. Watson, that you interfere with my affairs to your own danger. You have your warning.

HOLMES: I'll make a note of it.

RYLOTT: And you refuse to tell me if Miss Stonor has been here?

HOLMES: Don't we seem to be travelling just a little in a circle?

RYLOTT *(picking up hat from table)*: Well, you can't prevent me from finding out from her.

HOLMES: Ah! there I must talk a little seriously to you, Dr. Grimesby Rylott. You have mentioned this young lady, and I know something of her circumstances. I hold you responsible. My eye is on you, sir, and the Lord help you — the Lord help you — if any harm befall her. Now leave this room, and take my warning with you.

RYLOTT: You cursèd fool! I may teach you both not to meddle with what does not concern you. Keep clear of Stoke Moran!

(RYLOTT *goes out, slamming the door.*)

HOLMES: I had a presentiment he would slam the door.

(WATSON *rises.*)

Stoke Moran must be less dull than many country villages. Quite a breezy old gentleman, Watson. Well, I must thank you for a very pretty problem. What the exact danger may be which destroyed one sister and now threatens the other may be suspected, but cannot yet be defined. That is why I must visit the room.

WATSON: I will come with you, Holmes.

HOLMES: My dear fellow, you are no longer an unattached knight-errant. Dangerous quests are forbidden. What would Miss Morstan say?

WATSON: She would say that the man who would desert his friend would never make a good husband.

HOLMES: Well, my dear Watson, it may be our last adventure together, so I welcome your co-operation.

WATSON: Well, I'll be off.

HOLMES: You will leave Victoria to-night at eleven fifteen, for Stoke Moran.

WATSON: Good-bye — I'll see you at the station.

HOLMES: Perhaps you will.

(WATSON *goes.*)

Perhaps you will! *(Rings.)* Perhaps you won't! *(Stands near fire.)*

(*Enter* BILLY.)

BILLY: Yes, sir.

HOLMES: Ever been in love, Billy?

BILLY: Not of late years, sir.

HOLMES: Too busy, eh?

BILLY: Yes, Mr. Holmes.

HOLMES: Same here. Got my bag there, Billy?

BILLY: Yes, sir. *(Puts it on table.)*

HOLMES: Put in that revolver.

BILLY: Yes, sir.

HOLMES: And the pipe and pouch.

BILLY *(takes it from table)*: Yes, sir.

HOLMES: Got the dark lantern?

BILLY: Yes, sir.

HOLMES: The lens and the tape?

BILLY: Yes, sir.

HOLMES: Plaster of Paris, for prints?

BILLY: Yes, sir.

HOLMES: Oh, and the cocaine. *(Hands it.)*

BILLY: Yes, sir. *(Throws it down.)*

HOLMES: You young villain! you've broken it. *(Takes his ear and turns his head round.)* You're a clever boy, Billy.

BILLY: Yes, Mr. Holmes.

CURTAIN.

ACT III

SCENE I. — *The Hall at Stoke Place.*

MRS. STAUNTON *is discovered at the back, reading a telegram.*

MRS. STAUNTON: Are you there, Rodgers?

(Enter RODGERS.)

RODGERS: Well, Mrs. Staunton.

MRS. STAUNTON: I've had a telegram from the master. He will be here presently. He is bringing the new butler with him, so you can hand over to-night.

RODGERS: To-night, Mrs. Staunton. It all seems very sudden.

MRS. STAUNTON: Peters will need your room. That's his name, Peters. He brings a young girl with him, his daughter. The attic will do for her. That will do, Rodgers.

(RODGERS *goes into the morning-room.)*

(Enter ENID *from the entrance hall.)*

ENID: Oh, Mrs. Staunton.

MRS. STAUNTON: Yes, Miss.

ENID: Has any message come in my absence?

MRS. STAUNTON: No, Miss.

ENID: Let me know at once if any comes.

(ENID *goes into the bedroom wing.)*

MRS. STAUNTON: Yes, Miss. A message! A message!

(Enter ALI, *hurriedly.)*

(To him.) Well?

ALI: Has she come back?

MRS. STAUNTON: Yes, she is in her room.

ALI: I see her meet Curtis Sahib. Then I lose her.

MRS. STAUNTON: Well, she has come back. I have heard from the master. She is not to go out any more. He will come soon. Until he does, we must hold her. She asked if there was a message

for her. Who can she expect a message from? Ah—stand back,
Ali, she's coming.

(ALI *stands at door to servants' hall.*)

(Re-enter ENID, *still dressed for walking.)*

MRS. STAUNTON: I beg pardon, Miss, but what are you going
to do?

ENID: I am going down to the village. *(Crosses towards entrance
hall.)*

MRS. STAUNTON: What for?

ENID: How dare you ask me such a question? What do you
mean by it?

MRS. STAUNTON: I thought it was something we could do for
you.

ENID: It was not.

MRS. STAUNTON: Then I am sorry, Miss, but it can't be done.
The Doctor didn't like you going to London to-day. His orders are
that you should not go out again.

ENID: How dare you? I am going out now.

MRS. STAUNTON: Get to the door, Ali! It's no use, Miss, we
must obey our orders. You don't budge from here.

ENID: What is the meaning of this?

MRS. STAUNTON: It is not for the likes of us to ask the meaning.
The Doctor is a good master, but his servants have to obey him.

ENID: I will go out. *(Tries to rush past.)*

MRS. STAUNTON: Lock the door, Ali.

(ALI *locks the door to the entrance hall.*)

The other locks are locked as well. You needn't try the windows,
for Siva is loose. All right, Ali, give me the key—you can go!

(ALI *goes into the servants' hall.*)

Now, Miss, do what the Doctor wishes. That's my advice to you.

(She exits into the servants' hall.)

(ENID *waits until she has gone; then she rushes across to the
writing-table and scribbles a telegram.)*

(RODGERS *enters from the morning-room.)*

ENID: Oh, Rodgers—

RODGERS: Yes, Miss.

ENID: Come here, Rodgers!

(RODGERS *comes down.*)

I want to speak to you. I hear that you are leaving us. I wanted to say how sorry I am.

RODGERS: God bless you, Miss Enid. My heart is sore to part with you. All the kindness I've ever had in this house has been from poor Miss Violet and you.

ENID: Rodgers, if ever I have done anything for you, you can repay it now a hundredfold.

RODGERS: Nothing against the master, Miss Enid! Don't ask me to do anything against the master.

ENID: How can you love him?

RODGERS: Love him! No, no, I don't love him, Miss Enid. But I fear him—oh! I fear him. One glance of his eyes seems to cut me—to pierce me like a sword. I wouldn't even listen to anything against him, for I feel it would come round to him, and then—then—!

ENID: What can he do to you?

RODGERS: Oh, I couldn't, Miss Enid—don't ask me. What a man! what a man! Has he a child in his room, Miss Enid?

ENID: A child?

RODGERS: Yes—the milk—who drinks the milk? He drinks no milk. Every morning I take up the jug of milk. And the music—who is it he plays the music to?

ENID: Music! You have heard it, too. I'm so frightened. I'm in danger. I know I'm in danger. *(Rising.)*

RODGERS: In danger, Miss Enid?

ENID: And you can save me.

RODGERS: Oh, Miss Enid, I couldn't—I couldn't—I have no nerve. I couldn't.

ENID: All I want you to do is to take a telegram.

RODGERS: A telegram, Miss Enid?

ENID: They won't let me out, and yet I must send it.

RODGERS: Perhaps they won't let me out.

ENID: You could wait a little, and then slip away to the post office.

RODGERS: What is the telegram, Miss Enid? Say it slowly. My poor old head is not as clear as it used to be.

ENID: Give it to the clerk.

RODGERS: No, no, I must be sure it is nothing against the master.

ENID: It is my business—only mine. Your master's name is not even mentioned. See—it is to Mr. Sherlock Holmes—he is a friend of mine—Baker Street, London. "Come to me as soon as you can. Please hurry." That is all. Dear Rodgers, it means so much to me—please—please take it for me.

RODGERS: I can't understand things like I used.

ENID: Oh! do take it, Rodgers! You said yourself that I had always been kind to you. You *will* take it, won't you? *(Holds out telegram to RODGERS.)*

RODGERS: Yes, yes, I will take it, Miss Enid. *(Takes telegram and puts it in his pocket.)*

ENID: Oh! you don't know what a service you are doing. It may save me—it may save my going all the way to town.

RODGERS: Well, well, of course I will take it. What's that?

(Wheels heard outside.)

(Enter MRS. STAUNTON and ALI.)

MRS. STAUNTON: Quick, Ali! get the door unlocked. He won't like to be kept waiting. Rodgers, be ready to receive your master.

ENID *(to RODGERS)*: Don't forget—as soon as you can.

(She goes into the bedroom wing, followed by MRS. STAUNTON.)

(Wheels stop.)

(ALI *throws open the hall door and salaams. Enter* RYLOTT, *followed by* HOLMES, *disguised as Peters, the new butler, who is followed by* BILLY, *disguised as a young girl, with a big hat-box.)*

RYLOTT *(taking off things and handing them to ALI)*: Where is Miss Enid? Did she return?

ALI: Yes, sir, she is in her room.

RYLOTT: Ah! *(To RODGERS.)* What! still here.

RODGERS: I had some hopes, sir—

RYLOTT: Get away! Lay the supper! I'll deal with you presently.

(RODGERS *goes into the servants' hall.*)

Ali, you can go also. Show this young girl to the kitchen. *(To* HOLMES.) What is her name?

HOLMES: Amelia — the same as her mother's.

RYLOTT: Go to the kitchen, child, and make yourself useful.

(ALI *goes out, followed by* BILLY.)

(To HOLMES.) Now, my man, we may as well understand each other first as last. I'm a man who stands no nonsense in my own house. I give good pay, but I exact good service. Do you understand?

HOLMES: Yes, sir.

RYLOTT: I've had a man for some time, but he is old and useless. I want a younger man to keep the place in order. Rodgers will show you the cellar and the other things you should know. You take over from to-morrow morning.

HOLMES: Very good, sir. I'm sure, sir, it was very good of you to take me with such an encumbrance as my poor little orphaned Amelia.

RYLOTT: I've taken you not only with a useless encumbrance, but without references and without a character. Why have I done that? Because I expect I shall get better service out of you. Where are you to find a place if you lose this one? Don't you forget it.

HOLMES: I won't forget, sir. I'll do all I can. If I can speak to your late butler, sir, I have no doubt he will soon show me my duties.

RYLOTT: Very good. *(Rings bell.)*

(Enter MRS. STAUNTON *from the bedroom wing.)*

Mrs. Staunton, tell Rodgers I want him. By the way, where is Siva?

MRS. STAUNTON: Loose in the park, sir.

(She goes into the servants' hall.)

RYLOTT: By the way, I had best warn you, Peters, not to go out till my boar-hound comes to know you. She's not safe with strangers — not very safe with any one but myself.

HOLMES: I'll remember, sir.

RYLOTT: Warn that girl of yours.

(Enter RODGERS.)

HOLMES: Yes, I will.

RYLOTT: Ah, Rodgers, you will hand your keys over to Peters. When you have done so, come to me in the study.

RODGERS: Yes, sir.

(RYLOTT *goes into his study.)*

HOLMES *(after looking round)*: Well, I'm not so sure that I think so much of this place. Maybe you are the lucky one after all. I hope I am not doing you out of your job. I'd chuck it for two pins. If it wasn't for Amelia I'd chuck it now.

RODGERS: If it wasn't you it would be some one else. Old Rodgers is finished — used up. But he said he wanted to see me in the study. What do you think he wants with me in the study?

HOLMES: Maybe to thank you for your service; maybe to make you a parting present.

RODGERS: His eyes were hard as steel. What can he want with me? I get nervous these days, Mr. Peters. What was it he hold me to do?

HOLMES: To hand over the keys. *(Taking his overcoat off.)*

RODGERS: Yes, yes, the keys. *(Taking out keys.)* They are here, Mr. Peters. That's the cellar key, Mr. Peters. Be careful about the cellar. That was the first time he struck me — when I mistook the claret for the Burgundy. He's often hasty, but he always kept his hands off till then.

HOLMES: But the more I see of this place the less I fancy it. I'd be off to-night, but it's not so easy these days to get a place if your papers ain't in order. See here, Mr. Rodgers, I'd like to know a little more about my duties. The study is there, ain't it?

RODGERS: Yes, he is there now, waiting — waiting for me.

HOLMES: Where is his room?

RODGERS: You see the passage yonder. Well, the first room you come to is the master's bedroom; the next is Miss Enid's —

HOLMES: I see. Well, now, could you take me along to the master's room and show me any duties I have there?

RODGERS: The master's room? No one ever goes into the master's room. All the time I've been here I've never put my head inside the door.

HOLMES *(surprised)*: What? no one at all?

RODGERS: Ali goes. Ali is the Indian valet. But no one else.

HOLMES: I wonder you never mistook the door and just walked in.

RODGERS: You couldn't do that, for the door is locked.

HOLMES: Oh! he locks his door, does he? Dear me! None of the keys here any use, I suppose?

RODGERS: Don't think of such a thing. What are you saying? Why should you wish to enter the master's room?

HOLMES: I don't want to enter it. The fewer rooms the less work. Why do you suppose he locks the door?

RODGERS: It is not for me, nor for you, to ask why the master does things. He chooses to do so. That is enough for us.

HOLMES: Well, Mr. Rodgers, if you'll excuse my saying so, this old 'ouse 'as taken some of the spirit out of you. I'm sure I don't wonder. I don't see myself staying here very long. Wasn't there some one died here not so long ago?

RODGERS: I'd rather not talk of it, Mr. Peters.

HOLMES: A woman died in the room next the doctor's. The cabman was telling me as we drove up.

RODGERS: Don't listen to them, Mr. Peters. The master would not like it. Here is Miss Enid, and the Doctor wants me.

(Enter ENID *from the bedroom wing.)*

ENID: Rodgers, can I have a word with you?

RODGERS: Very sorry, Miss Enid, the master wants me.

(RODGERS *goes into the study.)*

ENID *(to* HOLMES): Are you — ?

HOLMES: I am Peters, Miss, the new butler.

ENID: Oh! *(Sits down beside table and writes.)*

(HOLMES *crosses and stands behind the table. Pause.)*

Why do you stand there? Are you a spy set to watch me? Am I never to have one moment of privacy?

HOLMES: I beg pardon, Miss.

ENID: I'm sorry if I have spoken bitterly. I have had enough to make me bitter.

HOLMES: I'm very sorry, Miss. I'm new to the place and don't quite know where I am yet. May I ask, Miss, if your name is Enid Stonor?

ENID: Yes. Why do you ask?

HOLMES: There was a lad at the station with a message for you.

ENID *(rising)*: A message for me! Oh! it is what I want of all things on earth! Why did you not take it?

HOLMES: I did take it, Miss, it is here. *(Hands her a note.)*

ENID *(tears it open, reads)*: "Fear nothing, and stay where you are. All will be right. Holmes." Oh! it is a ray of sunshine in the darkness—such darkness. Tell me, Peters, who was this boy?

HOLMES: I don't know, Miss—just a very ordinary nipper. The Doctor had gone on to the cab, and the boy touched my sleeve and asked me to give you this note in your own hand.

ENID: You said nothing to the Doctor.

HOLMES: Well, Miss, it seemed to be your business, not his. I just took it, and there it is.

ENID: God bless you for it. *(She conceals the note in her bosom.)*

HOLMES: I'm only a servant, Miss, but if I can be of any help to you, you must let me know.

(HOLMES *goes into the bedroom wing.)*

(ENID *takes the note out of her bosom, reads it again, then hurriedly replaces it as* RYLOTT *and* RODGERS *re-enter.)*

RYLOTT: Very good. You can go and pack your box.

RODGERS *(cringing)*: Yes, sir. You won't—

RYLOTT: That's enough. Get away!

(RODGERS *goes into the servants' hall.)*

(ENID *sits at the tea-table.)*

(Comes over to ENID.) There you are! I want a word or two with you. What the devil do you mean by slipping off to London the moment my back was turned? And what did you do when you got there?

ENID: I went there on my own business.

RYLOTT: Oh! on your own business, was it? Perhaps what you call your own business may prove to be my business also. Who did you see? Come, woman, tell me!

ENID: It was my own business. I am of age. You have no claim to control me.

RYLOTT: I know exactly where you went. You went to the rooms of Mr. Sherlock Holmes, where to met Dr. Watson, who had advised you to go there. Was it not so?

ENID: I will answer no questions. If I did as you say I was within my rights.

RYLOTT: What have you been saying about me? What did you go to consult Mr. Holmes about?

(ENID *remains silent.*)

D'you hear? What did you go about? By God, I'll find a way to make you speak! *(Seizes her by the arm.)* Come!

(Enter HOLMES.)

HOLMES: Yes, sir.

RYLOTT: I did not ring for you.

HOLMES: I thought you called.

RYLOTT: Get out of this! What do you mean?

HOLMES: I beg your pardon, sir.

(He goes into the servants' hall.)

(RYLOTT *goes to the door of the servants' hall, looks through, and then returns.)*

RYLOTT: Look here, Enid, let us be sensible. I was too hot just now. But you must realize the situation. Your wisest and safest course is complete submission. If you do what I tell you there need be no friction between us.

ENID: What do you wish me to do?

RYLOTT: Your marriage will complicate the arrangement which was come to at your mother's death. I want you, of your own free will, to bind yourself to respect it. Come, Enid, you would not wish that your happiness should cause loss and even penury to me. I am an elderly man. I have had losses, too, which make it the more necessary that I should preserve what is left. If you will sign a little deed it will be best for both of us.

ENID: I have promised to sign nothing until a lawyer has seen it.

RYLOTT: Promised. Promised whom?

ENID: I promised my fiancé.

RYLOTT: Oh! you did, did you? But why should lawyers come between you and me, Enid? I beg you—I urge you to do what I ask. *(Opening out papers before her.)*

ENID: No, no, I cannot. I will not.

RYLOTT: Very good! Tell me the truth, Enid. I won't be angry. What are your suspicions of me?

ENID: I have no suspicions.

RYLOTT: Did I not receive your fiancé with civility?

ENID: Yes, you did.

RYLOTT: Have I not, on the whole, been kind to you all this winter?

ENID: Yes, you have.

RYLOTT: Then, tell me, child, why do you suspect me?

ENID: I don't suspect you.

RYLOTT: Why do you send out messages to get help against me?

ENID: I don't understand you.

RYLOTT: Don't you send out for help? Tell me the truth, child.

ENID: No.

RYLOTT *(with a yell)*: You damned little liar! *(Bangs the telegram down before her.)* What was this telegram that you gave to Rodgers?

(ENID *sinks back, half fainting.*)

Ah! you infernal young hypocrite. Shall I read it to you? "Come to me as soon as you can. Please hurry." What did you mean by that? What did you mean, I say? *(Clutching her arm.)* None of your lies —out with it.

ENID: Keep your hands off me, you coward!

RYLOTT: Answer me—answer me, then!

ENID: I will answer you! I believe that you murdered my mother by your neglect. I believe that in some way you drove my sister to her grave. Now, I am certain that you mean to do the same to me. You're a murderer—a murderer! We were left to your care— helpless girls. You have ill-used us—you have tortured us—now you have murdered one of us, and you would do the same to me. You are a coward, a monster, a man fit only for the gallows!

RYLOTT: You'll pay for this, you little devil! Get to your room.

ENID: I will. I'm not without friends, as you may find.

RYLOTT: You've got some plot against me. What have you been arranging in London? What is it? *(Clutches her.)*

ENID: Let me go!

RYLOTT: What did you tell them? By God, I'll twist your head off your shoulders if you cross me! *(Seizes her by the neck.)*

ENID: Help! Help!

(Enter HOLMES.)

HOLMES: Hands off, Dr. Rylott.

(RYLOTT *releases* ENID.)

You had best go to your room, young lady. I'll see that you are not molested. Go at once, I tell you, go.

RYLOTT: You infernal villain. I'll soon settle you.

(After ENID goes out, he runs to a rack at the side, gets a whip, opens the.hall door, stands near it with his whip.)

Now, then, out you go! By George, you'll remember Stoke Moran.

HOLMES: Excuse me, sir, but is that a whip?

RYLOTT: You'll soon see what it is.

HOLMES: I am afraid I must ask you to put it down.

RYLOTT: Oh, indeed! must you? *(Comes forward to him.)*

HOLMES *(taking out a revolver)*: Yes, sir! You'll please put down that whip.

RYLOTT *(falling back)*: You villain!

HOLMES: Stand right back, sir. I'll take no risks with a man like you. Right back, I say! Thank you, sir.

RYLOTT: Rodgers! Ali! My gun!

(He runs into his study.)

HOLMES: Hurry up, Billy! No time to lose.

(Enter BILLY, as Amelia, from the servants' hall.)

BILLY: Yes, Mr. Holmes.

(HOLMES *and* BILLY *go out through the entrance hall.)*

(Several shots are heard outside. RYLOTT rushes in from his study with his gun.)

(Enter ALI — running in from outside.)

ALI: Stop, Sahib, stop!

RYLOTT: What were those shots?

ALI: The new butler, sir. He shoot Siva!

RYLOTT: Shot my dog! By God,.I'll teach him! *(Rushes towards door.)*

ALI: No, no, Sahib. He gone in darkness. What do you do? People come. Police come.

RYLOTT: You're right. *(Puts gun down.)* We have another game; Ali, you will watch outside Miss Enid's window to-night.

ALI: Yes, Sahib, shall I watch all night?

RYLOTT: All night? No, not all night! You will learn when you may cease your watch.

CURTAIN.

SCENE II. — ENID'S *bedroom.*

ENID *is discovered seated near the lamp at a small table near the window. A knock is heard at the door.*

ENID: Who is there?

RYLOTT *(off)*: It is I.

ENID: What do you want?

RYLOTT: Why is your light still burning?

ENID: I have been reading.

RYLOTT: You are not in bed, then?

ENID: Not yet.

RYLOTT: Then I desire to come in.

ENID: But it is so late.

RYLOTT *(rattles door)*: Come, come, let me in this instant.

ENID: No, no, I cannot!

RYLOTT: Must I break the door in?

ENID: I will open it, I will open it. *(Opens door.)* Why do you persecute me so?

(RYLOTT *enters, in his dressing-gown.*)

RYLOTT: Why are you so childish and so suspicious? Your mind has brooded upon your poor sister's death until you have built up these fantastic suspicions against me. Tell me now, Enid — I'm not such a bad sort, you know, if you only deal frankly with me. Tell me, have you any idea of your own about how your sister died? Was that what you went to Mr. Holmes about this morning? Couldn't you take me into your confidence as well as him? Is it not natural that I should feel hurt when I see you turn to a stranger for advice?

ENID: How my poor sister met her death only your own wicked heart can know. I am as sure that it came to her through you as if I had seen you strike her down. You may kill me, if you like, but I *will* tell you what I think.

RYLOTT: My dear child, you are overwrought and hysterical. What can have put such wild ideas into your head? After all, I may have a hasty temper — I have often deplored it to you — but what excuse have I ever given you for such monstrous suspicions?

ENID: You think that by a few smooth words you can make me forget all your past looks, your acts. You cannot deceive me. I know the danger, and I face it.

RYLOTT: What, then, is the danger?

ENID: It is near me to-night, whatever it is.

RYLOTT: Why do you think so?

ENID: Why is that Indian watching in the darkness? I opened my window just now, and there he was. Why is he there?

RYLOTT: To prevent your making a public fool of yourself. You are capable of getting loose and making a scandal.

ENID: He is there to keep me in my room until you come to murder me.

RYLOTT: Upon my word, I think your brain is unhinged. Now, look here, Enid, be reasonable for a moment.

ENID: What's that?

RYLOTT: What is it, then?

ENID: I thought I heard a cry.

RYLOTT: It's the howling of the wind. Listen to me. If there is friction between us — and I don't for a moment deny that there is — why is it? You think I mean to hurt you. I could only have one possible motive for hurting you. Why not remove that motive? Then you could no longer work yourself into these terrors. Here is that legal paper I spoke of. Mrs. Staunton could witness it. All I want is your signature.

ENID: No, never.

RYLOTT: Never!

ENID: Unless my lawyer advises it.

RYLOTT: Is that final?

ENID *(springing up)*: Yes, it is. I will never sign it.

RYLOTT: Well, I have done my best for you. It was your last chance.

ENID: Ah! then you do mean murder.

RYLOTT: The last chance of regaining my favour. You — *(Pause.)* Get to your bed and may you wake in a more rational mood to-morrow. You will not be permitted to make a scandal. Ali will be at his post outside, and I shall sit in the hall; so you may reconcile yourself to being quiet. Nothing more to say to me?

(He goes out.)

(When he has gone, ENID listens to his departing footsteps. Then she locks the door once again, and looks round her.)

ENID: What is that tapping? Surely I heard tapping! Perhaps it is the pulse within my own brain?

(Tapping.)

Yes! there it is again! Where was it? Is it the signal of death? *(Looks wildly round the walls.)* Ah! it grows louder. It is the window. *(Goes towards window.)* A man! a man crouching in the darkness. Still tapping. It's not Ali! The face was white. Ah!

(The window opens and HOLMES *enters.)*

HOLMES: My dear young lady, I trust that I don't intrude.

ENID: Oh, Mr. Holmes, I'm so glad to see you! Save me! save me! Mr. Holmes, they mean to murder me.

HOLMES: Tut, tut! we mean that they shall do nothing of the sort.

ENID: I had given up all hope of your coming.

HOLMES: These old-fashioned window-catches are most inefficient.

ENID: How did you pass the Indian and the dog?

HOLMES: Well, as to the Indian, we chloroformed him. Watson is busy tying him up in the arbour at the present moment. The dog I was compelled to shoot at an earlier stage of the proceedings.

ENID: You shot Siva!

HOLMES: I might have been forced to shoot her master also. It was after I sent you to your room. He threatened me with a whip.

ENID: You were—you were Peters, the butler.

HOLMES *(feeling the walls)*: I wanted to be near you. So this is the famous room, is it? Dear me! very much as I had pictured it. You will excuse me for not discovering myself to you, but any cry or agitation upon your part would have betrayed me.

ENID: But your daughter Amelia?

HOLMES: Ah, yes, I take Billy when I can. Billy as messenger is invaluable.

ENID: Then you intended to watch over me till night?

HOLMES: Exactly. But the man's brutality caused me to show my hand too soon. However, I have never been far from your window. I gather the matter is pressing.

ENID: He means to murder me to-night.

HOLMES: He is certainly in an ugly humour. He is not in his room at present.

ENID: No, he is in the hall.

HOLMES: So we can talk with safety. What has become of the excellent Watson? *(Approaches window.)* Come in, Watson, come in!

(Enter WATSON *from window.)*

How is our Indian friend?

WATSON: He is coming out of the chloroform; but he can neither move nor speak. Good evening, Miss Stonor, what a night it is.

ENID: How can I thank you for coming?

HOLMES: You'll find Dr. Watson a useful companion on such an occasion. He has a natural turn for violence — some survival of his surgical training. The wind is good. Its howling will cover all sounds. Just sit in the window, Watson, and see that our retreat is safe. With your leave, I will inspect the room a little more closely. Now, my dear young lady, I can see that you are frightened to death, and no wonder. Your courage, so far, has been admirable. Sit over here by the fire.

ENID: If he should come —!

HOLMES: In that case answer him. Say that you have gone to bed. *(Takes lamp from table.)* A most interesting old room — very quaint indeed! Old-fashioned comfort without modern luxury. The passage is, as I understand, immediately outside?

ENID: Yes.

HOLMES: Mr. Peters made two attempts to explore the ground, but without avail. By the way, I gather that you tried to send me a message, and that old Rodgers gave it to your stepfather.

ENID: Yes, he did.

HOLMES: He is not to be blamed. His master controls him. He *had* to betray you. *(Placing lamp down.)*

ENID: It was my fault.

HOLMES: Well, well, it was an indiscretion, but it didn't matter. Let me see now, on this side is the room under repair. Quite so. Only one door. This leads into the passage?

ENID: Yes.

HOLMES: And that passage to the hall?

ENID: Yes.

HOLMES: Here is where the genial old gentleman sleeps when he is so innocently employed. Where is his door?

ENID: Down the passage.

HOLMES: Surely I heard him —

(A step is heard in the passage.)

ENID: Yes, it's his step.

(HOLMES *holds his hat over the light. There is a knock at the door.)*

RYLOTT *(outside door)*: Enid!

ENID: What is it?

RYLOTT: Are you in bed?

ENID: Yes.

RYLOTT: Are you still of the same mind?

ENID: Yes, I am.

(Pause. They all listen.)

HOLMES *(whispering)*: Has he gone into his room?

ENID *(crossing to door, listening)*: No, he's gone down the passage again to the hall.

HOLMES: Then we must make the most of the time. Might I trouble you, Watson, for the gimlet and the yard measure? Thank you! The lantern also. Thank you! You can turn up the lamp. I am interested in this partition wall. *(Standing on the bed.)* No little surprise, I suppose? No trap-doors and sliding panels? Funny folk, our ancestors, with a quaint taste in practical joking. *(Gets on bed and fingers the wall.)* No, it seems solid enough. Dear me! and yet you say your sister fastened both door and window. Remarkable. My lens, Watson. A perfectly respectable wall — in fact, a commonplace wall. Trap-door in the floor? *(Kneels at one side of the bed, then the other.)* No, nothing suspicious in that direction. Ancient carpeting — *(crossing round bed)* — oak wain-scot — nothing more. Hullo! *(Pulling at bed-post.)*

WATSON: Why, what is it?

HOLMES: Why is your bed clamped to the floor?

ENID: I really don't know.

HOLMES: Was the bed in your other room clamped?

ENID: No, I don't think it was.

HOLMES: Very interesting. Most interesting and instructive. And this bell-pull — where does it communicate with?

ENID: It does not work.

HOLMES: But if you want to ring?

ENID: There is another over here.

HOLMES: Then why this one?

ENID: I don't know. There were some changes after we came here.

HOLMES: Quite a burst of activity, apparently. It took some strange shapes. *(Standing on the bed.)* You may be interested to know that the bell-rope ends in a brass hook. No wire attachment; it is a dummy. Dear me! how very singular. I see a small screen above it, which covers a ventilator, I suppose?

ENID: Yes, Mr. Holmes, there is a ventilator.

HOLMES: Curious fad to ventilate one room into another when one could as well get the open air. Most original man, the architect. Very singular indeed. There is no means of opening the flap from here; it must open on the other side.

WATSON: What do you make of it, Holmes?

HOLMES: Suggestive, my dear Watson, very suggestive. Might I trouble you for your knife? With your permission, Miss Stonor, I will make a slight alteration. *(Stands on bed-head and cuts the bell-pull.)*

WATSON: Why do you do that, Holmes?

HOLMES: Dangerous, Watson, dangerous. Bear in mind that this opening, concealed by a flap of wood, leads into the room of our cheery Anglo-Indian neighbour. I repeat the adjective, Watson—Anglo-Indian.

WATSON: Well, Holmes?

HOLMES: The bed is clamped so that it cannot be shifted. He has a dummy bell-pull which leads to the bed. He has a hole above it which opens on his room. He is an Anglo-Indian doctor. Do you make nothing of all this? The music, too? The music. What is the music?

WATSON: A signal, Holmes.

HOLMES: A signal! A signal to whom?

WATSON: An accomplice.

HOLMES: Exactly. An accomplice who could enter a room with locked doors—an accomplice who could give a sure death which leaves no trace. An accomplice who can only be attracted back by music.

ENID: Hush! he is gone to his room.

(A door is heard to close outside.)

Listen! The door is shut.

HOLMES *(as* WATSON *is about to take up lamp)*: Keep the lamp covered, so that if the ventilator is opened no light will show. He must think the girl is asleep. Keep the dark lantern handy. We must wait in the dark. I fancy we shall not have long to wait.

ENID: I am so frightened.

HOLMES: It is too much for you.

WATSON: Can I do anything, Holmes?

HOLMES: You can hand me my hunting-crop. Hush! What's that?

(Flute music is heard.)

My stick, Watson — quick, be quick! Now take the lantern. Have you got it? When I cry, "Now!" turn it full blaze upon the top of the bell-rope. Do you understand?

WATSON: Yes.

HOLMES: Down that bell-rope comes the messenger of death. It guides it to the girl's pillow. Hush! the flap!

(The flap opens, disclosing a small square of light. This light is obscured. Music a good deal louder.)

(Cries sharply.) Now!

(WATSON *turns the lantern full on to the bell-rope. A snake is seen half through the hole.* HOLMES *lashes at it with his stick. It disappears backwards.)*

(The flute music stops.)

WATSON: It has gone.

HOLMES: Yes, it has gone, but we know the truth.

(A loud cry is heard.)

WATSON: What is that?

HOLMES: I believe the devil has turned on its master.

(Another cry.)

It is in the passage. *(Throws open the door.)*

(In the doorway is seen DR. RYLOTT *in shirt and trousers, the snake round his head and neck.)*

RYLOTT: Save me! save me!

(RYLOTT *rushes in and falls on the floor.* WATSON *strikes at the snake as it writhes across the room.)*

WATSON *(looking at the snake)*: The brute is dead.
HOLMES *(looking at* RYLOTT): So is the other.

(They both run to support the fainting lady.)

Miss Stonor, there is no more danger for you under this roof.

CURTAIN.

The Crown Diamond
An Evening with Sherlock Holmes

Characters

MR. SHERLOCK HOLMES
The famous Detective.

DR. WATSON
His Friend.

BILLY
Page to MR. HOLMES.

COL. SEBASTIAN MORAN
An intellectual Criminal.

SAM MERTON
A Boxer.

SCENE. — MR. HOLMES'S *room in Baker Street. It presents the usual features, but there is a deep bow window to it, and across there is drawn a curtain running upon a brass rod fastened across eight feet above the ground, and enclosing the recess of the window.*

Enter WATSON *and* BILLY.

WATSON: Well, Billy, when will he be back?

BILLY: I'm sure I couldn't say, sir.

WATSON: When did you see him last?

BILLY: I really couldn't tell you.

WATSON: What, you couldn't tell me?

BILLY: No, sir. There was a clergyman looked in yesterday, and there was an old bookmaker, and there was a workman.

WATSON: Well?

BILLY: But I'm not sure they weren't *all* Mr. Holmes. You see, he's very hot on a chase just now.

WATSON: Oh!

BILLY: He neither eats nor sleeps. Well, you've lived with him same as me. You know what he's like when he's after some one.

WATSON: I know.

BILLY: He's a responsibility, sir, that he is. It's a real worry to me sometimes. When I asked him if he would order dinner, he said, "Yes, I'll have chops and mashed potatoes at 7.30 the day after to-morrow." "Won't you eat before then, sir?" I asked. "I haven't time, Billy, I'm busy," said he. He gets thinner and paler, and his eyes get brighter. It's awful to see him.

WATSON: Tut, tut, this will never do. I must certainly stop and see him.

BILLY: Yes, sir, it will ease my mind.

WATSON: But what is he after?

BILLY: It's this case of the Crown Diamond.

WATSON: What, the hundred thousand pound burglary?

BILLY: Yes, sir. They must get it back, sir. Why, we had the Prime Minister and the Home Secretary both sitting on that very sofa. Mr. Holmes promised he'd do his very best for them. Quite nice he was to them. Put them at their ease in a moment.

278

WATSON: Dear me! I've read about it in the paper. But I say, Billy, what have you been doing to the room? What's this curtain?

BILLY: I don't know, sir. Mr. Holmes had it put there three days ago. But we've got something funny behind it.

WATSON: Something funny?

BILLY *(laughing)*: Yes, sir. He had it made.

(BILLY *goes to the curtain and draws it across, disclosing a wax image of Holmes seated in a chair, back to the audience.*)

WATSON: Good heavens, Billy!

BILLY: Yes, sir. It's like him, sir. *(Picks the head off and exhibits it.)*

WATSON: It's wonderful! But what's it for, Billy?

BILLY: You see, sir, he's anxious that those who watch him should think he's at home sometimes when he isn't. There's the bell, sir. *(Replaces head, draws curtain.)* I must go.

(BILLY *goes out.*)

(WATSON *sits down, lights a cigarette, and opens a paper. Enter a tall, bent* OLD WOMAN *in black with veil and side-curls.*)

WATSON *(rising)*: Good day, Ma'm.

WOMAN: You're not Mr. Holmes?

WATSON: No, Ma'm. I'm his friend, Dr. Watson.

WOMAN: I knew you couldn't be Mr. Holmes. I'd always heard *he* was a handsome man.

WATSON *(aside)*: Upon my word!

WOMAN: But I must see him at once.

WATSON: I assure you he is not in.

WOMAN: I don't believe you.

WATSON: What!

WOMAN: You have a sly, deceitful face—oh, yes, a wicked, scheming face. Come, young man, where is he?

WATSON: Really, Madam . . . !

WOMAN: Very well, I'll find him for myself. He's in there, I believe. *(Walks toward bedroom door.)*

WATSON *(rising and crossing)*: That is his bedroom. Really, Madam, this is outrageous!

WOMAN: I wonder what he keeps in this safe.

(She approaches it, and as she does so the lights go out, and the room is in darkness save for "DON'T TOUCH" *in red fire over the safe. Four red lights spring up, and between them the inscription* "DON'T TOUCH!" *After a few seconds the lights go on again, and* HOLMES *is standing beside* WATSON.)

WATSON: Good heavens, Holmes!

HOLMES: Neat little alarm, is it not, Watson? My own invention. You tread on a loose plank and so connect the circuit, or I can turn it on myself. It prevents inquisitive people becoming too inquisitive. When I come back I know if any one has been fooling with my things. It switches off again automatically, as you saw.

WATSON: But my dear fellow, why this disguise?

HOLMES: A little comic relief, Watson. When I saw you sitting there looking so solemn, I really couldn't help it. But I assure you, there is nothing comic in the business I am engaged upon. Good heavens! *(Rushes across room, and draws curtain, which has been left partly open.)*

WATSON: Why, what is it?

HOLMES: Danger, Watson. Airguns, Watson. I'm expecting something this evening.

WATSON: Expecting what, Holmes?

HOLMES *(lighting pipe)*: Expecting to be murdered, Watson.

WATSON: No, no, you are joking, Holmes!

HOLMES: Even my limited sense of humour could evolve a better joke than that, Watson. No, it is a fact. And in case it should come off—it's about a two to one chance—it would perhaps be as well that you should burden your memory with the name and address of the murderer.

WATSON: Holmes!

HOLMES: You can give it to Scotland Yard with my love and a parting blessing. Moran is the name. Colonel Sebastian Moran. Write it down, Watson, write it down! 136, Moorside Gardens, N.W. Got it?

WATSON: But surely something can be done, Holmes. Couldn't you have this fellow arrested?

HOLMES: Yes, Watson, I could. That's what's worrying him so.

WATSON: But why don't you?

HOLMES: Because I don't know where the diamond is.

WATSON: What diamond?

HOLMES: Yes, yes, the great yellow Crown Diamond, seventy-seven carats, lad, and without flaw. I have two fish in the net. But I haven't got the stone there. And what's the use of taking *them?* It's the stone I'm after.

WATSON: Is this Colonel Moran one of the fish in the net?

HOLMES: Yes, and he's a shark. He bites. The other is Sam Merton the boxer. Not a bad fellow, Sam, but the Colonel has used him. Sam's not a shark. He's a big silly gudgeon. But he's flopping about in my net, all the same.

WATSON: Where is this Colonel Moran?

HOLMES: I've been at his elbow all morning. Once he picked up my parasol. "By your leave, Ma'm," said he. Life is full of whimsical happenings. I followed him to old Straubenzee's workshop in the Minories. Straubenzee made the airgun — fine bit of work, I understand.

WATSON: An airgun?

HOLMES: The idea was to shoot me through the window. I had to put up that curtain. By the way, have you seen the dummy? *(Draws curtain.)*

(WATSON nods.)

Ah! Billy has been showing you the sights. It may get a bullet through its beautiful wax head at any moment.

(Enter BILLY.)

Well, Billy?

BILLY: Colonel Sebastian Moran, sir.

HOLMES: Ah! the man himself. I rather expected it. Grasp the nettle, Watson. A man of nerve! He felt my toe on his heels. *(Looks out of window.)* And there is Sam Merton in the street — the faithful but fatuous Sam. Where is the Colonel, Billy?

BILLY: Waiting-room, sir.

HOLMES: Show him up when I ring.

BILLY: Yes, sir.

HOLMES: Oh, by the way, Billy, if I am not in the room show him in just the same.

BILLY: Very good, sir.

(BILLY goes out.)

WATSON: I'll stay with you, Holmes.

HOLMES: No, my dear fellow, you would be horribly in the way. *(Goes to the table and scribbles a note.)*

WATSON: He may murder you.

HOLMES: I shouldn't be surprised.

WATSON: I can't possibly leave you.

HOLMES: Yes, you can, my dear Watson, for you've always played the game, and I am very sure that you will play it to the end. Take this note to Scotland Yard. Come back with the police. The fellow's arrest will follow.

WATSON: I'll do that with joy.

HOLMES: And before you return I have just time to find out where the diamond is. *(Rings bell.)* This way, Watson. We'll go together. I rather want to see my shark without his seeing me.

(WATSON and HOLMES go into the bedroom.)

(Enter BILLY and COLONEL SEBASTIAN MORAN, who is a fierce, big man, flashily dressed, with a heavy cudgel.)

BILLY: Colonel Sebastian Moran.

(BILLY goes out.)

(COLONEL MORAN looks round, advances slowly into the room, and starts as he sees the dummy figure sitting in the window. He stares at it, then crouches, grips his stick, and advances on tip-toe. When close to the figure he raises his stick. HOLMES comes quickly out of the bedroom door.)

HOLMES: Don't break it, Colonel, don't break it.

COLONEL *(staggering back)*: Good Lord!

HOLMES: It's such a pretty little thing. Tavernier, the French modeller, made it. He is as good at waxwork as Straubenzee is at airguns. *(Shuts curtains.)*

COLONEL: Airguns, sir. Airguns! What do you mean?

HOLMES: Put your hat and stick on the side table. Thank you. Pray take a seat. Would you care to put your revolver out also? Oh, very good, if you prefer to sit upon it.

(The COLONEL sits down.)

I wanted to have five minutes' chat with you.

COLONEL: I wanted to have five minutes' chat with *you.*

(HOLMES *sits down near him and crosses his leg.)*

I won't deny that I intended to assault you just now.

HOLMES: It struck me that some idea of that sort had crossed your mind.

COLONEL: And with reason, sir, with reason.

HOLMES: But why this attention?

COLONEL: Because you have gone out of your way to annoy me. Because you have put your creatures on my track.

HOLMES: My creatures?

COLONEL: I have had them followed. I know that they come to report to you here.

HOLMES: No, I assure you.

COLONEL: Tut, sir! Other people can observe as well as you. Yesterday there was an old sporting man; to-day it was an elderly lady. They held me in view all day.

HOLMES: Really, sir, you compliment me! Old Baron Dowson, before he was hanged at Newgate, was good enough to say that in my case what the law had gained the stage had lost. And now you come along with your kindly words. In the name of the elderly lady and of the sporting gentleman I thank you. There was also an out-of-work plumber who was an artistic dream — you seem to have overlooked him.

COLONEL: It was you . . . you!

HOLMES: Your humble servant! If you doubt it, you can see the parasol upon the settee which you so politely handed to me this morning down in the Minories.

COLONEL: If I had known you might never —

HOLMES: Never have seen this humble home again. I was well aware of it. But it happens you didn't know, and here we are, quite chatty and comfortable.

COLONEL: What you say only makes matters worse. It was not your agents, but you yourself, who have dogged me. Why have you done this?

HOLMES: You used to shoot tigers?

COLONEL: Yes, sir.

HOLMES: But why?

COLONEL: Pshaw! Why does any man shoot a tiger? The excitement. The danger.

HOLMES: And no doubt the satisfaction of freeing the country from a pest, which devastates it and lives on the population.

COLONEL: Exactly.

HOLMES: My reasons in a nutshell.

COLONEL *(springing to his feet)*: Insolent!

HOLMES: Sit down, sir, sit down! There was another more practical reason.

COLONEL: Well?

HOLMES: I want that yellow Crown Diamond.

COLONEL: Upon my word! Well, go on.

HOLMES: You knew that I was after you for that. The real reason why you are here to-night is to find out how much I know about the matter. Well, you can take it that I know *all* about it save one thing, which you are about to tell me.

COLONEL *(sneering)*: And, pray, what is that?

HOLMES: Where the diamond is.

COLONEL: Oh, you want to know that, do you? How the devil should I know where it is?

HOLMES: You not only know, but you are about to tell me.

COLONEL: Oh, indeed!

HOLMES: You can't bluff me, Colonel. You're absolute plate glass. I see to the very back of your mind.

COLONEL: Then of course you see where the diamond is.

HOLMES: Ah! then you do know. You have admitted it.

COLONEL: I admit nothing.

HOLMES: Now, Colonel, if you will be reasonable we can do business together. If not you may get hurt.

COLONEL: And *you* talk about bluff!

HOLMES *(raising a book from the table)*: Do you know what I keep inside this book?

COLONEL: No, sir, I do not.

HOLMES: You.

COLONEL: Me!

HOLMES: Yes, sir, *you.* You're all here, every action of your vile and dangerous life.

COLONEL: Damn you, Holmes! Don't go too far.

HOLMES: Some interesting details, Colonel. The real facts as to the death of Miss Minnie Warrender of Laburnum Grove. All here, Colonel.

COLONEL: You—you devil!

HOLMES: And the story of young Arbothnot, who was found drowned in the Regents Canal just before his intended exposure of you for cheating at cards.

COLONEL: I—I never hurt the boy.

HOLMES: But he died at a very seasonable time. Do you want some more, Colonel? Plenty of it here. How about the robbery in the train deluxe to the Riviera, February 13th, 1892? How about the forged cheque on the Credit Lyonnais the same year?

COLONEL: No, you're wrong there.

HOLMES: Then I'm right on the others. Now, Colonel, you are a card-player. When the other fellow holds all the trumps it saves time to throw down your hand.

COLONEL: If there was a word of truth in all this, would I have been a free man all these years?

HOLMES: I was not consulted. There were missing links in the police case. But I have a way of finding missing links. You may take it from me that I could do so.

COLONEL: Bluff! Mr. Holmes, bluff!

HOLMES: Oh, you wish me to prove my words! Well, if I touch this bell it means the police, and from that instant the matter is out of my hands. Shall I?

COLONEL: What has all this to do with the jewel you speak of?

HOLMES: Gently, Colonel! Restrain that eager mind. Let me get to the point in my own hum-drum way. I have all this against you, and I also have a clear case against both you and your fighting bully in this case of the Crown Diamond.

COLONEL: Indeed!

HOLMES: I have the cabman who took you to Whitehall, and the cabman who brought you away. I have the commissionaire who saw you beside the case. I have Ikey Cohen who refused to cut it up for you. Ikey has peached, and the game is up.

COLONEL: Hell!

HOLMES: That's the hand I play from. But there's one card missing. I don't know where this king of diamonds is.

COLONEL: You never shall know.

HOLMES: Tut! tut! don't turn nasty. Now, consider. You're going to be locked up for twenty years. So is Sam Merton. What good are you going to get out of your diamond? None in the world. But if you let me know where it is. . . well, I'll compound a felony. We don't want you or Sam. We want the stone. Give that up, and so far as I am concerned you can go free so long as you behave yourself in the future. If you make another slip, then God help you. But this time my commission is to get the stone, not you. *(Rings bell.)*

COLONEL: But if I refuse?

HOLMES: Then, alas, it must be you, not the stone.

(Enter BILLY.)

BILLY: Yes, sir.

HOLMES *(to the* COLONEL*)*: I think we had better have your friend Sam at this conference. Billy, you will see a large and very ugly gentleman outside the front door. Ask him to come up, will you?

BILLY: Yes, sir. Suppose he won't come, sir?

HOLMES: No force, Billy! Don't be rough with him. If you tell him Colonel Moran wants him, he will come.

BILLY: Yes, sir.

(BILLY goes out.)

COLONEL: What's the meaning of this, then?

HOLMES: My friend Watson was with me just now. I told him that I had a shark and a gudgeon in my net. Now, I'm drawing the net and up they come together.

COLONEL *(leaning forward)*: You won't die in your bed, Holmes!

HOLMES: D'you know, I have often had the same idea. For that matter, your own finish is more likely to be perpendicular than horizontal. But these anticipations are morbid. Let us give ourselves up to the unrestrained enjoyment of the present. No good fingering your revolver, my friend, for you know perfectly well that you dare not use it. Nasty, noisy things, revolvers. Better stick to airguns, Colonel Moran. Ah!. . .I think I hear the fairy footsteps of your estimable partner.

(Enter BILLY.*)*

BILLY: Mr. Sam Merton.

(Enter SAM MERTON, *in check suit and loud necktie, yellow overcoat.)*

HOLMES: Good day, Mr. Merton. Rather damp in the street, is it not?

(BILLY *goes out.)*

MERTON *(to the* COLONEL*)*: What's the game? What's up?

HOLMES: If I may put it in a nutshell, Mr. Merton, I should say it is *all* up.

MERTON *(to the* COLONEL*)*: Is this cove tryin' to be funny — or what? I'm not in the funny mood myself.

HOLMES: You'll feel even less humourous as the evening advances, I think I can promise you that. Now, look here, Colonel. I'm a busy man and I can't waste time. I'm going into the bedroom. Pray make yourselves entirely at home in my absence. You can explain to your friend how the matter lies. I shall try over the Barcarolle upon my violin. *(Looks at watch.)* In five minutes I shall return for your final answer. You quite grasp the alternative, don't you? Shall we take you, or shall we have the stone?

(HOLMES *goes into his bedroom, taking his violin with him.)*

MERTON: What's that? He knows about the stone!

COLONEL: Yes, he knows a dashed sight too much about it. I'm not sure that he doesn't know *all* about it.

MERTON: Good Lord!

COLONEL: Ikey Cohen has split.

MERTON: He has, has he? I'll do him down a thick 'un for that.

COLONEL: But that won't help us. We've got to make up our minds what to do.

MERTON: Half a mo'. He's not listening, is he? *(Approaches bedroom door.)* No, it's shut. Look to me as if it was locked.

(Music begins.)

Ah! there he is, safe enough. *(Goes to curtain.)* Here, I say! *(Draws it back, disclosing the figure.)* Here's that cove again, blast him!

COLONEL: Tut! it's a dummy. Never mind it.

MERTON: A fake, is it? *(Examines it, and turns the head.)* By. Gosh, I wish I could twist his own as easy. Well, strike me! Madame Tussaud ain't in it!

(As MERTON *returns towards the* COLONEL, *the lights suddenly go out, and the red* "DON'T TOUCH" *signal goes up. After a few seconds the lights readjust themselves. Figures must transpose at that moment.)*

Well, dash my buttons! Look 'ere, Guv'nor, this is gettin' on my nerves. Is it unsweetened gin, or what?

COLONEL: Tut! it is some childish hanky-panky of this fellow Holmes, a spring or an alarm or something. Look here, there's no time to lose. He can lag us for the diamond.

MERTON: The hell he can!

COLONEL: But he'll let us slip if we only tell him where the stone is.

MERTON: What, give up the swag! Give up a hundred thousand!

COLONEL: It's one or the other.

MERTON: No way out? You've got the brains, Guv'nor. Surely you can think a way out of it.

COLONEL: Wait a bit! I've fooled better men than he. Here's the stone in my secret pocket. It can be out of England to-night, and cut into four pieces in Amsterdam before Saturday. He knows nothing of Van Seddor.

MERTON: I thought Van Seddor was to wait till next week.

COLONEL: Yes, he *was.* But now he must get the next boat. One or other of us must slip round with the stone to the "Excelsior" and tell him.

MERTON: But the false bottom ain't in the hat-box yet!

COLONEL: Well, he must take it as it is and chance it. There's not a moment to lose. As to Holmes, we can fool him easily enough. You see, he won't arrest us if he thinks he can get the stone. We'll put him on the wrong track about it, and before he finds it *is* the wrong track, the stone will be in Amsterdam, and we out of the country.

MERTON: That's prime.

COLONEL: You go off now, and tell Van Seddor to get a move on him. I'll see this sucker and fill him up with a bogus confession. The stone's in Liverpool—that's what I'll tell him. By the time he finds it isn't, there won't be much of it left, and we'll be on blue water. *(He looks carefully round him, then draws a small leather box from his pocket, and holds it out.)* Here is the Crown Diamond.

HOLMES *(taking it, as he rises from his chair)*: I thank you.

COLONEL *(staggering back)*: Curse you, Holmes! *(Puts hand in pocket.)*

MERTON: To hell with him!

HOLMES: No violence, gentlemen; no violence, I beg of you. It must be very clear to you that your position is an impossible one. The police are waiting below.

COLONEL: You—you devil! How did you get there?

HOLMES: The device is obvious but effective; lights off for a moment and the rest is common sense. It gave me a chance of listening to your racy conversation which would have been painfully constrained by a knowledge of my presence. No, Colonel, no. I am covering you with a .450 Derringer through the pocket of my dressing-gown. *(Rings bell.)*

(Enter BILLY.)

Send them up, Billy.

(BILLY *goes out.)*

COLONEL: Well, you've got us, damn you!

MERTON: A fair cop. . . . But I say, what about that bloomin' fiddle?

HOLMES: Ah, yes, these modern gramophones! Wonderful invention. Wonderful!

CURTAIN.

An Outline

In 1942, while researching his book CONAN DOYLE: HIS LIFE AND ART, *Hesketh Pearson made two important discoveries among Sir Arthur's papers. One was the typescript of "The Case of the Man Who Was Wanted." The other was an outline for an unwritten Sherlock Holmes story.*

Doyle worked out each Holmes adventure with methodical care, Pearson wrote, "first of all thinking out the problem and its solution, then sketching the main outline, then writing the story." The plot sketch which he found had not been written into a story, for Doyle must have realized it was not up to standard. Still, it is an enjoyable insight into the author's methods. Pearson seems to have been of the opinion that it dated from about 1892.

Plot for Sherlock Holmes Story

A girl calls on Sherlock Holmes in great distress. A murder has been committed in her village — her uncle has been found shot in his bedroom, apparently through the open window. Her lover has been arrested. He is suspected on several grounds.

(1) He has had a violent quarrel with the old man, who has threatened to alter his will, which is in the girl's favour, if she ever speaks to her lover again.

(2) A revolver has been found in his house, with his initials scratched on the butt, and one chamber discharged. The bullet found in the dead man's body fits this revolver.

(3) He possesses a light ladder, the only one in the village, and there are the marks of the foot of such a ladder on the soil below the bedroom window, while similar soil (fresh) has been found on the feet of the ladder.

His only reply is that he never possessed a revolver, and that it has been discovered in a drawer of the hatstand in his hall, where it would be easy for anyone to place it. As for the mould on the ladder (which he has not used for a month) he has no explanation whatever.

Notwithstanding these damning proofs, however, the girl persists in believing her lover to be perfectly innocent, while she suspects another man, who has also been making love to her, though she has no evidence whatever against him, except that she feels by instinct that he is a villain who would stick at nothing.

Sherlock and Watson go down to the village and inspect the spot, together with the detective in charge of the case. The marks of the ladder attract Holmes's special attention. He ponders — looks about him — inquires if there is any place where anything bulky could be concealed. There is — a disused well, which has not been searched because apparently nothing is missing. Sherlock, however, insists on the well being explored. A village boy consents to be lowered into it, with a candle. Before he goes down Holmes whispers something in his ear — he appears surprised. The boy is

295

lowered and, on his signal, pulled up again. He brings to the surface *a pair of stilts!*

"Good Lord!" cries the detective, "who on earth could have expected this?" — "I did," replies Holmes. — "But why?" — "Because the marks on the garden soil were made by two perpendicular poles — the feet of a ladder, which is on the slope, would have made depressions slanting towards the wall."

(N.B. The soil was a strip beside a gravel path on which the stilts left no impression.)

This discovery lessened the weight of the evidence of the ladder, though the other evidence remained.

The next step was to trace the user of the stilts, if possible. But he had been too wary, and after two days nothing had been discovered. At the inquest the young man was found guilty of murder. But Holmes is convinced of his innocence. In these circumstances, and as a last hope, he resolves on a sensational strategem.

He goes up to London, and, returning on the evening of the day when the old man is buried, he and Watson and the detective go to the cottage of the man whom the girl suspects, taking with them a man whom Holmes has brought from London, who has a disguise which makes him the living image of the murdered man, wizened body, grey shrivelled face, skull-cap, and all. They have also with them the pair of stilts. On reaching the cottage, the disguised man mounts the stilts and stalks up the path towards the man's open bedroom window, at the same time crying out his name in a ghastly sepulchral voice. The man, who is already half mad with guilty terrors, rushes to the window and beholds in the moonlight the terrific spectacle of his victim stalking towards him. He reels back with a scream as the apparition, advancing to the window, calls in the same unearthly voice — "As you came for me, I have come for you!" When the party rush upstairs into his room he darts to them, clinging to them, gasping, and, pointing to the window, where the dead man's face is glaring in, shrieks out, "Save me! My God! He has come for me as I came for him."

Collapsing after this dramatic scene, he makes a full confession. He has marked the revolver, and concealed it where it was found — he has also smeared the ladder-foot with soil from the old man's garden. His object was to put his rival out of the way, in the hope of gaining possession of the girl and her money.

The Discovery

For many, "The Case of the Man Who Was Wanted" is the most fascinating of all the published Apocrypha. It was not written by Sir Arthur Conan Doyle. It was written by an unemployed architect named Arthur Whitaker. Yet it was published in Sir Arthur's name by his heirs in the innocent belief that it was genuine.

The story was composed and sent to Conan Doyle in 1910, in the desperate hope that Doyle might consider a collaboration. Sir Arthur understandably declined to collaborate, but, in a most courteous letter to Whitaker, he praised the tale and suggested that Whitaker rewrite it with characters of his own. Failing that, he offered £10 for the use of the plot, though he could not undertake to guarantee he would ever use it. The impoverished Whitaker preferred the immediate prospect of the £10, and his typescript went in among Doyle's papers. The idea was never used.

Sir Arthur died on 7 July 1930, and his papers lay undisturbed for many years. Hesketh Pearson, in 1942, became the first to go through them, and he discovered "The Man Who Was Wanted."

The Sherlockian world was electrified. A heretofore unknown Sherlock Holmes adventure! Pressure from many sources immediately came to bear on the Conan Doyle Estate to publish the piece. A paragraph or two were printed in Pearson's 1943 biography of Doyle, but the Estate resisted the many offers for its publication, preferring to wait until the end of the Second World War and a more favourable literary climate.

At last, COSMOPOLITAN made a satisfactory offer, and "The Case of the Man Who Was Wanted" appeared in the August 1948 issue of that magazine, as well as in Britain's THE SUNDAY DISPATCH during January 1949.

Then the truth came out. Arthur Whitaker, now retired, was still living. He contacted the Estate and was able to produce his *carbon copy of the typescript as well as Conan Doyle's hand-written letter, dated thirty-eight years earlier, in which Doyle had offered to purchase the plot.*

The Estate was embarrassed, to be sure. Some of THE SUNDAY DISPATCH'S *money had to be refunded. Whitaker himself was bought off for £150 and died soon after, and the whole thing was hushed up. No statement of correction was ever printed by* COSMOPOLITAN, *and the Conan Doyle Estate never issued any comment on the affair whatever. "The Case of the Man Who Was Wanted" was suppressed. It is reprinted here for the first time anywhere.*

In hindsight, of course, it is difficult to understand how anyone could have believed that "The Man Who Was Wanted" was written by Doyle. The first clue should have been the typewritten manuscript. Doyle's works were almost invariably handwritten, either by himself or his secretary, Major Alfred Wood. They were seldom typed. Beyond that, the tale is well crafted, and in general its tone rings true, but the diction, especially in the dialogue, is nothing like Doyle's. Its progression, too, its "procedural" detail, is subtly off colour.

These points aside, however, Whitaker's story is one of the best serious pastiches of Sherlock Holmes ever written. He has captured Holmes's personality to a hair (even if Gillette's cushions do creep in at the beginning), and the clues presented, and Holmes's inferences from them, are as authentically "Sherlockian" as anything Doyle wrote. So is the opening scene in the Baker Street rooms, with its conversation over stairways and vacation plans (though the British Museum theft is a bit much), as well as the detective's petulance against Mr. Jervis the bank manager and his remarks on the apparent foolishness of the culprit. Whitaker is wider of the mark with Watson, whose uncharacteristic quotation of Dickens's Sam Weller is a little jolting, and he does not even come close to an accurate portrayal of Inspector Lestrade. The plot twist and the long closing scene with Lestrade, though, are just the sorts of things Doyle might have concocted.

There are several minor "Watsonisms"—the good doctor was a widower in 1895, and in medical retirement, not a married man with a thriving practice, and the dates of Jabez Booth's residence at Mrs. Purnell's lodging house are "hopelessly discordant," in the words of one commentator—but the severer criticisms which have been levelled against the work are spurious ones. The samples of Booth's handwriting might well have been procured at the earlier visit to the Sheffield police or from Mr. Jervis. Holmes's eight or ten hours by himself were more than adequate to locate "Mr. Winter's" lodgings. Booth's dual imposture aboard the EMPRESS QUEEN *is no more improbable than are the incidents in Doyle's own adventures of "A Case of Identity" or "The Five Orange Pips." Whitaker's tale holds together without a flaw.*

In sum, then, "The Case of the Man Who Was Wanted" is as good as most of the "Canonical" Sherlock Holmes stories and is better than some. Doyle did not write it, but he might have. And had he done so, he need not have been in the least ashamed of it.

The Case of
the Man Who Was Wanted

by Arthur Whitaker

During the late autumn of 'ninety-five a fortunate chance
enabled me to take some part in another of my friend Sherlock
Holmes's fascinating cases.

My wife not having been well for some time, I had at last
persuaded her to take a holiday in Switzerland in the company of
her old school friend Kate Whitney, whose name may be
remembered in connection with the strange case I have already
chronicled under the title of "The Man with the Twisted Lip." My
practice had grown much, and I had been working very hard for
many months and never felt in more need myself of a rest and a
holiday. Unfortunately I dared not absent myself for a long
enough period to warrant a visit to the Alps. I promised my wife,
however, that I would get a week or ten days' holiday in somehow,
and it was only on this understanding that she consented to the
Swiss tour I was so anxious for her to take. One of my best patients
was in a very critical state at the time, and it was not until August
was gone that he passed the crisis and began to recover. Feeling
then that I could leave my patient in the hands of a *locum tenens,*
I began to wonder where and how I should best find the rest and
change I needed.

Almost at once the idea came to my mind that I would hunt up
my old friend Sherlock Holmes, of whom I had seen nothing for
several months. If he had no important inquiry in hand, I would
do my uttermost to persuade him to join me.

Within half an hour of coming to this resolution I was standing
in the doorway of the familiar old room in Baker Street.

Holmes was stretched upon the couch with his back towards
me, the familiar dressing gown and old brier pipe as much in
evidence as of yore.

"Come in, Watson," he cried, without glancing round. "Come
in and tell me what good wind blows you here?"

"What an ear you have, Holmes," I said. "I don't think that I could have recognized your tread so easily."

"Nor I yours," said he, "if you hadn't come up my badly lighted staircase taking the steps two at a time with all the familiarity of an old fellow lodger; even then I might not have been sure who it was, but when you stumbled over the new mat outside the door which has been there for nearly three months, you needed no further announcement."

Holmes pulled out two or three of the cushions from the pile he was lying on and threw them across into the armchair. "Sit down, Watson, and make yourself comfortable; you'll find cigarettes in a box behind the clock."

As I proceeded to comply, Holmes glanced whimsically across at me. "I'm afraid I shall have to disappoint you, my boy," he said. "I had a wire only half an hour ago which will prevent me from joining in any little trip you may have been about to propose."

"Really, Holmes," I said, "don't you think this is going a little *too* far? I begin to fear you are a fraud and pretend to discover things by observation, when all the time you really do it by pure out-and-out clairvoyance!"

Holmes chuckled. "Knowing you as I do, it's absurdly simple," said he. "Your surgery hours are from five to seven, yet at six o'clock you walk smiling into my rooms. Therefore you must have a *locum* in. You are looking well, though tired, so the obvious reason is that you are having, or about to have, a holiday. The clinical thermometer, peeping out of your pocket, proclaims that you have been on your rounds to-day, hence it's pretty evident that your real holiday begins to-morrow. When, under these circumstances, you come hurrying into my rooms—which, by the way, Watson, you haven't visited for nearly three months—with a new Bradshaw and a timetable of excursion bookings bulging out of your coat pocket, then it's more than probable you have come with the idea of suggesting some joint expedition."

"It's all perfectly true," I said, and explained to him, in a few words, my plans. "And I'm more disappointed than I can tell you," I concluded, "that you are not able to fall in with my little scheme."

Holmes picked up a telegram from the table and looked at it thoughtfully. "If only the inquiry this refers to promised to be of anything like the interest of some we have gone into together, nothing would have delighted me more than to have persuaded you to throw your lot in with mine for a time; but really I'm afraid to do so, for it sounds a particularly commonplace affair," and he crumpled the paper into a ball and tossed it over to me.

I smoothed it out and read: "To Holmes, 221B Baker Street, London, S.W. Please come to Sheffield at once to inquire into case of forgery. Jervis, Manager British Consolidated Bank."

"I've wired back to say I shall go up to Sheffield by the one-thirty-A.M. express from St. Pancras," said Holmes. "I can't go sooner as I have an interesting little appointment to fulfill to-night down in the East End, which should give me the last information I need to trace home a daring robbery from the British Museum to its instigator—who possesses one of the oldest titles and finest houses in the country, along with a most insatiable greed, almost mania, for collecting ancient documents. Before discussing the Sheffield affair any further, however, we had perhaps better see what the evening paper has to say about it," continued Holmes, as his boy entered with the *Evening News, Standard, Globe* and *Star.* "Ah, this must be it," he said, pointing to a paragraph headed: "Daring Forger's Remarkable Exploits in Sheffield."

"Whilst going to press we have been informed that a series of most cleverly forged cheques have been successfully used to swindle the Sheffield banks out of a sum which cannot be less than six thousand pounds. The full extent of the fraud has not yet been ascertained, and the managers of the different banks concerned, who have been interviewed by our Sheffield correspondent, are very reticent.

"It appears that a gentleman named Mr. Jabez Booth, who resides at Broomhill, Sheffield, and has been an employee since January, 1881, at the British Consolidated Bank in Sheffield, yesterday succeeded in cashing quite a number of cleverly forged cheques at twelve of the principal banks in the city and absconding with the proceeds.

"The crime appears to have been a strikingly deliberate and well-thought-out one. Mr. Booth had, of course, in his position in one of the principal banks in Sheffield, excellent opportunities of studying the various signatures which he forged, and he greatly facilitated his chances of easily and successfully obtaining cash for the cheques by opening banking accounts last year at each of the twelve banks at which he presented the forged cheques, and by this means becoming personally known at each.

"He still further disarmed suspicion by crossing each of the forged cheques and paying them into his account, while, at the same time, he drew and cashed a cheque of his own for about half the amount of the forged cheque paid in.

"It was not until early this morning, Thursday, that the fraud was discovered, which means that the rascal has had some twenty hours in which to make good his escape. In spite of this we have little doubt but that he will soon be laid by the heels, for we are informed that the finest detectives from Scotland Yard are already upon his track, and it is also whispered that Mr. Sherlock Holmes, the well-known and almost world-famed criminal expert of Baker Street, has been asked to assist in hunting down this daring forger."

"Then there follows a lengthy description of the fellow, which I needn't read but will keep for future use," said Holmes, folding the paper and looking across at me. "It seems to have been a pretty smart affair. This Booth may not be easily caught for, though he hasn't had a long time in which to make his escape, we mustn't lose sight of the fact that he's had twelve months in which to plan how he would do the vanishing trick when the time came. Well! What do you say, Watson? Some of the little problems we have gone into in the past should at least have taught us that the most interesting cases do not always present the most bizarre features at the outset."

" 'So far from it, on the contrary, quite the reverse,' to quote Sam Weller," I replied. "Personally nothing would be more to my taste than to join you."

"Then we'll consider it settled," said my friend. "And now I must go and attend to that other little matter of business I spoke to you about. Remember," he said, as we parted, "one-thirty at St. Pancras."

I was on the platform in good time, but it was not until the hands of the great station clock indicated the very moment due for our departure, and the porters were beginning to slam the carriage doors noisily, that I caught the familiar sight of Holmes's tall figure.

"Ah! here you are, Watson," he cried cheerily. "I fear you must have thought I was going to be too late. I've had a very busy evening and no time to waste; however, I've succeeded in putting into practice Phileas Fogg's theory that 'a well-used minimum suffices for everything,' and here I am."

"About the last thing I should expect of you," I said as we settled down into two opposite corners of an otherwise empty first-class carriage, "would be that you should do such an unmethodical thing as to miss a train. The only thing which would surprise me more, in fact, would be to see you at the station ten minutes before time."

"I should consider that the greatest evil of the two," said Holmes sententiously. "But now we must sleep; we have every prospect of a heavy day."

It was one of Holmes's characteristics that he could command sleep at will; unfortunately he could resist it at will also, and often have I had to remonstrate with him on the harm he must be doing himself, when, deeply engrossed in one of his strange or baffling problems, he would go for several consecutive days and nights without one wink of sleep.

He put the shades over the lamps, leaned back in his corner, and in less than two minutes his regular breathing told me he was fast asleep. Not being blessed with the same gift myself, I lay back in my corner for some time, nodding to the rhythmical throb of the express as it hurled itself forward through the darkness. Now and again as we shot through some brilliantly illuminated station or past a line of flaming furnaces, I caught for an instant a glimpse of Holmes's figure coiled up snugly in the far corner with his head sunk upon his breast.

It was not until after we had passed Nottingham that I really fell asleep and, when a more than usually violent lurch of the train over some points woke me again, it was broad daylight, and Holmes was sitting up, busy with a Bradshaw and boat timetable. As I moved, he glanced across at me.

"If I'm not mistaken, Watson, that was the Dore and Totley tunnel through which we have just come, and if so we shall be in Sheffield in a few minutes. As you see I've not been wasting my time altogether, but studying my Bradshaw, which, by the way,

Watson, is the most useful book published, without exception, to anyone of my calling."

"How can it possibly help you now?" I asked in some surprise.

"Well, it may or it may not," said Holmes thoughtfully. "But in any case it's well to have at one's finger tips all knowledge which may be of use. It's quite possible that this Jabez Booth may have decided to leave the country and, if this supposition is correct, he would undoubtedly time his little escapade in conformity with information contained in this useful volume. Now I learn from this Sheffield *Telegraph* which I obtained at Leicester, by the way, when you were fast asleep, that Mr. Booth cashed the last of his forged cheques at the North British Bank in Saville Street at precisely two-fifteen P.M. on Wednesday last. He made the round of the various banks he visited in a hansom, and it would take him about three minutes only to get from this bank to the G.C. station. From what I gather of the order in which the different banks were visited, he made a circuit, finishing at the nearest point to the G.C. station, at which he could arrive at about two-eighteen. Now I find that at two-twenty-two a boat express would leave Sheffield G.C., due in Liverpool at four-twenty, and in connection with it the White Star liner *Empress Queen* should have sailed from Liverpool docks at six-thirty for New York. Or again at two-forty-five a boat train would leave Sheffield for Hull, at which town it was due at four-thirty in time to make a connection with the Holland steam packet, *Comet,* sailing at six-thirty for Amsterdam.

"Here we are provided with two not unlikely means of escape, the former being the most probable; but both worth bearing in mind."

Holmes had scarcely finished speaking when the train drew up.

"Nearly five past four," I remarked.

"Yes," said Holmes, "we are exactly one and a half minutes behind time. And now I propose a good breakfast and a cup of strong coffee, for we have at least a couple of hours to spare."

After breakfast we visited first the police station where we learned that no further developments had taken place in the matter we had come to investigate. Mr. Lestrade of Scotland Yard had arrived the previous evening and had taken the case in hand officially.

We obtained the address of Mr. Jervis, the manager of the bank at which Booth had been an employee, and also that of his landlady at Broomhill.

A hansom landed us at Mr. Jervis's house at Fulwood at seven-thirty. Holmes insisted upon my accompanying him, and we were both shown into a spacious drawing room and asked to wait until the banker could see us.

Mr. Jervis, a stout, florid gentleman of about fifty, came puffing into the room in a very short time. An atmosphere of prosperity seemed to envelop, if not actually to emanate from him.

"Pardon me for keeping you waiting, gentlemen," he said, "but the hour is an early one."

"Indeed, Mr. Jervis," said Holmes, "no apology is needed unless it be on our part. It is, however, necessary that I should ask you a few questions concerning this affair of Mr. Booth, before I can proceed in the matter, and that must be our excuse for paying you such an untimely visit."

"I shall be most happy to answer your questions as far as it lies in my power to do so," said the banker, his fat fingers playing with a bunch of seals at the end of his massive gold watch chain.

"When did Mr. Booth first enter your bank?" said Holmes.

"In January 1881."

"Do you know where he lived when he first came to Sheffield?"

"He took lodgings at Ashgate Road, and has, I believe, lived there ever since."

"Do you know anything of his history or life before he came to you?"

"Very little, I fear; beyond that his parents were both dead, and that he came to us with the best testimonials from one of the Leeds branches of our bank, I know nothing."

"Did you find him quick and reliable?"

"He was one of the best and smartest men I have ever had in my employ."

"Do you know whether he was conversant with any other language besides English?"

"I feel pretty sure he wasn't. We have one clerk who attends to any foreign correspondence we may have, and I know that Booth has repeatedly passed letters and papers on to him."

"With your experience of banking matters, Mr. Jervis, how long a time do you think he might reasonably have calculated would elapse between the presentation of the forged cheques and their detection?"

"Well, that would depend very largely upon circumstances," said Mr. Jervis. "In the case of a single cheque it might be a week or two, unless the amounts were so large as to call for special inquiry, in which case it would probably never be cashed at all until such inquiry had been made. In the present case, when there were a dozen forged cheques, it was most unlikely that some one of them should not be detected within twenty-four hours and so lead to the discovery of the fraud. No sane person would dare to presume upon the crime remaining undetected for a longer period than that."

"Thanks," said Holmes, rising. "Those were the chief points I wished to speak to you about. I will communicate to you any news of importance I may have."

"I am deeply obliged to you, Mr. Holmes. The case is naturally causing us great anxiety. We leave it entirely to your discretion to take whatever steps you may consider best. Oh, by the way, I sent instructions to Booth's landlady to disturb nothing in his rooms until you had had an opportunity of examining them."

"That was a very wise thing to do," said Holmes, "and may be the means of helping us materially."

"I am also instructed by my company," said the banker, as he bowed us politely out, "to ask you to make a note of any expenses incurred, which they will of course immediately defray."

A few moments later we were ringing the bell of the house in Ashgate Road, Broomhill, at which Mr. Booth had been a lodger for over seven years. It was answered by a maid who informed us that Mrs. Purnell was engaged with a gentleman upstairs. When we explained our errand she showed us at once up to Mr. Booth's rooms, on the first floor, where we found Mrs. Purnell, a plump, voluble, little lady of about forty, in conversation with Mr. Lestrade, who appeared to be just concluding his examination of the rooms.

"Good morning, Holmes," said the detective, with a very self-satisfied air. "You arrive on the scene a little too late; I fancy I have already got all the information needed to catch our man!"

"I'm delighted to hear it," said Holmes dryly, "and must indeed congratulate you, if this is actually the case. Perhaps after I've made a little tour of inspection we can compare notes."

"Just as you please," said Lestrade, with the air of one who can afford to be gracious. "Candidly I think you will be wasting time, and so would you if you knew what I've discovered."

"Still I must ask you to humour my little whim," said Holmes, leaning against the mantelpiece and whistling softly as he looked round the room.

After a moment he turned to Mrs. Purnell. "The furniture of this room belongs, of course, to you?"

Mrs. Purnell assented.

"The picture that was taken down from over the mantelpiece last Wednesday morning," continued Holmes, "that belonged to Mr. Booth, I presume?"

I followed Holmes's glance across to where an unfaded patch on the wallpaper clearly indicated that a picture had recently been hanging. Well as I knew my friend's methods of reasoning, however, I did not realize for a moment that the little bits of spiderweb which had been behind the picture, and were still clinging to the wall, had told him that the picture could only have been taken down immediately before Mrs. Purnell had received orders to disturb nothing in the room; otherwise her brush, evidently busy enough elsewhere, would not have spared them.

The good lady stared at Sherlock Holmes in open-mouthed astonishment. "Mr. Booth took it down himself on Wednesday morning," she said. "It was a picture he had painted himself, and he thought no end of it. He wrapped it up and took it out with him, remarking that he was going to give it to a friend. I was very much surprised at the time, for I knew he valued it very much; in fact he once told me that he wouldn't part with it for anything. Of course, it's easy to see now why he got rid of it."

"Yes," said Holmes. "It wasn't a large picture, I see. Was it a water colour?"

"Yes, a painting of a stretch of moorland, with three or four large rocks arranged like a big table on a bare hilltop. Druidicals, Mr. Booth called them, or something like that."

"Did Mr. Booth do much painting, then?" enquired Holmes.

"None, whilst he's been here, sir. He has told me he used to do a good deal as a lad, but he had given it up."

Holmes's eyes were glancing round the room again, and an

exclamation of surprise escaped him as they encountered a photo standing on the piano.

"Surely that's a photograph of Mr. Booth," he said. "It exactly resembles the description I have of him?"

"Yes," said Mrs. Purnell, "and a very good one it is too."

"How long has it been taken?" asked Holmes, picking it up.

"Oh, only a few weeks, sir. I was here when the boy from the photographer's brought them up. Mr. Booth opened the packet whilst I was in the room. There were only two photos, that one and another which he gave to me."

"You interest me exceedingly," said Holmes. "This striped lounge suit he is wearing. Is it the same that he had on when he left Wednesday morning?"

"Yes, he was dressed just like that, as far as I can remember."

"Do you recollect anything of importance that Mr. Booth said to you last Wednesday before he went out?"

"Not very much, I'm afraid, sir. When I took his cup of chocolate up to his bedroom, he said — "

"One moment," interrupted Holmes. "Did Mr. Booth usually have a cup of chocolate in the morning?"

"Oh, yes, sir, summer and winter alike. He was very particular about it and would ring for it as soon as ever he waked. I believe he'd rather have gone without his breakfast almost than have missed his cup of chocolate. Well, as I was saying, sir, I took it up to him myself on Wednesday morning, and he made some remark about the weather and then, just as I was leaving the room, he said, 'Oh, by the way, Mrs. Purnell, I shall be going away to-night for a couple of weeks. I've packed my bag and will call for it this afternoon.' "

"No doubt you were very much surprised at this sudden announcement?" queried Holmes.

"Not very much, sir. Ever since he's had this auditing work to do for the branch banks, there's been no knowing when he would be away. Of course, he'd never been off for two weeks at a stretch, except at holiday times, but he had so often been away for a few days at a time that I had got used to his popping off with hardly a moment's notice."

"Let me see, how long has he had this extra work at the bank — several months, hasn't he?"

"More. It was about last Christmas, I believe, when they gave it to him."

"Oh, yes, of course," said Holmes carelessly, "and this work naturally took him from home a good deal?"

"Yes, indeed, and it seemed to quite tire him, so much evening and night work too, you see, sir. It was enough to knock him out, for he was always such a very quiet, retiring gentleman and hardly ever used to go out in the evenings before."

"Has Mr. Booth left many of his possessions behind him?" asked Holmes.

"Very few, indeed, and what he has are mostly old useless things. But he's a most honest thief, sir," said Mrs. Purnell paradoxically, "and paid me his rent, before he went out on Wednesday morning, right up to next Saturday, because he wouldn't be back by then."

"That was good of him," said Holmes, smiling thoughtfully. "By the way, do you happen to know if he gave away any other treasures before he left?"

"Well, not *just* before, but during the last few months he's taken away most of his books and sold them, I think, a few at a time. He had rather a fancy for old books and has told me that some editions he had were worth quite a lot."

During this conversation, Lestrade had been sitting drumming his fingers impatiently on the table. Now he got up. "Really, I fear I shall have to leave you to this gossip," he said. "I must go and wire instructions for the arrest of Mr. Booth. If only you would have looked before at this old blotter, which I found in the wastebasket, you would have saved yourself a good deal of unnecessary trouble, Mr. Holmes," and he triumphantly slapped down a sheet of well-used blotting paper on the table.

Holmes picked it up and held it in front of a mirror over the sideboard. Looking over his shoulder I could plainly read the reflected impression of a note written in Mr. Booth's handwriting, of which Holmes had procured samples.

It was to a booking agency in Liverpool, giving instructions to them to book a first-class private cabin and passage on board the *Empress Queen* from Liverpool to New York. Parts of the note were slightly obliterated by other impressions, but it went on to say that a cheque was enclosed to pay for tickets, etc., and it was signed by J. Booth.

Holmes stood silently scrutinizing the paper for several minutes.

It was a well-used sheet, but fortunately the impression of the note was well in the centre, and hardly obliterated at all by the other marks and blots, which were all round the outer circumference of the paper. In one corner the address of the Liverpool booking agency was plainly decipherable, the paper evidently having been used to blot the envelope with also.

"My dear Lestrade, you have indeed been more fortunate than I had imagined," said Holmes at length, handing the paper back to him. "May I ask what steps you propose to take next?"

"I shall cable at once to the New York police to arrest the fellow as soon as he arrives," said Lestrade, "but first I must make quite certain the boat doesn't touch at Queenstown or anywhere and give him a chance of slipping through our fingers."

"It doesn't," said Holmes quietly. "I had already looked to see as I thought it not unlikely, at first, that Mr. Booth might have intended to sail by the *Empress Queen.*"

Lestrade gave me a wink for which I would dearly have liked to have knocked him down, for I could see that he disbelieved my friend. I felt a keen pang of disappointment that Holmes's foresight should have been eclipsed in this way by what, after all, was mere good luck on Lestrade's part.

Holmes had turned to Mrs. Purnell and was thanking her.

"Don't mention it, sir," she said. "Mr. Booth deserves to be caught, though I must say he's always been a gentleman to me. I only wish I could have given you some more useful information."

"On the contrary," said Holmes, "I can assure you that what you have told us has been of the utmost importance and will very materially help us. It's just occurred to me, by the way, to wonder if you could possibly put up my friend Dr. Watson and myself for a few days, until we have had time to look into this little matter?"

"Certainly, sir, I shall be most happy."

"Good," said Holmes. "Then you may expect us back to dinner about seven."

When we got outside, Lestrade at once announced his intention of going to the police office and arranging for the necessary orders for Booth's detention and arrest to be cabled to the head of the New York police; Holmes retained an enigmatical silence as to what he purposed to do but expressed his determination to remain at Broomhill and make a few further inquiries. He insisted, however, upon going alone.

"Remember, Watson, you are here for a rest and holiday and I can assure you that if you did remain with me you would only find my programme a dull one. Therefore, I insist upon your finding some more entertaining way of spending the remainder of the day."

Past experience told me that it was quite useless to remonstrate or argue with Holmes when once his mind was made up, so I consented with the best grace I could, and leaving Holmes, drove off in the hansom, which he assured me he would not require further.

I passed a few hours in the art gallery and museum and then, after lunch, had a brisk walk out on the Manchester Road and enjoyed the fresh air and moorland scenery, returning to Ashgate Road at seven with better appetite than I had been blessed with for months.

Holmes had not returned, and it was nearly half past seven before he came in. I could see at once that he was in one of his most reticent moods, and all my inquiries failed to elicit any particulars of how he had passed his time or what he thought about the case.

The whole evening he remained coiled up in an easy chair puffing at his pipe and hardly a word could I get from him.

His inscrutable countenance and persistent silence gave me no clue whatever as to his thought on the inquiry he had in hand, although I could see his whole mind was concentrated upon it.

Next morning, just as we had finished breakfast, the maid entered with a note. "From Mr. Jervis, sir; there's no answer," she said.

Holmes tore open the envelope and scanned the note hurriedly and, as he did so, I noticed a flush of annoyance spread over his usually pale face.

"Confound his impudence," he muttered. "Read that, Watson. I don't ever remember to have been treated so badly in a case before."

The note was a brief one:

"The Cedars, Fulwood.

"September sixth.

"Mr. Jervis, on behalf of the directors of the British Consolidated Bank, begs to thank Mr. Sherlock Holmes for his prompt attention and valued services in the matter concerning the fraud and disappearance of their ex-employee, Mr. Jabez Booth.

"Mr. Lestrade, of Scotland Yard, informs us that he has succeeded in tracking the individual in question who will be arrested shortly. Under these circumstances they feel it unnecessary to take up any more of Mr. Holmes's valuable time."

"Rather cool, eh, Watson? I'm much mistaken if they don't have cause to regret their action when it's too late. After this I shall certainly refuse to act for them any further in the case, even if they ask me to do so. In a way I'm sorry because the matter presented some distinctly interesting features and is by no means the simple affair our friend Lestrade thinks."

"Why, don't you think he is on the right scent?" I exclaimed.

"Wait and see, Watson," said Holmes mysteriously. "Mr. Booth hasn't been caught yet, remember." And that was all that I could get out of him.

One result of the summary way in which the banker had dispensed with my friend's services was that Holmes and I spent a most restful and enjoyable week in the small village of Hathersage, on the edge of the Derbyshire moors, and returned to London feeling better for our long moorland rambles.

Holmes having very little work in hand at the time, and my wife not yet having returned from her Swiss holiday, I prevailed upon him, though not without considerable difficulty, to pass the next few weeks with me instead of returning to his rooms at Baker Street.

Of course, we watched the development of the Sheffield forgery case with the keenest interest. Somehow the particulars of Lestrade's discoveries got into the papers, and the day after we left Sheffield they were full of the exciting chase of Mr. Booth, the man wanted for the Sheffield bank frauds.

They spoke of "the guilty man restlessly pacing the desk of the *Empress Queen,* as she ploughed her way majestically across the solitary wastes of the Atlantic, all unconscious that the inexorable hand of justice could stretch over the ocean and was already waiting to seize him on his arrival in the New World." And Holmes after reading these sensational paragraphs would always lay down the paper with one of his enigmatical smiles.

At last the day on which the *Empress Queen* was due at New York arrived, and I could not help but notice that even Holmes's usually inscrutable face wore a look of suppressed excitement as he unfolded the evening paper. But our surprise was doomed to be prolonged still further. There was a brief paragraph to say that the *Empress Queen* had arrived off Long Island at six A.M. after a good passage. There was, however, a case of cholera on board, and the New York authorities had consequently been compelled to put the boat in quarantine, and none of the passengers or crew would be allowed to leave her for a period of twelve days.

Two days later there was a full column in the papers stating that it had been definitely ascertained that Mr. Booth was really on board the *Empress Queen.* He had been identified and spoken to by one of the sanitary inspectors who had had to visit the boat. He was being kept under close observation, and there was no possible chance of his escaping. Mr. Lestrade of Scotland Yard, by whom Booth had been so cleverly tracked down and his escape forestalled, had taken passage on the *Oceania,* due in New York on the tenth, and would personally arrest Mr. Booth when he was allowed to land.

Never before or since have I seen my friend Holmes so astonished as when he had finished reading this announcement. I could see that he was thoroughly mystified, though why he should be so was quite a puzzle to me. All day he sat coiled up in an easy chair, with his brows drawn down into two hard lines and his eyes half closed as he puffed away at his oldest brier in silence.

"Watson," he said once, glancing across at me. "It's perhaps a good thing that I was asked to drop that Sheffield case. As things are turning out I fancy I should only have made a fool of myself."

"Why?" I asked.

"Because I began by assuming that somebody else wasn't one — and now it looks as though I had been mistaken."

For the next few days Holmes seemed quite depressed, for nothing annoyed him more than to feel that he had made any mistake in his deductions or got onto a false line of reasoning.

At last the fatal tenth of September, the day on which Booth was to be arrested. Eagerly but in vain we scanned the evening papers. The morning of the eleventh came and still brought no news of the arrest, but in the evening papers of that day there was a short paragraph hinting that the criminal had escaped again.

For several days the papers were full of the most conflicting rumours and conjectures as to what had actually taken place, but all were agreed in affirming that Mr. Lestrade was on his way home alone and would be back in Liverpool on the seventeenth or eighteenth.

On the evening of the last named day Holmes and I sat smoking in his Baker Street rooms, when his boy came in to announce that Mr. Lestrade of Scotland Yard was below and would like the favour of a few minutes' conversation.

"Show him up, show him up," said Holmes, rubbing his hands together with an excitement quite unusual to him.

Lestrade entered the room and sat down in the seat to which Holmes waved him, with a most dejected air.

"It's not often I'm at fault, Mr. Holmes," he began, "but in this Sheffield business I've been beaten hollow."

"Dear me," said Holmes pleasantly, "you surely don't mean to tell me that you haven't got your man yet."

"I do," said Lestrade. "What's more, I don't think he ever will be caught!"

"Don't despair so soon," said Holmes encouragingly. "After you have told us all that's already happened, it's just within the bounds of possibility that I may be able to help you with some little suggestions."

Thus encouraged, Lestrade began his strange story, to which we both listened with breathless interest.

"It's quite unnecessary for me to dwell upon incidents which are already familiar," he said. "You know of the discovery I made in Sheffield which, of course, convinced me that the man I wanted had sailed for New York on the *Empress Queen*. I was in a fever of impatience for his arrest, and when I heard that the boat he had taken passage on had been placed in quarantine, I set off at once in order that I might actually lay hands upon him myself. Never have five days seemed so long.

"We reached New York on the evening of the ninth, and I rushed off at once to the head of the New York police and from him learned that there was no doubt whatever that Mr. Jabez Booth was indeed on board the *Empress Queen*. One of the sanitary inspectors who had had to visit the boat had not only seen but actually spoken to him. The man exactly answered the description of Booth which had appeared in the papers. One of the New York detectives had been sent on board to make a few inquiries and to inform the captain privately of the pending arrest. He found that Mr. Jabez Booth had actually had the audacity to book his passage and travel under his real name without even attempting to disguise himself in any way. He had a private first-class cabin, and the purser declared that he had been suspicious of the man from the first. He had kept himself shut up in his cabin nearly all the time, posing as an eccentric semi-invalid person who must not be disturbed on any account. Most of his meals had been sent down to his cabin, and he had been seen on deck but seldom and hardly ever dined with the rest of the passengers. It was quite evident that he had been trying to keep out of sight, and to attract as little attention as possible. The stewards and some of the passengers who were approached on the subject later were all agreed that this was the case.

"It was decided that during the time the boat was in quarantine nothing should be said to Booth to arouse his suspicions but that the pursers, stewards and captain, who were the only persons in the secret, should between them keep him under observation until the tenth, the day on which passengers would be allowed to leave the boat. On that day he should be arrested."

Here we were interrupted by Holmes's boy, who came in with a telegram. Holmes glanced at it with a faint smile.

"No answer," he said, slipping it in his waistcoat pocket. "Pray continue your very interesting story, Lestrade."

"Well, on the afternoon of the tenth, accompanied by the New York chief inspector of police and detective Forsyth," resumed Lestrade, "I went on board the *Empress Queen* half an hour before she was due to come up to the landing stage to allow passengers to disembark.

"The purser informed us that Mr. Booth had been on deck and that he had been in conversation with him about fifteen minutes before our arrival. He had then gone down to his cabin and the purser, making some excuse to go down also, had actually seen him enter it. He had been standing near the top of the companionway since then and was sure Booth had not come up on deck again since.

" 'At last,' I muttered to myself, as we all went down below, led by the purser who took us straight to Booth's cabin. We knocked but, getting no answer, tried the door and found it locked. The purser assured us, however, that this was nothing unusual. Mr. Booth had had his cabin door locked a good deal and, often, even his meals had been left on a tray outside. We held a hurried consultation and, as time was short, decided to force the door. Two good blows with a heavy hammer broke it from the hinges, and we all rushed in. You can picture our astonishment when we found the cabin empty. We searched it thoroughly, and Booth was certainly not there."

"One moment," interrupted Holmes. "The key of the door— was it on the inside of the lock or not?"

"It was nowhere to be seen," said Lestrade. "I was getting frantic for, by this time, I could feel the vibration of the engines and hear the first churning sound of the screw as the great boat began to slide slowly down towards the landing stage.

"We were at our wits' end; Mr. Booth must be hiding some-where on board, but there was now no time to make a proper search for him, and in a very few minutes passengers would be leaving the boat. At last the captain promised us that, under the circumstances, only one landing gangway should be run out and, in company with the purser and stewards, I should stand by it with a complete list of passengers, ticking off each one as he or she left. By this means it would be quite impossible for Booth to escape us even if he attempted some disguise, for no person whatever would be allowed to cross the gangway until identified by the purser or one of the stewards.

"I was delighted with the arrangement, for there was now no way by which Booth could give me the slip.

"One by one the passengers crossed the gangway and joined the jostling crowd on the landing stage and each one was identified and his or her name crossed off my list. There were one hundred and ninety-three first-class passengers on board the *Empress Queen*, including Booth, and, when one hundred and ninety-two had disembarked, his was the only name which remained!

"You can scarcely realize what a fever of impatience we were in," said Lestrade, mopping his brow at the very recollection, "nor how interminable the time seemed as we slowly but carefully ticked off one by one the whole of the three hundred and twenty-four second-class passengers and the three hundred and ten steerage from my list. Every passenger except Mr. Booth crossed that gangway, but he certainly did not do so. There was no possible room for doubt on that point.

"He must therefore be still on the boat, we agreed, but I was getting panic-stricken and wondered if there were any possibility of his getting smuggled off in some of the luggage which the great cranes were now beginning to swing up onto the pier.

"I hinted my fear to detective Forsyth, and he at once arranged that every trunk or box in which there was any chance for a man to hide should be opened and examined by the customs officers.

"It was a tedious business, but they didn't shirk it, and at the end of two hours were able to assure us that by no possibility could Booth have been smuggled off the boat in this way.

"This left only one possible solution to the mystery. He *must* be still in hiding somewhere on board. We had had the boat kept under the closest observation ever since she came up to the landing stage, and now the superintendent of police lent us a staff of twenty men and, with the consent of the captain and the assistance of the pursers and stewards, etc., the *Empress Queen* was searched and re-searched from stem to stern. We didn't leave unexamined a place in which a cat could have hidden, but the missing man wasn't there. Of that I'm certain—and there you have the whole mystery in a nutshell, Mr. Holmes. Mr. Booth certainly *was* on board the *Empress Queen* up to, and at, eleven o'clock on the morning of the tenth, and although he could not by any possibility have left it, we are nevertheless face to face with the fact that he wasn't there at five o'clock in the afternoon."

Lestrade's face as he concluded his curious and mysterious narrative bore a look of the most hopeless bewilderment I ever saw, and I fancy my own must have pretty well matched it, but Holmes threw himself back in his easy chair, with his long thin legs stuck straight out in front of him, his whole frame literally shaking with silent laughter. "What conclusion have you come to?" he gasped at length. "What steps do you propose to take next?"

"I've no idea. Who could know what to do? The whole thing is impossible, perfectly impossible; it's an insoluble mystery. I came to you to see if you could, by any chance, suggest some entirely fresh line of inquiry upon which I might begin to work."

"Well," said Holmes, cocking his eye mischievously at the bewildered Lestrade, "I can give you Booth's present address, if it will be of any use to you?"

"His what!" cried Lestrade.

"His present address," repeated Holmes quietly. "But before I do so, my dear Lestrade, I must make one stipulation. Mr. Jervis has treated me very shabbily in the matter, and I don't desire that my name shall be associated with it any further. Whatever you do you must not hint the source from which any information I may give you has come. You promise?"

"Yes," murmured Lestrade, who was in a state of bewildered excitement.

Holmes tore a leaf from his pocket book and scribbled on it: "Mr. A. Winter, c/o Mrs. Thackary, Glossop Road, Broomhill, Sheffield."

"You will find there the present name and address of the man you are in search of," he said, handing the paper across to Lestrade. "I should strongly advise you to lose no time in getting hold of him, for though the wire I received a short time ago — which unfortunately interrupted your most interesting narrative — was to tell me that Mr. Winter had arrived back home again after a temporary absence, still it's more than probable that he will leave there, for good, at an early date. I can't say how soon — not for a few days, I should think."

Lestrade rose. "Mr. Holmes, you're a brick," he said, with more real feeling than I have ever seen him show before. "You've saved my reputation in this job just when I was beginning to look like a perfect fool, and now you're forcing me to take all the credit, when I don't deserve one atom. As to how you have found this out, it's as great a mystery to me as Booth's disappearance was."

"Well, as to that," said Holmes airily, "I can't be sure of all the facts myself, for of course I've never looked properly into the case. But they are pretty easy to conjecture, and I shall be most happy to give you my idea of Booth's trip to New York on some future occasion when you have more time to spare.

"By the way," called out Holmes, as Lestrade was leaving the room, "I shouldn't be surprised if you find Mr. Jabez Booth, *alias*

Mr. Archibald Winter, a slight acquaintance of yours, for he would undoubtedly be a fellow passenger of yours, on your homeward journey from America. He reached Sheffield a few hours before you arrived in London and, as he has certainly just returned from New York, like yourself, it's evident you must have crossed on the same boat. He would be wearing smoked glasses and have a heavy dark moustache."

"Ah!" said Lestrade, "there *was* a man called Winter on board who answered to that description. I believe it must have been he, and I'll lose no more time," and Lestrade hurried off.

"Well, Watson, my boy, you look nearly as bewildered as our friend Lestrade," said Holmes, leaning back in his chair and looking roguishly across at me, as he lighted his old brier pipe.

"I must confess that none of the problems you have had to solve, in the past, seemed more inexplicable to me than Lestrade's account of Booth's disappearance from the *Empress Queen.*"

"Yes, that part of the story is decidedly neat," chuckled Holmes, "but I'll tell you how I got at the solution of the mystery. I see you are ready to listen.

"The first thing to do in any case is to gauge the intelligence and cunning of the criminal. Now, Mr. Booth was undoubtedly a clever man. Mr. Jervis himself, you remember, assured us as much. The fact that he opened banking accounts in preparation for the crime twelve months before he committed it proves it to have been a long-premeditated one. I began the case, therefore, with the knowledge that I had a clever man to catch, who had had twelve months in which to plan his escape.

"My first real clues came from Mrs. Purnell," said Holmes. "Most important were her remarks about Booth auditing work which kept him from home so many days and nights, often consecutively. I felt certain at once, and inquiry confirmed, that Mr. Booth had had no such extra work at all. Why then had he invented lies to explain these absences to his landlady? Probably because they were in some way connected, either with the crime, or with his plans for escaping after he had committed it. It was inconceivable that so much mysterious outdoor occupation could be directly connected with the forgery, and I at once deduced that this time had been spent by Booth in paving the way for his escape.

"Almost at once the idea that he had been living a double life occurred to me, his intention doubtless being to quietly drop one individuality after committing the crime and permanently take up the other—a far safer and less clumsy expedient than the usual one of assuming a new disguise just at the very moment when everybody is expecting and looking for you to do so.

"Then there were the interesting facts relating to Booth's picture and books. I tried to put myself in his place. He valued these possessions highly; they were light and portable, and there was really no reason whatever why he should part with them. Doubtless, then, he had taken them away by degrees and put them someplace where he could lay hands on them again. If I could find out where this place was, I felt sure there would be every chance I could catch him when he attempted to recover them.

"The picture couldn't have gone far for he had taken it out with him on the very day of the crime. . . . I needn't bore you with details. . . . I was two hours making inquiries before I found the house at which he had called and left it—which was none other than Mrs. Thackary's in Glossop Road.

"I made a pretext for calling there and found Mrs. T. one of the most easy mortals in the world to pump. In less than half an hour I knew that she had a boarder named Winter, that he professed to be a commercial traveller and was from home most of the time. His description resembled Booth's save that he had a moustache, wore glasses.

"As I've often tried to impress upon you before, Watson, details are the most important things of all, and it gave me a real thrill of pleasure to learn that Mr. Winter had a cup of chocolate brought up to his bedroom every morning. A gentleman called on the Wednesday morning and left a parcel, saying it was a picture he had promised for Mr. Winter, and asking Mrs. Thackary to give it to Winter when he returned. Mr. Winter had taken the rooms the previous December. He had a good many books which he had brought in from time to time. All these facts taken in conjunction made me certain that I was on the right scent. Winter and Booth were one and the same person, and as soon as Booth had put all his pursuers off the track he would return, as Winter, and repossess his treasures.

"The newly taken photo and the old blotter with its telltale note were too obviously intentional means of drawing the police onto Booth's track. The blotter, I could see almost at once, was a fraud, for not only would it be almost impossible to use one in the ordinary way so much without the central part becoming undecipherable, but I could see where it had been touched up.

"I concluded therefore that Booth, *alias* Winter, never actually intended to sail on the *Empress Queen*, but in that I underestimated his ingenuity. Evidently he booked *two* berths on the boat, one in his real, and one in his assumed name, and managed very cleverly to successfully keep up the two characters throughout the voyage, appearing first as one individual and then as the other. Most of the time he posed as Winter, and for this purpose Booth became the eccentric semi-invalid passenger who remained locked up in his cabin for such a large part of his time. This, of course, would answer his purpose well; his eccentricity would only draw attention to his presence on board and so make him one of the best-known passengers on the boat, although he showed so little of himself.

"I had left instructions with Mrs. Thackary to send me a wire as soon as Winter returned. When Booth had led his pursuers to New York, and there thrown them off the scent, he had nothing more to do but to take the first boat back. Very naturally it chanced to be the same as that on which our friend Lestrade returned, and that was how Mrs. Thackary's wire arrived at the opportune moment it did."